copy on
winnet
mar. '92

NF.   980611

3 FEB 1974		20. MAY 1989
	13. APR. 1976	24. JUN. 1989
21 FEB 1974		
15 MAR 1974	14. MAY 19	IDL FROM UB
	24. JUN. 1976	TO ...... PS ......
23 MAR 1974	-7. AUG. 1976	D.B. 8.12.89
24 APR 19	25. SEP. 1976	16 DEC 1989
29 APR 1974	-5. JUL 1977	18. DEC. 1990
30 MAY 1974	16. FEB. 1978	2/3 2/95
14 JUN 1974	19. APR. 1978	0 FEB 201
19 JUL 1974	28. DEC. 1978	
9 AUG 74	18. MAY 1981	
2 MAY 1975	8. JUN 198	
11 OCT 1975	-6. JAN. 19 8	
-2. JAN 1976	27. JAN. 19 8	
	12. MAR. 19 8	BASEMENT

The Key

By the same Author

THE INDESTRUCTIBLE IRISH

The Key

by John Philip Cohane

Preface by CYRUS H. GORDON
Professor of Mediterranean Studies
Brandeis University

TURNSTONE BOOKS, LONDON

02252333

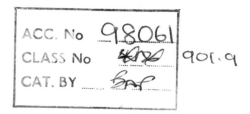
© 1969, 1973 by John Philip Cohane
First American edition 1971
First British Commonwealth edition 1973

Turnstone Press Ltd
37 Upper Addison Gardens,
London W14 8AJ

ISBN 0 85500 006 6

Set in Linotype Janson
Printed in Great Britain by
Lowe & Brydone (Printers) Ltd
Thetford, Norfolk

"For as God was the help of our reason to illuminate us, so should we likewise turn it every way, that we may be more capable of understanding His mysteries; provided only that the mind be enlarged, according to its capacity, to the grandeur of the mysteries, and not the mysteries contracted to the narrowness of the mind."

FRANCIS BACON

To four splendid Baconians:

Herman W. Liebert—LIBRARIAN, THE BEINECKE RARE BOOK AND MANUSCRIPT LIBRARY, YALE UNIVERSITY

Dr. Frederick L. Santee—FORMER PROFESSOR OF CLASSICS, KENYON COLLEGE

Dr. Professor Johannes Rahder (Retired)—HALL OF GRADUATE STUDIES, YALE UNIVERSITY

David McDowell—CROWN PUBLISHERS, INC.

And above all, to Rosalind Cole

Acknowledgments

I wish to express my gratitude to: J. Donald Rawlings, my lawyer and old friend, who with his wife, Eleanor, patiently read hundreds of pages of research and preliminary drafts of the material; Admiral H. B. Miller, USN (Ret.), who was an enthusiast from the beginning; Charles J. Haughey, Minister for Finance, Republic of Ireland, who on a score of occasions lent his support and encouragement to the project; Doris Bryen, of London, who brought together most of the photographs; Warren Potter, of Crown Publishers, whose meticulous copy editing contributed immeasurably to the accuracy of the text; and to the staffs of the Bibliothèque Nationale, Paris; the British Council Library, Rome; the British Museum Library, London; the Jewish Museum Library, New York; the Library of Congress, Washington, D.C.; the Limerick Public Library, Ireland; the Museum of the American Indian, Heye Foundation Library, New York; the National Library, Dublin, the New York Public Library—with special thanks to Norwood Vail, First Assistant, Map Division; the Royal Astronomical Society Library, London; the Royal Hibernian Society Library, Dublin; the Royal Statistical Society Library, London; the Trinity College Library, Dublin; the Wiedener Library, Harvard University; and the Yale University Library, Beinecke Rare Book and Manuscript Library, New Haven.

Contents

List of Illustrations

8

And the whole earth was of one language, and of one speech.

Genesis 11:1

Preface

There is abundant evidence pointing to nautical contacts between the Old and New worlds going back to the Bronze Age. Exact dates elude us, but by 1500 B.C., the process already had a long history. By that time, one of the most important factors of civilization on the world scene was the international and intercontinental network of merchant mariners. They were not composed of one ethnic group; but *a* dominant, if not *the* dominant, element was Northwest Semitic, closely akin to the Phoenicians in language, religion, and way of life. To those mariners we owe much of our civilization, including the alphabet.

How they developed and spread civilization is illustrated by the Bronze Age shipwreck excavated by George Bass at Gelidonya off the coast of Turkey. The vessel, operating in the Aegean with Minoan-Mycenaean cargo, was made of Syrian wood, and its captain bore a Syrian seal. Thus the ship and its leadership were from the Northwest Semitic sphere. On the ship were the bronze tools of craftsmen, reflecting the fact that such vessels moved not only merchandise but also carried the people who actually practiced the arts and crafts.

The metallurgy of pre-Columbian Mesoamerica belonged, not to the Iron Age, but to the Bronze Age, showing that the technological pattern had been set before the later Phoenicians,

Greeks, Romans, and others appeared on the stage of history, let alone reached America.

Mankind cherishes history but often lapses into collective amnesia. The Egyptians forgot how to read their ancestors' hieroglyphs; and the Persians lost their knowledge not only of the script but also of the history and of the very names of Cyrus, Cambyses, and Xerxes who made their ancestors the rulers of the world. The forgotten systems of writing had to be rediscovered, and their messages revealed, through decipherment in the nineteenth century. What seems strange is that Persian history had been preserved in the ancient Greek and Hebrew classics unbeknown to the Persians themselves.

Much the same thing has happened to us Americans. We are interested in our hemisphere but believe, at least tacitly, that white men did not come to America before Columbus' discovery of our continent in 1492—or certainly not before the Vikings around A.D. 1000. And yet—to say nothing of Plato's Atlantis— the Greek author Theopompus in the fourth century B.C. wrote of an enormous land inhabited by a race quite unlike the Greeks. Three centuries later, Diodorus of Sicily described a great land, with navigable rivers, west of Africa, discovered by Phoenicians blown across the ocean by strong winds. Diodorus also tells that the Tyrians wanted to establish a colony there but were prevented from doing so by the Carthaginians, who wished to reserve that great land in the west for themselves in case Carthage should ever be vanquished. In the second century A.D., Claudius Aelianus reports that the land in the west was still remembered by the Carthaginians or Phoenicians of Cadiz.

We are the victims of collective amnesia concerning our own country—but we do not have to remain so. There is no dearth of facts reflecting the transoceanic contacts of America, from the east and west, throughout millennia before Columbus. One of the lines of investigation is the plethora of place-names dotting the globe. Those names reflect important data out of which world history—including the history of pre-Columbian America —will be reconstructed.

Names are tricky. Like all words, they are subject to phonetic law. To understand them, we must control the morphology of their elements, and the meaning of their parts as well as their meaning as a whole. When we deal with names that have always been in the same well-known milieu, there is little difficulty. "New Haven" means just that: "a new haven." And the same holds for a name that follows any known patterns; thus "Philadelphia" contains the Greek words *phil*—'love"—and *adelph*—"sibling"—so that the current interpretation "City of Brotherly Love" is correct.

When, however, a name has been transmitted from one speech group to another, we run into problems, especially when the original language of the name is unfamiliar. "Egypt" comes from *h.t-k³-pth*, "House of the Soul of Ptah" (pronounced around 1400 B.C. *Hikuptah*), the name of the sacred area of Memphis, after which the country came to be named. An Egyptologist knows that *E* goes back to the word for "house"; *gy*, to the word for "soul"; and *pt* to "Ptah."

Once we run into the problem of *The Key*, we are confronted with multiple complications. There are many languages involved —too many for any linguist to know. Some of the languages are extinct. The channels of transmission are manifold, and for the most part still obscure. Without knowing the linguistic identity of the channels, it is impossible to formulate the "phonetic laws" that are involved. When *frater* (as in "fraternity") occurs in English, it is borrowed directly from Latin; the native English cognate is "brother" according to well-established phonetic law; "friar" comes into English from Norman French (compare modern French *frère*). Here we are dealing with familiar West European languages. Such is not the case, for example, when we grapple with American Indian names of problematic origin. The complexities scare off the professional linguists who are all too aware of their own inadequacies.

John Philip Cohane knows the pitfalls of his subject. He does not pretend to know what only the professional linguists know, let alone what they do not know. As a Semitist, with some additional competence in Egyptian and Indo-European languages, I have corrected some of the author's errors in the languages that I happen to know. I cannot impart wisdom concerning the countless languages of which I am ignorant. But one thing is certain: *The Key* deals with a vital problem that must sooner or later be stated, and it takes an intelligent amateur with wide perspective and ability to communicate it interestingly, to make a start. John Cohane is opening the subject and bringing it to the attention of a wide public. Specialists in scores of fields will and should criticize the aspects that they control in detail from the sources.

It is books like *The Key* that help bring about important re-valuations. The refinements, which come later, would never come at all unless authors like John Philip Cohane wrote books like *The Key* to open new horizons.

Cyrus H. Gordon
Professor of Mediterranean Studies
Brandeis University

Chapter 1

OVER EIGHT YEARS ago I took into the British Council Library in Rome, all unsuspecting as to what was about to happen, two place-names that are discussed in Michael Harrison's *London Beneath the Pavement*.[1] The names are world famous—the Thames River and Berkshire County. Since then, those two place-names have led me by way of maps and the printed page several times around the globe, into out-of-the-way corners of the earth, and finally made me wonder whether unwittingly I might have stumbled onto the key to much of mankind's prehistory. If so, it was Michael Harrison who first handed me the key.

I was not especially prepared for such an odyssey. I am not a professional etymologist, although a good part of my adult years has been spent working with words and the origin of words. My knowledge of ancient languages is nil except for Latin. As the research piled up, overflowing from desk drawers and files into corners of my library, I felt at times as though I had been condemned for some unknown offense to cleaning out the Augean stables, and I have more than once been tempted to throw the whole mess into the fireplace and begin on something less nebulous.

And yet, at other times, I have felt as though I were standing

[1] London: (Peter) Davies, 1961.

before a gigantic jigsaw puzzle into which a surprisingly large number of pieces seemed to fit into the right places. Several months ago, an older and far wiser man than myself expressed the opinion that I would very likely be engaged on this project for the rest of my life. Having reached the mid-fifties, and having not the slightest intention of spending what time remains to me on this planet working on further research, I am going to try to set down on paper just as simply as possible the conclusions I have reached. I will leave it to the reader to decide whether my time has been wasted or well spent.

The twin adjacent starting points given to me by Michael Harrison, the Thames River and Berkshire County, are both names generally believed to have been brought into the British Isles prior to the arrival about 400 B.C. of the Celts. Both these names figure in the pages that follow; in fact, if I have interpreted the evidence correctly, they were actually carried to England by two different though related groups of pre-Celtic people. But while exploring their ramifications, I came upon other names that appear to be of greater significance, or at least where research adds up to more positive conclusions.

Although I realize that the surface has been only lightly scraped, sufficient evidence in my opinion has been collected to indicate a strong likelihood that in ancient times, before the Phoenicians, the Carthaginians, the Egyptians, the Greeks, and the Romans, certain key names and words were taken out in all directions from the Mediterranean, in some instances by water routes, and that these same names and words can still be found, in spite of corruptions, in the names of rivers, mountains, volcanoes, and waterfalls, lakes, islands, regions, towns and cities, scattered all across the face of the earth. Further, that in many instances these same key names and words are to be found in personal and tribal names, in mythological and deified names, in the names of animals, birds, fish, flowers, trees, foods, parts of the body, and are half concealed in the spoken and written languages of widely separated peoples.

After five or six months, I began to search for a more specific source for these key names and words than the Mediterranean basin. Within a relatively short time, it became apparent that, for better or worse, all of them figure prominently in ancient Semitic legends and mythology. Most of them are to be found in the Old Testament, notably in Genesis. This is not to say there may not be a more logical, even earlier, point of origin than the Semites, but if so I have not been able to find it. On the basis of the evidence it would seem that a high percentage of the people on earth today are far more closely related than is generally assumed and that they are bound together by at least one early bloodstream that is Semitic in origin.

I should hasten to add that if someone had unfolded such a basic premise to me five years ago, I would have greeted it with as much skepticism as the average "educated" person. During the past forty years I have looked on the Bible as a collection of myths and folktales containing little of scientific value. Starting with no preconceived theories or opinions, objectively sorting out and assembling data, I could not have been more astonished where the chain of facts led me. I am also the first to agree that the research methods used are, to say the least, highly unorthodox. Two principal objections immediately come to mind, and they have been tossed at me by semiliterates and brilliant scholars alike during the past few years. First, with human beings capable of making only a limited number of sounds, there is bound to be an enormous duplication in the pronunciation and/or spelling of place-names in any two given areas on the face of the earth. Second—and it is this objection that makes some etymologists throw up their hands in horror at any comparative study conducted along these lines—there are only a limited number of instances where the meanings of these key names and words are today the same in different parts of the world.

Examining the first objection, I believe it will emerge from these pages that certain simple sounds, no easier to pronounce and in some cases more difficult to pronounce than equally simple sounds, actually do appear in prehistoric, pre-Europeanized place-names far above what the laws of chance, the mathematical possibilities, would call for, while others played relatively insignificant roles. On the second objection, it seems at least plausible that if certain key names and words *were* taken out several thousand years ago from a common point, with the passage of time and the lack of any appreciable communication between areas their original meanings could have been forgotten, changed, or corrupted, while the original sounds, especially in the names of rivers, mountains, lakes, waterfalls, volcanoes, islands, and regions could have survived in reasonably pure forms. This process of forgetting, of change and corruption in meaning, will be traced in some historic instances.

In spite of these two morale-building reflections, and in spite of the fact that a number of reputable scholars have encouraged me in this effort, the chances are I would long since have abandoned the entire undertaking if a second, far more provocative, development had not taken place in the research. It slowly became apparent that some of the most important names and words in question had been subtly blended together within many individual names and had been woven together in combination with one another to form the same names, or astonishingly similar names, in widely separated parts of the world.

This development naturally put a far greater strain on the laws of chance than had the repetition of single sounds or elements. In the majority of cases, two of these elements would appear together, but occasionally three, four, or in a few instances five elements would be blended within a single place-name. Sometimes the order of the elements would be the same from one name to another. At other times they would be reversed or appear in a different sequence. The same key elements also began to turn up in combination within mythological names, personal and tribal names, and in words of unique significance. Some of these appeared so dramatically, in such unexpected areas, that alone they afforded considerable food for speculation.

As the tide grew, as the same blended elements continued to emerge over and over again in all parts of the world, in spite of the fact that recurring waves of doubt engulfed me—and still do engulf me—I gradually became convinced that it was less likely these combinations or blendings had happened *by accident* than that they had resulted from *intelligent design*. The very fact that, according to authorities on both sides of the Atlantic, no one had ever focused attention on these widely separated, often repeated combinations also kept me pushing along the shadowy track that lay ahead.

During the past year another major fact has become apparent. The key names have broken down into two groups on a geographical basis. The names in the first group, which appears to be older, are to be found in *all* parts of the world. Those in the second group are to be found on a more intensified level but in a *limited* portion of the world. This latter set of names permeates the Mediterranean basin, Europe, Africa, and parts of Asia, moves across the Atlantic into the West Indies, into Brazil, and are found along the gulf coast of Central America and up the East Coast of North America. They are not, however, to be found in any significant degree on the continent of North America, in Central America, Mexico, Peru, or Chile. They are also strikingly absent from China and in the Pacific, from and including the Hawaiian Islands.

If one puts a charted overlay containing only the first group of names on top of a map of the world, and then puts on top of that another charted overlay containing only the second group of names, the most logical conclusion is that in prehistoric times instead of one there were two dispersions from the Mediterranean, the first truly worldwide, the second petering out along the eastern coast of the Americas in one direction, in Japan, the Philippines, Australia, and New Zealand in the other direction. Again, there may be a more logical conclusion to be drawn from the data, but if so, I have not been able to think of one. And again, for better or worse, all the key names in *both* groups have prominent origin points in Semitic legends and mythology, as well as in known Semitic place-names.

Last, an additional outside source of encouragement became available. Along the way I discovered that work being done by

highly qualified scholars on a number of different fronts tends
to support my basic premise. Viewed against the backdrop of
this work, some completed in the past, some continuing at the
present moment, the overall conclusions offered up in this book
do not seem as far out to me as they would have seven or eight
years ago. The work has been primarily in the fields of language
(etymology), archaeology, and anthropology. Supplementing
this, on a less scientific level, there exist, in practically all parts
of the world, deep-seated, persistent convictions based on ancient
mythology and folklore that the original settlers, or early visitors,
in many instances the ancestors of the present inhabitants, were
"white" gods, men or supermen, who had arrived "by ship,
from overseas." Since you are undoubtedly approaching what
follows in a spirit of healthy—I trust open-minded—skepticism,
it should be worthwhile before unfolding my own research to
discuss in several chapters some of the highlights, scientific and
legendary, that tend to support a prehistoric dispersion or dispersions of peoples, Semitic or otherwise, from the Mediterranean.

Chapter 2

THE UNTIMELY DEATH of Dr. Morris Swadesh, generally regarded as America's most distinguished etymologist, occurred in the spring of 1968. Formerly of Columbia University, Dr. Swadesh had been engaged for several years before his death at the National University of Mexico in a comparative study in depth between, on one hand, the Aztec and Mayan dialects and, on the other, the Hebrew language. The most recently published summary of this study indicates a relationship of approximately 20 percent between the two native dialects and Hebrew, an extraordinarily high figure in view of the geographic and time factors involved.

Dr. Swadesh's etymological research was only part of a broad continuing project in the fields of archaeology and anthropology being carried on by the New World Foundation of Orinda, California, to establish possible links between Europe and the Americas. To date these studies, according to the foundation, have revealed over five hundred specific examples of cultural similarities between the Mediterranean and the Mexican/Central American part of the world (tribal customs and ceremonies, articles of clothing, household utensils and furnishings, knowledge of the sciences and the arts, with particular emphasis on decorative and architectural details). Dovetailing with Dr. Swadesh's findings, a high percentage of the relationships appear to be of common Semitic origin.

23

These current activities represent a massive, concentrated effort to settle once and for all a question that has puzzled Europeans ever since Cortez led his conquistadores into Mexico. It is an accepted historic fact that one of the reasons, if not the chief reason, for the downfall of Montezuma's well-organized Aztec Empire was the belief held by the natives, rulers and ruled alike, from time immemorial that the founders of their ancient civilization had been "bearded white gods" who had first appeared in sailing ships "from the east." The tradition had been handed down from generation to generation that these strangers, having passed on their wisdom and scientific knowledge to the Mexicans, had departed with the promise that they would someday return.

Montezuma and his people clung until it was too late to the belief that the Spaniards were these same "gods" or their descendants fulfilling their promise to come back. Legends of an almost identical nature proved to be a vital factor in Pizarro's swift conquest of the even more highly developed Inca Empire in Peru. In Mexico the legends concerned primarily Quetzalcoatl, "white-skinned and full-bearded." In Peru, Viracocha was the supreme deity of the Quechua Indians, and *viracocha* is still the Peruvian word for "white man." The Aymara tribe also claimed that their ancestors were white.

Within a matter of months after the subjugation of the Aztecs, Spanish monks who had accompanied Cortez, having set about the task of "Christianizing" the natives, were struck by the vivid similarities between local legends and major episodes contained in the Old Testament. A number of these legends were set down verbatim by the monks. Alfred Maury[1] commented in regard to some of them: "There is scarcely a prominent fact in the opening chapters of the Book of Genesis that cannot be duplicated from the legends of the American nations, and scarcely a custom known to the Jews that does not find its counterpart among the people of the New World. It is a very remarkable

---

[1] "Déluge," *La Encyclopédie moderne* (Paris, 1860).

fact that we find in America, traditions of the Deluge coming nearer to that of the Bible and the Chaldean religion than among any people of the Old World."

In the opinion of Maury and other scholars, the Mexican versions differed less both in expression and in details of events from the earliest known versions than did the European, including the Spanish versions. The "teachers" were unwittingly being "taught" by the "pupils," as later comparative research between texts revealed. Other native legends told of the Garden of Eden, of the expulsion of Adam and Eve, complete to the temptation by a serpent and the sharing of a forbidden fruit. The same familiar legend was also pictorialized in native art that predated the advent of the Spaniards.

Edward King, Viscount Kingsborough, the eighteenth-century explorer and writer, whose ten huge volumes, *Antiquities of Mexico*,[2] first depicted in illustrations and texts the newly discovered Western civilization, was convinced as a result of his research in Mexico that he had come upon a "lost" Hebrew culture. Of another native myth Kingsborough stated that it was "a clearly established legend which singularly resembles the Bible record of the Tower of Babel." The portrayal of this same pre-Columbian legend was acted out by "The Indian Flyers" in front of the Mexican Pavilion at the New York World's Fair some years ago, a breathtaking performance witnessed by over five million spectators and to which *Life* devoted one of its cover stories.

In North America, although they did not play such a fatal role as those in Mexico and Peru, widespread Indian legends told of "white" ancestors and gods, of superhuman visitors and beneficiaries who had first appeared from across the sea to the east. These, too, were recorded by early European missionaries and explorers, and several of them will be discussed in some detail in connection with certain key names and words. The enormous amount of research compiled by Ignatius Donnelly, Republican

[2] London, 1830–1848.

PLATE 1. Mexico: four Huaztec statues. The one second from the right resembles Easter Island images (see Plates 11 and 12), while those on either side bear marked Semitic facial characteristics.

Photo: the Mansell Collection

Congressman from Minnesota in the mid-nineteenth century, has been until recently disregarded by the academic world because Donnelly used it to support in his best-selling book *Atlantis*, first published in 1889, the theory that there had once been a "Lost Continent" between Europe and the Americas. Donnelly, working his way around the entire perimeter of the Atlantic Ocean, spent so much time on his opus at the Smithsonian Institution that the Republican Party finally refused to back his candidacy for reelection. He amassed over six hundred and fifty pieces of evidence tending to support a common origin for Old World and New World cultures. These ranged from language and mythological similarities, through tribal customs and religious beliefs, to a large number of fruits, vegetables, and animals that could have been transported in different directions from a common source during prehistoric times.

Donnelly based his conviction that this common source was a "Lost Continent of Atlantis" primarily on his disbelief that ancient man was capable of crossing long stretches of open ocean by sailing ship and that therefore he could not have reached the Americas from the, Mediterranean. If the evidence herein is valid, then such voyages were made at far earlier dates than has been generally accepted. Aside from the question of whether the Mediterranean or a hypothetical Atlantis was the common point of origin, much of Donnelly's research tends to support the major premise of this book. Dr. Edgerton Sykes, Fellow of the Royal Geographical, Central Asian, and Indian societies speaks in the preface to a new edition of *Atlantis,* published in 1949 and 1962, of "the great influence which he exercised on the thought of the United States in particular and on that of the European culture complex in general."

Predating the work of Dr. Swadesh in Mexico, there were a number of etymological studies that drew comparisons between Hebrew and certain North American Indian dialects. Notably *The American Nations,* by Constantine S. Rafinesque of the University of Pennsylvania,[4] in which vocabulary comparisons were noted between Taino, the West Indian dialect, and Semitic. In addition, A. C. M. Leesberg published, at Leiden, in 1903, a paper, *Comparative Philology: A Comparison Between Semitic and American Languages.*

It has also been intriguing to read reports during the past few years by several etymologists of top rank who, after research covering long periods of time, have claimed to find similarities between, first, what is known of the Etruscan language and native dialects in the West Indies and along the east coast of South America, notably in Surinam; second, between Portuguese personal names and Indian personal names in New England, and, more recently, between Insular Celtic, Welsh and Irish,

[4] Philadelphia, 1836.

and certain North American Indian dialects. Again, these are the kinds of findings one would expect to emerge if one common language *were* taken out during prehistoric times from one point of origin.

Along these same general lines, the most significant work on the European side of the Atlantic is currently being conducted by a small group of embattled but extremely well-positioned authorities spearheaded by Dr. H. H. Wagner, head of Celtic Studies at Queen's University, Belfast, and Dr. Professor Julius Pokorny, who at eighty-five, is still active as Professor Emeritus of Comparative Linguistics at the University of Zurich.

These authorities, following a course first charted at the turn of the century by the Welsh etymologist John Morris-Jones, claim that both English and Insular Celtic share a common substratum that is closely related to the Hamito-Semitic languages, including the Berber dialects and Egyptian, and to Hebrew. This is not a claim that has been greeted with open arms in either England or Ireland. Working more or less in their own vacuums on either side of the Irish Sea, neither Celtophiles nor Anglophiles have been anxious to acknowledge that any significant common bloodstream exists between the traditional adversaries, the Irish and the English, let alone wanting to have anything to do with the Mediterranean or, above all, with the Hebrews. Yet it is no more possible to shrug off the work being done by this group of men than that done by the late Dr. Swadesh in Mexico.

While the bulk of etymologists in both England and Ireland have been standing staunchly by their traditional guns, a large number of British archaeologists and anthropologists, probably a majority of them, have, unlike their Irish compeers, now agreed that at least one broad early bloodstream in England came from the Mediterranean. Without engaging in the controversy as to whether or not they were Semites, they believe that the people who settled in Ireland and Britain about two thousand years before Christ, who planted barley on the southern plains of England and who built Stonehenge, were related culturally and ethnically to the Homeric civilization of Mycenae and Crete. Much of the evidence supporting this view centers upon the two great prehistoric complexes twelve miles apart on the Salisbury Plain in Wiltshire, Avebury and Stonehenge. The workmanship at Stonehenge is itself of primary importance. The lintel stones that lie across the great upright stones are curved to form the overall circle, with each stone tongued and grooved to one another, as well as being jointed with mortise and tenons to the upright stones. This technique is identical to the one employed in the building of the famous Postern Gate at Mycenae, and is found nowhere else in Europe in buildings dating back to this period, approximately 1650 B.C. In addition, the upper ends of the supporting stones are broader than the lower ends. Thus when viewed from the ground they appear to be of the same width from top to bottom.

Dramatically confirming a close relationship between the Homeric civilization and Stonehenge, one of the most important archaeological discoveries ever made in the British Isles took place in 1953. Professor R. J. C. Atkinson observed on one of the inner circle of upright stones, facing directly toward the visitors' entrance, a carved hilt dagger identical to those buried in the shaft graves of Mycenae but again unknown elsewhere in Europe. On the same and adjacent stones are also carved about thirty axheads similar to those manufactured only in Ireland at that period. Further linking the British Isles to the Mediterranean are the large number of faïence beads, made from a composition material similar to glass, that have been found in graves around Stonehenge and Avebury. The trails of these beads, manufactured in both Egypt and Greece, are in themselves tangible clues to the routes taken by prehistoric man out of the Mediterranean basin. The trail leading to the Salisbury Plain proceeds up the west coast of Spain and France to Brittany and to the coasts of both Ireland and England, hence via Dorset to Stonehenge and Avebury. Other trails begin in the eastern Mediterranean and follow the Volga and Ural rivers deep into Siberia and along the Danube into Poland. Another has been traced up

PLATE 2. Wiltshire, England: an aerial view of Stonehenge showing
the extent of the surrounding bank and ditch. Fifty-six circular pits
(white dots), when excavated, were found to contain cremated
bones, some with grave goods. Ditch, bank, and pits date to approximately 1900 B.C.; the inner stones are 100 to 200 years later. Each
massive upright weighs 26 tons.

Photo: Aerofilms Limited

PLATE 3. Wiltshire, England: inner circle at Stonehenge with curved and grooved horizontal lintels. "Myceneaen" hilt dagger discovered in 1953 by Professor R. J. C. Atkinson is on stone 53. The stones are wider at the top than at the bottom, creating the illusion of straight lines when viewed from ground.

Photo: A. F. Kersting

31

PLATE 4. Mycenae, Greece: Postern Gate in north wall of Citadel.
The details of workmanship are as at Stonehenge, both dating to the
same approximate period, and unique in Europe.

Photo: the Mansell Collection

PLATE 5. Mycenae, Greece: Schliemann's Grave Circle (Grave Circle A). Here were found bronze daggers similar to one carved on a stone at Stonehenge. Circular enclosure wall is built of limestone slabs and horizontal cover slabs. The view is from the Lion Gate, looking toward the Gulf of Mauplia.

Photo: the Mansell Collection

the Nile far into Africa. All these routes are pertinent to the
subject at hand.

Dramatic archaeological links between the Mediterranean and
Ireland also exist in the Irish passage graves at Knowth (ex-
cavated four years ago) and New Grange, both on the Boyne
River, which closely resemble in a number of details those at
Mycenae, as well as those on Crete, and in Spain and Portugal.
Far more than words, the visual evidence in Plates 5–7, 15–17,
and 19 points up these similarities. See also Plates 20–22, 26, 27,
39, and 40 for the relationship between Malta and the Aran
Islands.

The die-hard attitude of the Dublin traditionalists toward a
Mediterranean ancestry is especially difficult to understand in
view of material contained in early Irish mythology. Various
legends, in particular the ninth-century *Lebòr Gabala Erenn*,
trace in minute detail the voyages of at least one group of early
Irish from Egypt and Libya to Crete and Sicily, thence to Spain
and on to Ireland. This is not only a journey that parallels the
trail of the faïence beads, but in one chapter, "From Ur to
Ireland," of his fascinating, well-documented book *Gold*,[5]
C. H. V. Sutherland maps out an identical course via crude
mining remains left by ancient explorers from the Mediterranean
whose search for this precious metal led them to the once-rich
deposits in County Wicklow, Ireland. Articles manufactured
from this supply were later not only traded extensively throughout Great Britain and all across the Continent but also back into
the Mediterranean. Sutherland's findings also lead up the Volga,
Ural, and Danube rivers, again following the trails of the faïence
beads.

[5] London: Thames and Hudson, 1959.

PLATE 6. Ireland: Knowth, near New Grange and the Boyne River.
After years of searching, excavations conducted by Dr. George
Eogan in 1968 brought to light the longest passage grave in Europe.
The view is of a passage leading to the burial chamber.
                          Photo: Irish National Monuments Branch

As to how these early wanderers reached Ireland and England, carvings on stones in the British Isles and along the northwest coast of Europe depict ships much like the Viking longboats, complete with crews of as many as thirty men, suggesting lengths of up to seventy feet or more. These carvings have been dated through carbon testing to as early as 2500 B.C. Their prototypes have been traced step by step back to the Mediterranean by Gale Sieveking of the British Museum in his chapter "Migration of the Megaliths" in *Vanished Civilizations of the Ancient World*.[6] In this connection it seems most significant that the first cycle of Irish mythology overflows with tales of long, epic voyages to distant islands across the sea, of great pilots and traders, as well as of demigods highly skilled in the creation of bronze and golden articles. The comparison to the tales of Ulysses and his companions, of Jason and the Argonauts and their search for the Golden Fleece, has been drawn by innumerable authors.

All this is in direct contrast to the second cycle of Irish mythology, the so-called "Heroic" or "Ulster" Cycle, which is agreed to be of Celtic origin. Here the chariot-drawn warriors, fond of individual combat, of boasting and roistering, members of a pastoral, dispersed society, are counterparts of the Celts as depicted on the Continent by Caesar and other classical writers. It is doubtful if the mythology of any people offers such positive evidence that their ancestry was composed of two divergent strains whose habits, customs, and pursuits were at opposite ends of the pole, with the first strain fitting in closely to an overseas, far-ranging, trading pattern.

The scientific carbon testing of archaeological remains has left one major gap in the academic world's former views on prehistory that drastically affects both the British Isles and the Mediterranean. For the past two hundred years, the Phoenicians have served as a convenient grab bag for any voyages or colonies predating the Carthaginians, the Egyptians, the Greeks, or the

[6] London: Thames and Hudson, 1963.

Romans. Any inexplicable ruins or traces of exploratory and trading activities have been more or less automatically credited to this hardy Semitic race. It has now been generally accepted (see *The Encyclopædia Britannica*) that the incredible seafaring era of the Phoenicians did not begin until the twelfth century B.C., that they never came nearer to the tin mines of Cornwall than the tin mines along the west coast of Spain, and that they never established any permanent contact with either Ireland or Great Britain. Without detracting in any way from their later accomplishments, and leaving aside the question of whether or not the Phoenicians' journeys took them across the Atlantic to the Americas, there are a number of important questions that appear to be unanswered.

Chapter 3

THREE MAJOR QUESTIONS raised by the updating of the Phoenicians' maritime activities to the twelfth century B.C. are:

1. The fabulous ruined temples on the island of Malta, with a number of associated Semitic inscriptions, have traditionally been attributed to the Phoenicians. Carbon testing, however, has established that the earliest of these temples date back to approximately five thousand B.C., almost *four thousand years* before the Phoenicians began their epic journeys.[1]

If not the Phoenicians, then what earlier, seafaring Semitic people did build these Maltese temples?

2. A number of specialists on the development of the Greek alphabet, which is accepted as Semitic in origin, are now of the opinion that the Phoenicians, who traditionally have been credited with the passing on of their own alphabet to the Greeks, did not enjoy a sufficiently long cultural stage to have invented such an alphabet, but, rather, that they received their alphabet from an unknown, earlier Semitic people and in turn passed it on with refinements to the Greeks.

The late R. A. Stewart Macalister, Professor of Celtic Archae-

[1] For a summary of pre-Phoenician seafaring activity involving Malta, Sardinia, the Balearic, Lipari, and other islands, see "The Western Mediterranean" in *The Concise Encyclopedia of Archaeology* (London: Hutchinson & Co., 1960), "In Malta, the temple-builders had disappeared by 1400 B.C." (page 312).

PLATE 7. Malta: ruins of Mnajdra. The origin of these great mega-lithic structures on Malta, predating Cnossus and Mycenae, as well as those in Ireland, by several thousand years, remains one of the most puzzling of prehistoric mysteries. Long ascribed to the Phoeni-cians, they now appear to be the work of a much earlier seafaring people.

Photo: the Mansell Collection

ology at University College, Dublin, presented this view in convincing detail during the course of three Schweich Lectures delivered before the British Academy in 1911. They were later published under the title *The Philistines, Their History and Civilization.*[2] Later scholars have amplified and clarified Macalister's opinions.

If this viewpoint is correct, who were these unknown, earlier Semitic people?

Recent archaeological evidence from Byblos on the Lebanese coast and Ras Shamra (ancient Ugarit) on the Syrian coast indicates that the Phoenicians actually employed two alphabets, both Semitic, one, with thirty characters, that did not survive; the other, of twenty-two characters, all consonants, which was the forerunner of the Greek alphabet. The lack of vowels prior to the Greek alphabet becomes of paramount importance in the data presented in subsequent chapters herein. (For a general summary on up-to-date authoritative opinion on the development of the Greek alphabet, from which stemmed the Roman and later European alphabets, see *The Encyclopædia Britannica.*)

3. It has traditionally been claimed that the Semitic owners of the tin mines in Cornwall, who were banished from England in the eleventh century, during a pogrom instituted by Edward the Confessor, but who had controlled and operated these mines since time immemorial, were direct descendants of Phoenician explorers and traders.[3] As mentioned a moment ago, however, it now would seem that the Phoenicians never reached the British Isles.

If this is so, who were the prehistoric, seafaring ancestors of these Semitic owner-operators of the Cornish tin mines banished during the reign of Edward the Confessor?

Interwoven with these three questions are two others that have never been satisfactorily answered:

[2] London: Oxford University Press, 1913.
[3] See *The Sunday Times* (London), September 25th, 1966, "Passport to Cornwall."

4. Who were the mysterious "Sea People," the Akhaiwa, who in the thirteenth century B.C., coming "from the west," created havoc throughout the Mediterranean. They smashed the Hittite Empire, and with the help of Libya almost defeated the Egyptians, releasing their stranglehold on the eastern Mediterranean. They may well have brought Cnossus and Mycenae down in flaming ruin. Did they come from inside the Mediterranean or from outside, and if the latter, from what direction? Were these "Sea People" Semites?

5. What part did the Philistines play in the prehistoric maritime development of the Mediterranean? In the Old Testament, Exodus 23:31, this great inland body of water is referred to as "The Sea of the Philistines," and their gods and coastal strongholds indicate they were once a naval power of awesome stature. Did they ever venture outside the Mediterranean, and in what direction? There is strong evidence from Egyptian inscriptions that the Philistines were allies of the "Sea People" and the Libyans in the attack on Egypt in the thirteenth century B.C. and that subsequently, their days of glory vanished, they settled down as bumptious, restless neighbors of the Israelites, giving their name to Palestine.[4] Throughout the Old Testament they are regarded as fellow Semites by the Israelites.[5]

On all five of these questions (the origin of the prehistoric ruins of Malta and other western Mediterranean islands, the Semitic roots of the Greek alphabet, the presence of early Semites in Cornwall, the roles of the Akhaiwa "Sea People" and the Philistines), the basic premise of this book, that before the Egyptian, Phoenician, Greek, and Carthaginian eras there were two major Semitic migrations or dispersions, will, I believe, shed some revealing light.[6]

[4] See A. R. Burn, *Minoans, Philistines, and Greeks* (London: Routledge, 1930), Chapters V and VI, "Egypt and Sea-Raiders" and "The Great Migrations: About 1210–1190 B.C."

[5] See *Atlas of the Bible*, Father L. H. Grollenberg (London: Thomas Nelson and Sons, 1956).

[6] Cyrus H. Gordon states: "Because scholars call certain people 'Phoenicians,' one can not assume this designation is realistic. Texts from

PLATE 8. Egypt: Temple of Medinet Habu. The mural records scenes of naval battles between the forces of Rameses III and the mysterious "Sea People" who in the thirteen and twelfth centuries B.C., as allies of the Libyans, attacked and nearly destroyed the Egyptian Empire. Known as the Akhaiwa, or Akhiyawa, they obliterated the Kingdom of the Hittites, created havoc throughout the eastern Mediterranean, and may have been responsible for the downfall of Cnossus and Mycenae.

Photo: the Mansell Collection

A word on navigation within the Mediterranean would not
be amiss. A few summers ago I spent a fortnight cruising in
those waters with a friend on board his 130-foot yacht complete with crew of eight. For seventeen hours we headed into
the teeth of a howling storm between the islands of Ponza and
Sardinia, but finally had to alter our course several degrees
until the force of the wind and waves abated. We were never
able to cruise off the west coast of Corsica because of the
weather. At the time my friend, who has been based at an
Italian port for over ten years and who has made two transatlantic round trips in the same yacht, told me that on the
average the weather was worse *inside* than *outside* the Mediterranean. The concept that those ancient navigators who reached
the seabound islands, built the ruins on Malta and elsewhere,
and who, judging from skeletal remains, transported elephants
to Malta, Cyprus, and Crete, were sailing around in sheltered
waters, does not fit the facts in the case.

From a standpoint of archaeological significance the excavation of the Bronze Age ship sunk off Cape Gelidonya, Turkey,
referred to by Cyrus Gordon in his preface, ranks on a
par with Professor Atkinson's discovery of the carved "Mycenaean" dagger at Stonehenge. The evidence gathered in this
laborious underwater excavation, conducted under the leadership
of George Bass,[7] established conclusively that at least as early as
1200 B.C. seafarers from the Syro-Palestinian region were engaged in active trade throughout the eastern Mediterranean.

The metal cargo salvaged from the wreck, first located by
Peter Throckmorton, proved to be "the largest hoard of pre-

Ugarit datable in the Late Bronze Age speak of Tyre and Sidon as old
established Northwest Semitic centers practicing Canaanite religion and
doubtless engaged in their nautical and commercial way of life. My own
researches have convinced me that a wide-ranging, seafaring people
with intercontinental contacts contributed to Mediterranean civilization
by the Middle Bronze Age and perhaps earlier."

[7] For a fuller description of the Gelidonya project and a number of
other monumental sub-marine excavations, see George Fletcher Bass,
Archaeology Under Water (London: Thames and Hudson, 1966). Dr.
Bass is director of the University of Pennsylvania Museum's Underwater
Section.

classical copper and bronze implements ever found in the Aegean area." A major portion was made up of four-handled copper ingots weighing approximately fifty-five pounds each, many stamped with signs in Cypro-Minoan script. (This type of ingot is found most frequently on Cyprus and Sardinia, two islands known to have later been colonized by Phoenicians.)

Bronze implements included hoes, picks, axes, adzes, chisels, knives, bowls, pins, spearheads, a shovel, and a spit. These had been broken up and packed in wicker baskets, apparently to be broken down into new tools and weapons. Other implements recovered indicate that metalworking was actually done aboard ship.

A study of pottery salvaged and other checks established the 1200 B.C. date, while stone balance-pan weights "proved" that the thirty-five-foot ship "could have traded with Egypt, Syria, Palestine, Cyprus, Troy, the Hittite Empire, Crete, and probably the Greek mainland." More detailed evidence "pointed to the Bronze Age ship having sailed from Syria to Cyprus, where it took on a cargo of scrap metal before its last tragic trip westward."

Although only a small amount of wood was preserved, it included "pieces of planks with tree-nails fitted into bored holes, just as in Homer's description of Odysseus [Ulysses]. The interior of the hull was lined with brushwood dunnage, the bark still well preserved, which finally explained the purpose of the brushwood used by Odysseus, a point which has caused Classicists trouble in translation and interpretation."

George Bass sums up: "Canaanite or Phoenicians were responsible for the cargo and the ship, and since there was no indication whatsoever that the ship was Greek or Cypriot, we must conclude that Phoenician sailors roamed the Mediterranean at the time of Odysseus."

Along the way during the past five years it came as a source of encouragement to discover that a great deal of etymological research has been done on two names that appear to bolster some of my own findings. One of these names, involving mythological names, as well as personal, river, and other names, has already forged what many experts look on as a strong chain between Great Britain, Ireland, the archaic Greeks, Egypt, and other lands in the Mediterranean area. The second, centered upon rivers, has forged a second, equally strong, universally accepted chain between Great Britain, Ireland, and the rest of the Indo-European part of the world.

Taking up the first name, Don/Dan, the place-name part of the picture offers no argument. Quoting from *The Concise Oxford Dictionary of English Place-Names*:

"Don is an old river-name, Brit *Dana*, which is related to the name DANUBE and is really an old word for 'water', found in Sanskr *danu*, 'rain, moisture.' "

Ranging from a number of *Don* and other rivers in England, Ireland, Scotland, and Wales through such rivers as the *Don*au (*Dan*ube), the Russian *Don*, the *Dn*ieper and *Dn*eister, the *Dan*, or, more popularly, the Jor*dan*, to the *Dhan*, *Dhon*, *Dhan*siri, and so on, in India, a huge network of rivers, it is agreed, derived their names from a common source. An impressively large group of authorities, notably C. Bonner (*A Study of the Danaid Myth*, Harvard Studies in Classical Philology) and Alwyn and Brinley Rees (*Celtic Heritage*[8]) believe the same Dan/Don element contained in these river names also figures prominently in a number of widely separated mythologies. As a fountainhead for all these legends they point to *Dan*aus, the ancestors of the *Dan*oi who were among the earliest settlers of Greece. Throughout the *Iliad* and the *Odyssey*, Danoi is one of the three regular name choices used.

Danaus is first encountered sharing the throne of Egypt with his half-brother Aegyptus. Driven out of Egypt by Aegyptus, Danaus with his fifty daughters, the Danaides, traveled via Rhodes to the Peloponnesus where he ascended the throne of Argos. These names, which figure so prominently in Mediter-

[8] London: Thames and Hudson, 1961.

ranean mythology, are believed by the Rees brothers, C. Bonner, and others to be closely related to the following names:

In Wales—*Don* is the mother of Aranshod, and the "Children of *Don*" constitute the royal house in Welsh mythology.

In Ireland—*Dan*aan (*Danu, Diann*an) is "the mother of all the Gods." The early settlers of Ireland were called "the children of *Dan*aan," the Tuatha De *Dan*aan, and the "royal House of Munster" was called "the House of *Donn*."

In India—*Danu*, consort of the mighty Asvins and Mitra-varuna, is also "the mother of the gods."

In Scandinavian and Teutonic mythology—*Donar* was the forerunner name for the Great *Thor* (hence our words "thunder" and "Thursday").

In Russia—*Denn*itsa supplants the sun as the wife of Myesyats, the male moon god. An early Russian prayer runs, "In the morning let us arise and pray to God and Dennitsa."

In classical Greek and Roman mythology such names as *Dione*, the mother of Venus; *Diana, Deian*era, the wife of Hercules; *Deione*, daughter of the Cretan Minos; and *Dion*ysus are held to be related or descended from the name *Dan*aus. The similarity between A*don*is in Roman mythology and *Dion* in Irish mythology, both of extraordinary beauty and both slain in youth by wild boars, has been commented on by a number of authors.

As the Rees brothers state somewhat plaintively in *Celtic Heritage*, while no one has convincingly related the names Danaan, Don, Donn, Danaids, Danaus, and Danu philologically to one another, "you will agree there's more than just a vague similarity." Eventually I shall offer what I believe is a possible earlier point of origin for these names than Danaus. In the meantime I have come across the names of two peoples that I find extremely provocative. In Siberia the earliest known inhabitants arrived from the Mongolian plateau in the third century A.D. Quoting *The Encyclopædia Britannica*: "To them must be assigned the remains from the Bronze period which are scattered over Southern Siberia. Iron was unknown to them, but they were expert in bronze, silver and gold work." The descendants of these people, with long, oval faces and fine hair, today live along the Yenissei River near Sumarokovo. They refer to themselves as the *"Din* People." The Navajo Indians in the American Southwest still refer to the former dwellers in their homeland as the *"Din*eh People."

The second major name that encouraged me in terms of what has been learned about it was the Thames river name. Here, unlike the Don/Dan name, nothing significant has been done on the mythological front. Due mainly to the monumental work of the German etymologist, Max Förster, however, who published three theses on the subject,[9] you will today find the following listed in *The Concise Oxford Dictionary of English Place-Names:*

"Thames . . . The name is a Brit river-name, cognate with Sanskr *Tamasa*, the name of a tributary to the Ganges, *tamasá*— 'dark,' Lat *tenebrae* etc. Cf. TAME. The name means 'dark river.' "

At the time when Caesar invaded England in 51 B.C., the Thames was called the *Tamesis*, and was so recorded by Caesar. It has been variously spelled since then—the *Tamesa, Tamensis, Tamisa, Temis*, and *Temes*. Today a gigantic network of Tem/Tam rivers of darkness, companions to the Don/Dan group, wind their way across the face of the Indo-European part of the world. In this case I am later going to offer what I believe was the true source of all these names. Further, I am going to try to convince you that as one of the six key names in a first "worldwide" dispersion from the Mediterranean, the Tem/Tam name, unlike the Don/Dan name, was taken out everywhere and that today it still permeates the mythological and place-name fabric of peoples scattered all over the face of the globe, on tiny, isolated islands as well as on great continents.

[9] *Keltisches Wortgut in Englischen* (Halle, 1921); *Der Flussname Themse und seine Sippe* (Munich, 1941); *Zur Geschichte des Reliquienkultus in Altengland* (Munich, 1943).

Chapter 4

Standing near the edge of the turquoise-blue waters of the Mediterranean in the desolate stretch of the northern Arabian desert, a few thousand years ago one of the most fruitful, lush garden spots on earth, it is almost impossible today to trace the swirling tides of migrations back and forth across the great land areas of Europe, Africa, and Asia. The tides have risen, ebbed, and surged upward again, in some cases beaten against one another. However, thanks to recent archaeological and anthropological discoveries, two gigantic prehistoric treks or movements are indicated.

During the early 1960s, the distinguished French explorer Dr. Henri Lhote conducted two expeditions, the Lhote Mission, into the Hoggar Region of southern Algeria, scene of fabulous prehistoric rock paintings. This mid-Sahara wilderness, like northern Arabia, once too was a fertile, broad pastureland, and the evidence collected by the Lhote expeditions indicates it was inhabited as early as six thousand years before Christ, with families settling down into more or less permanent abodes about 3000 B.C., perhaps earlier. Lhote and his associates believe these ancient people originally came westward, from Arabia, across Egypt and on into the heartland of Africa. Later, some time after 2000 B.C. they were apparently driven out of their homeland by a "Chariot People" from the north, down into southern Africa, into Niger and Nigeria, and in other directions, their white blood mingled today with other darker strains.

Here again, as in the case of Anglophiles and Celtophiles, there are nationalist party liners in such countries as Rhodesia and South Africa who bitterly resist any indications that white men have been in these areas before them. But aside from the highly regarded, objective findings of the French archaeologists, I believe the place-name and tribal-name evidence indicate that *both* Semitic dispersions flooded across the whole African continent thousands of years before Christ, as well as invading it from coastal regions.

Looking southeastward from northern Arabia, it is now generally believed that two great movements took place into India: one from the north, down through Iran and Iraq, and Afghanistan; the second based on the island of Ceylon, fanning out into southern India, a penetration that most likely came from a seafaring people. In Ceylon one picks up a thread that winds in a highly dramatic fashion across thousands of miles of open water. Specialists in the anthropological background of Asia and the Southwest Pacific believe there are strong blood ties between the Vedda culture in Ceylon, the aborigines of Australia, and the Ainu people of the Japanese islands, survivors of a prehistoric "white" Caucausian race. One has only to glance at a map to appreciate what sort of navigational experience must have been involved in such journeys, and the exceptional small-boat skills of the natives in such places as the Maldive Islands, in the islands of Melanesia, off the coasts of Borneo and Tasmania, give further food for speculation whether ancient man traveled more readily and more swiftly by water or by land.

The Ainu people, today mainly herded onto Hokkaido Island in north-central Japan, represent a source of embarrassment to the national authorities, since the Japanese official religion and their mythology teach that when their ancestors first descended from heaven the islands were uninhabited. The evidence is powerful, however, that the Ainus are descended from the so-called early Jomon people whose huge mounds and jade ornaments are

PLATES 9 and 10. Japan: the Ainu people, descendants of an ancient Caucasian "white" race, apparently the earliest inhabitants of Japanese islands. Today dwelling mainly on Hokkaido Island, they are fiercely conservative, and cling to traditional customs, dress, and

religious beliefs centering upon an elaborate Cult of the Bear. On the left, two Ainus exchange formalities as a prelude to negotiating a business transaction. On the right, three neighbors stand by as witnesses to the conference.

Photos: Radio Times Hulton Picture Library

found throughout the islands. Until lately, practically no out-side excavating was allowed at these sites, but now some of the younger Japanese scientists claim that they, as well as the Ainu people, are descended from the Jomon people.

Of particular interest is the early jade ornamentation, since no source of supply has ever been discovered in the islands. The nearest known source is halfway across the USSR, in the Lake Baikal region, within the heart of the Buryat-Mongol Republic. Also worthy of note, when the Ainu people first came under close observation by the Japanese in the late nineteenth century, their religion and to a great extent their entire social life cen-tered upon an elaborate cult of the Bear. This is of special sig-nificance since in Switzerland, the Scandinavian countries, and in Russia the bear since earliest times has occupied a semi-religious, ritualistic position. Among the Ainu each spring a bear cub would be taken alive, raised in captivity until full grown, and then, amid elaborate apologies and assurances that he was being sent to join the spirits of his forefathers, he would be sacrificed and eaten at a great festival.

Examining the various bits of evidence, it seems possible to draw a tenuous thread around the coast of Asia from Ceylon to Australia, from Australia into the Japanese islands, and from there across Russia into Europe. The vast stretches of the Pacific from the Asian mainland to the west coast of Central and South America are also offering up a mounting number of clues that mankind negotiated this journey back and forth, probably in both directions, during prehistoric times.

Of prime importance, pottery found recently in South Amer-ica indicates trading communication and artistic influence be-tween Ecuador and Japan as early as 2,500 years before Christ. The most dramatic, and what may prove to be the most illumi-nating, discovery was made in 1967, that of the Ch'u Silk Manu-script. Originally stolen in 1934 from a tomb in China's Middle Yangtze region, this 2,500-year-old "ragged" piece of "slimy" silk was traded between buyers for thirty years until purchased by the New York psychiatrist and art collector Arthur Sackler. Having since been examined by more than forty leading Sinologists, anthropologists, archaeologists, and art experts, the consensus of opinion is that it may not only unlock the door to much of China's past but will also clarify that country's prehistoric communication with other parts of the world, in particular with South America.

Among twelve creatures pictured along the borders of the manuscript are what appear to be deities with antlers and long, protruding tongues. These are almost identical to symbolic creatures featured in South American art from the same period. Speaking cautiously on the subject, Dr. Douglas Fraser, Columbia Associate Professor of Art History and Archaeology, stated in a news interview in 1968: "This is the first evidence we've had that some of South America's high cultures and civilization developed similarly to that of the Chinese."

It is impossible to pass through this part of the world without drawing attention to the monumental achievements of Thor Heyerdahl, the Norwegian scientist, explorer, and writer who, in addition to his best-selling books *Kon-Tiki* and *Aku-Aku*, has written a number of more specialized anthropological and archaeological pamphlets dealing with the Pacific area. In his most recent book, *Sea Routes to Polynesia*,[1] Heyerdahl presents convincing evidence that the prehistoric Peruvians must have been capable of sailing into the wind, that they made frequent journeys back and forth between the mainland and the islands of the Pacific, a point of vital significance in terms of the key name research which follows.

There are three other landmark books dealing with this part of the world, each of which combines meticulous research with great human interest: Constance Irwin's *Fair Gods and Stone Faces*,[2] Alma Reed's *The Ancient Past of Mexico*,[3] and Eric

[1] London: Allen and Unwin, 1965.
[2] London: W. H. Allen, 1964.
[3] London: Hamlyn, 1966.

de Bisschop's *Tahiti Nui*,[4] in which the author builds a strong case that the primary migrations in the Pacific were from east to west. Miss Reed dwells at considerable length on evidence that indicates that the prehistoric inhabitants of Mexico and Central America were Semites, sharing close cultural and ethnic ties to the Mediterranean. In the aggregate the three books help to explain why the still "officially" accepted viewpoint that the early civilizations of the New World were indigenous has come in for increasingly serious examination.

One of the most fascinating points covered in *Aku-Aku* is that excavations on Easter Island revealed, to quote Heyerdahl, "a clear-cut substratum of two distinct cultural epochs that antedated the final period of unrest and decadence concurring with the late arrival of the present population. Contrary to former suppositions, the history of Easter Island was not a brief explosive bloom of one coherent culture, but a restless exchange of three predeveloped cultural systems ending with complete decay."

Excavations at Easter Island also revealed, contrary to what might have been expected, that the highest architectural developments stemmed from the *first* settlers, "whereas the two subsequent cultural periods yielded superimposed structures of ·entirely different and inferior types." It has also been proved genetically by botanists that Peruvian sweet potatoes, Peruvian cotton species, and Peruvian gourds were transported in the remote past over long stretches of open ocean to various Polynesian islands. The significance of this has been discussed at considerable length by both Heyerdahl and de Bisschop.

Which brings us to a number of products, weapons, animals, and so on, whose shadowy prehistories individually and collectively support the theory that our forgotten ancestors were as courageous, restless, and indomitable in their exploration of this earth as some human beings are proving today in terms of outer space.

London: Collins, 1962.

PLATE 11. Easter Island, South Pacific: statue of the god Hoa-Haka-Nana-Ia, presented to Queen Victoria in 1869. The name Hoa-Haka-Nana-Ia is interpreted in the text as a blending of Hoa/Ok/Ana/Ana/Aya, with Hoa (Hawwah) and Ok as two most important names throughout the world in prehistoric times.

Photo: British Museum

55

PLATES 12 and 13. Easter Island, South Pacific: On the left, an eighteenth-century print shows figure standing on a platform, or *ahu*, of cut, grooved, and polished stones once used for funeral rites. The workmanship is the same as that employed in prehistoric Peru. (See

Plates 32, 33, 36, and 37.) The first settlers arrived already expert in cyclopean masonry. On the right are images outside the crater of the Rano Raraku. Over 400 of these gigantic figures, cut from single blocks of stone, have been found on this lonely island, two thousand miles off the coast of Chile, and about the same distance from the nearest Polynesian island.

Photos: Plate 12, Radio Times Hulton Picture Library;
Plate 13, Paul Popper, Ltd.

Chapter 5

WHILE SEARCHING FOR evidence supporting the theory that mankind sprang from a common point of origin, I was struck time and again by the vast amount of research obviously engaged in by many scholars working in many widely separated fields during the past several centuries. It is possible here only to skim lightly over the surface of this material. Those who would like to study the question in greater depth are strongly recommended to read Kaj Birket-Smith's *The Paths of Culture*.

In terms of fruits that have been enjoyed by the human race on this planet, the banana appears to have been not only the first cultivated species but also the one that was transported the farthest and to the largest number of places. The consensus of opinion is that the name "banana" is African and that it was indigenous to that continent. At the same time, one reads in Alphonse de Candolle's *The History of Cultivated Plants* (Paris, 1883) that in 1563 the explorer de Orta stated flatly, " 'Banana' is the native name in Guiana, on the coast of South America." Yet only thirty-four years later, in 1597, the explorer Antonio Pigafetta declared just as flatly that "banana" was the native name in the Congo. It is difficult to explain how the name could have been on both sides of the Atlantic before historic explorations began unless someone had crossed the ocean bearing the name with them.

Called by the Arabs the *mouz*, the banana became the *musa* in India. Pliny wrote that the soldiers of Alexander encountered it in that country. De Candolle states: "The cultivation of varieties dates in India, in China, and in the Archipelago, Java, Indonesia, etc., from an epoch impossible to realize; it even spread formerly into the islands of the South Pacific and to the West Coast of Africa. Varieties bore distinct names in the most separate Asiatic languages, such as Sanskrit, Chinese and Malay, again indicating great antiquity of culture."

The early worldwide migrations of the boomerang are in their own way as significant as those of the banana. The word comes from the Turuwal tribal language in New South Wales, Australia, but the ingeniously designed instrument, a masterpiece of aerodynamics, is depicted in Semito-Egyptian art of five thousand years ago. Besides its extensive use throughout Australia, it is found today in southern India, and in California and Arizona where certain Indian tribes still kill birds, rabbits, and other small animals with the boomerang.

Another classic argument in favor of the theory that mankind fanned out across the face of the earth from one common origin point is the *chark*. Of great importance in the destiny of mankind, undoubtedly one of the four or five key inventions of all time, the chark consists of a stick, usually made from the straight-grained, hard but elastic ash, with one sharp-pointed end fitted into a hollow in a flat piece of wood. Around the stick two cords are ingeniously wound in opposite directions. By pulling on the ends of the two cords, the stick can be spun back and forth at such speed the friction will set fire to leaves or other dry material placed in the hollow of the board. The chark is still used in such widely separated places as South America, Australia, Sumatra, and among the Veddas in Ceylon (thus linking together two of the ethnic groups mentioned above). Russian explorers found it as standard "household" equipment among tribes on the Kamchatka Peninsula in Siberia, across the Bering Straits from Alaska. It was formerly used throughout North and Central America as well as in South America.

In Hindu mythology the chark appears in a vital symbolic

PLATE 14. North America: a Cherokee Indian making fire with a simplified version of the chark. By twisting a round, pliable stick in the hollow of a flat board, a blaze can be obtained in less than half a minute. A more highly developed form of chark was used in such widely separated regions as Siberia, South America, and India.

Photo: Paul Popper, Ltd.

role. The two warring groups of gods, the Asuras and the Devas, having made a truce, wind the fabled giant snake Sesha around Mount Mandara. The Asuras pull at his head, the Devas at his tail, thus churning the ocean to create the drink of Immortality. The dual relationship of the ash tree and the serpent in mythologies throughout the world may stem from the use of the ash in the chark. The part played by fire, created by the chark, in keeping off snakes at night must have given the wood of this particular tree a special place in the minds and hearts of early man. Pliny advised his readers that if they drew a circle around themselves on the ground with an ash stick, no snake would dare to come within the circle. The identical superstition was prevalent among the North American Indians. As recently as the 1880s, reasonably well-educated white people in the Middle West stoutly maintained that a rattlesnake "would sooner go through fire" than creep over ash leaves or enter into the shade of the ash tree.

In Irish mythology three of the five sacred trees are ash trees. The other two are an oak and a yew. The mother of Phoroneus, the first man in earliest Greek mythology (later Prometheus, credited with stealing fire from heaven), was an ash tree. Norse gods created their first man out of Yggdrasill, an ash tree, and similar legends are told of Catequil, the mighty Thunder God of Peru. Putting ashes on the forehead was a custom prevalent throughout the Eastern world centuries before the Roman Catholics. Since the dawn of history, people have been doing it as a token of repentance, grief, and mourning. The very use of the word "ash" for all charred embers indicates the paramount role of this tree.

Branches of the ash tree were placed over the doors of houses and barns in the British Isles to ward off evil spirits and to keep away the witches and fairies. Young girls in Lancashire wore ash leaves on their breasts at night to learn of their suitors' attentions, and a branch of the ash tree was preferred as a divining rod. In some parts of Cornwall it is still believed a blow with an ash stick will instantly kill a snake, and until the last century Cornish children were passed through holes in ash trees to cure them of hernia. Elsewhere in England ash rods were used to cure diseased sheep, cows, and horses, especially of snakebite. The same practice is common among Swedish peasants.

We come next to one of the earliest known and most widely traded products—ivory. Here again we read that ivory, having been used for sculpture and decoration by the Egyptians from at least as early as 3000 B.C., was introduced to the Greeks by the Phoenicians. The fact, however, that Homer refers to ivory would once more indicate the benefactors of the Greeks were an earlier maritime people. In addition to elephant ivory, the inhabitants of North Africa and the Near East had access in prehistoric times to walrus ivory. Ivory carving became a highly developed art at undetermined dates in India, Burma, Java, Japan, Bali, Sumatra, and Borneo, while in both China and Babylonia it was probably practiced earlier than in Egypt.

The North American Indians also carved in ivory, but a more revealing example in terms of an interhemispheral relationship is represented by the Eskimos. Ivory needle cases of a winged type go back at least a thousand years, and they stem from earlier types. The oldest school featured graceful curves, scrolls, and concentric circles—"many of the concentric circles with incised dots are so accurate they seem hardly traceable without compasses."[1] Experts declare the Eskimo designs to be almost identical to the art as practiced by the Maoris and Melanesians in the South Seas. One cannot look at either school without being reminded of the carved scrollwork found at New Grange in Ireland, which in turn has been compared by specialists to decorations on gold objects unearthed at Mycenae and Crete.

One of the most intriguing threads encountered during the past five years has to do with the Eskimos. A barrister from Winnipeg, Canada, B. Shukett, advised me not too long ago that

[1] *The Encyclopædia Britannica.*

his former rabbi, **Dr. Nathan Cheil**, now located in **New Haven**, Connecticut, knew of startling similarities between Eskimo and Jewish customs. Pursuing this further with Rabbi Cheil, I learned that these similarities had been observed by a number of non-Jewish health officers working with the Eskimos and that they had been described in some detail in 1965 in *The Protagonist*, a well-known Canadian publication. Among a number of facts cited is the practice of the circumcision of Eskimo males.

In the field of weapons one cannot overlook two "pagan" favorites: the bow and arrow and the slingshot. The Cretans traditionally were the inventors of the bow and arrow. These inseparable companions are featured in early art throughout the Mediterranean area, found their way to Japan and the Americas long before the Europeans, and references are common in ancient Irish mythology, which, it should be remembered, developed outside the orbit of classical Greece and Rome. A quiverful of arrows was part of the standard equipment of the prehistoric Irish warrior. A number of specialists have drawn attention to striking similarities between the flint arrowheads and axheads found all over America and in profusion along the Ohio and Mississippi rivers and their tributaries and those found in equal profusion in Ireland.

The slingshot was a special favorite of the Semites, as witness David's destruction of Goliath. The seven hundred warriors of Gilead were trained to use either hand with equal dexterity. The slingshot found its way westward to the Balearic Islands, where the natives customarily carried three slings, one for long dis-

(See pages 64–65)
PLATE 15. Ireland: burial chamber at New Grange. Built approximately 1,000 years before the "Treasury of Atreus," the same beehive overlapping technique was employed in the construction of the roof. The chamber is also characteristic of similar structures in Crete, Spain, and Portugal.

Photo: Irish National Monuments Branch

PLATE 16. Malta: Temple of Hal Tarxien, circa 4000 B.C. In addition to the megalithic construction, note spiral design (center), as in Plate 15 at New Grange, Ireland. Also, the loose-stone wall in the background is characteristic of prehistoric ruins on the Aran Islands off the Irish west coast. See also plates 19, 20, 21, and 22.

Photo: the Mansell Collection

PLATE 17. Mycenae, Greece: burial chamber in the "Treasury of Atreus"; the interior view of the roof shows overlapping circular courses of stones. Projecting edges were cut away to provide smooth surfaces.

Photo: the Mansell Collection

tances, worn as a girdle around the waist; a shorter one worn as
a headband for middle-distance shooting; and a third, even
shorter one, carried in the hand in case of sudden attack. There
is a fascinating link between the name Balearic and that of Balor,
the awesome Irish giant who was slain by a slingball shot through
his huge single eye. The early Irish legends are full of descriptions of slingballs thudding against the shields of the warriors,
of brain balls—a mixture of lime, magic potions, and the brains
of slain enemies. King Conchobar died from the effects of a
slingball lodged in his head for seven years. The Irish countryside is covered with round slingballs ranging in size from prunes
to grapefruits, but on the Continent similar ammunition has
been found only along the coast of Brittany, and the consensus
of opinion is they were brought there by sea. Another telltale
path leads from place to place and side by side with the trail of
the faïence beads.

On the ornithological front it is worth reflecting a moment
on the cuckoo. Closely associated with the oak tree and the
mistletoe, both ancient symbols of fertility, the cuckoo was
regarded from earliest pagan times in England, Ireland, Scotland,
and Wales as a sacred bird. In remote parts of the British Isles
young children still dress in masquerade on St. Stephen's Day,
the day after Christmas, and go out in bands to "hunt the cuckoo." The same bird was held sacred in India, Malaysia, Japan,
Australia, and in other outlying corners of the earth. Its name,
possibly based on the sound it makes, appears closely related
throughout—in Old English, *cuccuk;* in Latin, *cuculus;* in Sanskrit, *kokila;* in India, Malaya, and Australia, *koel.*

There are two primary sources of food that in close relationship to each other have played enormous roles in our prehistory
and history, the pig and barley, both originally called in English
by the same name—*bar.* What is known about the pig and barley
indicates that our prehistoric ancestors were exploring and trading along the waterways of the world thousands of years before
the conventional dates that have been engrained in our minds
since childhood.

Chapter 6

THERE IS NO pig on the face of the earth today that does not have in its veins some strain of Chinese blood. At an unknown date, someone took the Chinese pig from Asia to Europe and crossed it with the European boar, thus producing the common pig. Or else brought the European boar to China and crossed it there with the Chinese pig. A bit more likely, in view of certain evidence, is that the marriage may have been arranged and consummated at a convenient place along this seven-thousand-mile route.

The pig, or *bar*, was introduced into the British Isles about 2000 B.C., and until the advent of Christianity it was there regarded as a sacred animal. It was forbidden to eat him until he had been castrated, an operation that was performed with elaborate, semireligious ceremony, after which he was called a "barrow," the same name used for the prehistoric graves of Britain. The fact that the "bier" on which the body of a dead person was laid was also called a *bar*, and that the board on which religious ceremonies and sacrifices were performed was also called a *bar*, gives an inkling of the high regard in which the pig was held. The bringing in of the "boar's" head at Christmas feasts is a carryover from those pagan times.

Although the pig was indigenous only to China, wherever European explorers sailed during the past five centuries they discovered that someone had brought pigs there before them. In some cases the pigs were still there, while the former residents had moved on or died off. Pigs were members of the welcoming committees in the Canary Islands, in Bermuda, Barbados, Puerto Rico (once Boriquén), and other West Indian islands, in the Americas, and all through the distant islands of the Pacific Ocean. On many isolated outposts the slaying, serving, and eating of the pig was, and in many cases still is, an occasion for festivities and elaborate ceremony, often religious in nature. One senses this in Hawaiian, Tahitian, and other pork dishes or recipes, with their specially concocted sauces, their combinations of pineapples and other exotic fruits. The pig was hardly a part of one's daily fare.

Barley was first thought to have been indigenous only to the dry lands of southwestern Asia, but further research points toward southeastern Asia. It was also very likely indigenous to the uplands of Ethiopia or may have been successfully transplanted there at an extremely early date. *In the beginning barley grew at no other known places in the world.* What is believed to be the oldest of all clay tablets, dating back nearly eight thousand years in Babylonia, depicts a priest preparing barley for brewing. Someone introduced the grain about five thousand years ago into Switzerland. A thousand years later barley was brought into Britain by the same people who brought the pig with them. Barley, too, was held to be a sacred product.

Just to the west of Stonehenge, linking that shattered edifice to barley and in turn to the pig, are four villages within a twenty-five-mile area that must have once been a single huge area devoted to the cultivation of barley. Their names—*Ber*wick Bassett, *Ber*wick St. John, *Ber*wick St. James, *Ber*wick St. Leonard (saintly appendages are often a dead giveaway that places were former centers of pagan activity)—mean literally "barley villages." The religious aspects of barley carried over into Christian times, with the monks supervising the tending of the grain and the brewing of the beer.

The key fact that barley was not introduced into China proper until 2000 B.C., the same time it was brought into Britain, strengthens the view that somewhere between China and the

Mediterranean there must have been a stepping-stone, an "overseas colony," that played a highly strategic part in the development and trading of both *bars*, barley and the pig—in other words, a cultural unit that had established a two-way contact between China and the Middle East. A considerable amount of evidence tends to support the island of Borneo as the center for such prehistoric activity. In the first recorded mention of Borneo, Ptolemy referred to it as "The Island of Barley." Placed off the corner of Southeast Asia, favored by monsoon and sailing winds, with a temperate climate and surrounded by navigable straits, Borneo is in an ideal situation for trade in both directions. As an additional attraction, gold was Borneo's principal export until the turn of this century, and it is still being mined at Bau. Hornbill ivory and other products indicate there has been an enormous amount of trade with China and elsewhere, stretching far back into the past.

Archaeological excavations beginning in 1947, including two expeditions sent out by Oxford University, have revealed that the whole island was once a single, highly integrated entity. The classic site to date is the great cave at Niah in western Borneo. Here a splendid set of wall drawings has been discovered with decorations showing the journey of a "ship of the dead" to the spirit world. Underneath the drawings on the stone floor of the cave, more than a hundred feet above the level of the valley, exquisitely carved model ships, which had been used as coffins, were also discovered. The relationship to the same type of ships of the dead that figured so prominently in the religion of the Egyptians and other neighboring Semitic peoples appears obvious. These are believed to have originated among the older Barabra tribes in the adjacent Nubian Valley of North Africa.

At the exact opposite end of the barley trail, in the last outpost of western Europe, in Ireland, an ancient ceremony was performed until the last half century that seems most relevant to those ships of the dead in Borneo and North Africa. Irish legends are full of descriptions of "voyages of the dead," and the most ribald part of the celebrated two-day and three-day wakes in rural areas was called "The Building of the Ship." A survival from pagan times, this was the portion of the wakes first eliminated after long and persistent effort by the Roman Catholic parish priests.

Further exploration and excavation in Borneo has revealed evidence of former large populations in the hitherto inaccessible uplands, long stone houses used for communal dwelling, traces of prehistoric grain cultivation, and hordes of wild pigs. These findings dovetail with the ancient myths of the lowland people that at one time their ancestors lived in the cooler, more productive uplands. Government plans are presently under way to repopulate these areas with families from the crowded lowlands.

Reflecting on barley and pigs, on long, hazardous sea voyages by ancient mariners from the Mediterranean, and on Ptolemy's reference to Borneo as "The Island of Barley," I am caught up by the lines from the *Odyssey* that describe Circe, the enchantress, whose name foreshadows Ceres, the Roman goddess, and our word "cereal," trapping the companions of Ulysses in her snare:

> "Inside she sat them on chairs, both
>   reclining and straight,
>   and mixed them a potion of Pramian wine
>   In which she mixed grated cheese, *barley* meal,
>   Yellow honey and a doze of her miserable drugs,
>   That they might completely forget their own country.
>   When she had served them the potion
>   and they
>   Had downed it, Circe, without more ado,
>   smote them all with her wand and
>   penned them up in the *pig* styes.
>   And sure enough they had the heads and bodies,
>   Bristles and voices of swine
>   But their minds were as human as ever."[1]

*   *   *

[1] Andrew Lang translation. Italics added.

And now, as a last prelude to what follows, I shall have to explain one process followed in arriving at certain conclusions. During the past two years I woke up to the fact that the mortality of initial vowels in many place-names and words had completely changed the original sense or meaning of those names and words. Further, I finally became convinced that this mortality, over the centuries and indiscriminately in every part of the world, was more the rule than the exception, that more names and words had lost initial vowels than had retained them. In order to prepare you for what is coming, and to show you what I mean, here are a few examples chosen from a wide assortment of times and places:

The Plain of Sharon, the fertile coastal area in ancient Palestine, had previously been called the Plain of Asharon. As Sharon, during historic times and by known, established channels, the name has been planted in many parts of the world. Any relationship to the name Asharon has been lost and forgotten.

Mount Carmel, or Mount Karmel, the mountain in northwest Israel, was once Mount Akkarmel. As Mount Carmel or Karmel, this name has also been bestowed on many communities during historic times and by known, established channels. Any relationship to Akkarmel has been lost.[2]

Of the five place-names I have come across in the Old Testament that in early times began with *Adam*, one site has been lost track of. Here is what has happened to the names of the other four:

Adami-nekeb was located in the Naphtali territory. Today it is Kn. ed-*Dam*iyeh.

Adam, or *Adom*, was the city on the bank of the Jordan where the waters were held back for the miraculous crossing. Today it is called Tell ed-*Dam*iyeh.

The *Adhaman* az Zaur watercourse in Iraq is today the *Damin* az Zawr watercourse.

[2] Cyrus H. Gordon notes that Asharon (Hebrew *hassārôn*) and Akkarmel (Hebrew *hakkarmel*) meant "*The* Sharon" and "*The* Carmel," as in the present-day "*The* Hague."

*Adam*ahi in Jordan has become *Dam*iya. In all four cases an initial *A* has been lost.

There is some evidence that even in biblical times, judging from certain extant place-names, the city of *Dam*as, *Dam*uz, Romanized into *Dam*ascus, believed to be the oldest continuously occupied site in the world, had *already* been shorn of an initial *A* and that it had earlier been called *Adam*as.

The El *Ouar Ouadi* (watercourse) in Syria during the past decade or so has had its name changed to the *Wa'r Wadi*. A *Ha*. initial sound or syllable, having apparently been lost in the pronunciation, has been removed from the spelling.

Otaheite is a name that may look unfamiliar to you. It is the way the name of the island of Tahiti in the South Pacific was spelled until the last century. The *O* in front has disappeared.

Ototeman is what the Ojibwa Indians called their "emblem of a family, clan or group." The white men not only knocked off the preceding *o*, but trimmed off the *an* ending. Today *ototeman* equals "totem" (pole).

In a move comparable to what recently happened to the El *Ouar Ouadi/Wa'r Wadi* (watercourse) in Syria, the *Oua*chita River in the Midwest is now given an alternate spelling, the Washita River, corresponding to the present pronunciation. The *Oua*chita Mountains, *Oua*chita Falls, and the city of *Oua*chita have long since been billed as *Wi*chita.

Shortly after the first European explorers arrived in North America, a group found themselves standing one day on the banks of the Awabasha River. Today they are the banks of the Wabash far away. An *a* has disappeared fore and aft.

The residents of Tascosa, Texas, have probably forgotten that their hometown was once called *A*tascosa. There is still, however, another town in Texas called Atascosa.

If someone asked you if you had ever seen an *arakunem* you might answer No. But that is what the Algonquin Indians called a raccoon. Only the middle part of the name has been preserved. "Raccoon" has evolved out of *rakun*.

These few examples out of hundreds should register the point. Internal vowels appearing and disappearing do not offer so much of a problem, but where they were positioned, and which vowels were selected by the first classical recorders of names, have resulted in some obvious blunders. To cite just one example:

Tarifa is the town in Spain closest to Africa. It was the first port taken by the Moors, and the last one they gave up. Because of duties on goods shipped through Tarifa, our word "tariff" evolved. Twenty miles north of Tarifa, on the Atlantic coast, is a place-name that, thanks to a great naval victory and a celebrated public square, has become forever England's—Cape Trafalgar.

The word "tariff" and the name Trafalgar would appear to have no relationship to each other, yet, examining the two place-names Tarifa and Trafalgar more closely, it would appear that someone at some point had failed to put a vowel between the *T* and the *r* in the second of the two names, that they should be:

    Tarifa
        and
    Tarifa-lgar;
or, conversely:
    Trafa
        and
    Trafalgar.

In other words, two names twenty miles apart that seem to have come from one common origin have lost all relationship to each other—to such a degree that as far as I could discover, while staying in this part of Spain recently, no one has ever focused attention on the similarity. Certain other such errors, some of paramount importance, will be examined in due course.

While the temptation to insert, remove, and change vowels indiscriminately in names and words has been at times overwhelming, I have tried to hold the process within bounds. I believe the reader will agree, however, that in a number of instances the experiment paid off in rich dividends. In fact, more than any other single factor, it was this simple procedure that eventually unlocked the doorway to our past.

Chapter 7

Cry "Havoc!" and let slip the dogs of war.
Julius Caesar, III, i

I NOW BELIEVE the most important word in the English language is "havoc," best known for its usage by Shakespeare in the above immortal line. Originally "havoc" was not a single word but two words or two *names*, Haue and Oc. In one of its earliest recorded usages a thirteenth-century writer refers to Haue and Oc as *Godys* (Gods), so that apparently seven hundred years ago they were thought to have been two forgotten pagan deities. The two names eventually became joined into one word, *hauoke* or *hauoc*; next by a more or less standard Greek/Latin change from *w* to *v*, into *havok*. And finally into the present accepted form "havoc."

"Haue Oc!" was a cry sounded on the battlefields of Britain after victory. It signaled that the fighting was over; the time for pillaging had arrived. In this context it would appear the warriors were offering up a shout of thanksgiving to two gods, Haue and Oc, who had helped them win the day.

Without straining, these two names would seem to fit the two most impressive, most mysterious prehistoric monuments in Europe—if not in the world—Stonehenge and, sixteen miles

PLATE 18. Wiltshire, England: Avebury, monolithic stones erected in three circles around the Sacred Enclosure. These, in the outer circle, some weighing over ninety tons, compose the largest stone circle in the world. Sixteen miles from Stonehenge, Avebury dates back to an earlier period.

Photo: A. F. Kersting

north-northwest of Stonehenge, the largest circle of upright stone pillars in existence, on which the village of Avebury has been built. Before the village, or *bury*, was erected on the gigantic ruins, a process that unfortunately involved the removal and use of some of the upright stones, the site was called plain Ave.

This name has been attributed to an "unknown woman named Afa"; but before the same standardization process that changed Haue into Hava in "havoc" took place at Avebury, the name of the site would have been identical to Haue. The exact same element appears in the word "*hav*oc" and in *Ave*bury. There is no etymological argument on this score, only the question of whether the same person or deity is referred to in both instances. There is a second related Ava/Haue name in the local picture. The so-called East *Avon* River flows across Salisbury Plain within a few miles of both Avebury and Stonehenge. The name Avon is pre–Anglo-Saxon. It means generically "water," and is found in a number of other river names, including the Ive, which etymologically is identical to Ave and which will come back into the spotlight again.

The possible relationship between the Ave in *Ave*bury and the Haue/Hav in "*hav*oc" appears more logical when one examines certain other place names in the immediate vicinity of Avebury and Stonehenge, an area unique in Britain as far as prehistoric remains are concerned.

There are in this area, between the Thames and a few miles south of Stonehenge, six place names which feature as their key element: Oc, the second element in "hav*oc*." The fact that "Haue" and "Oc", those ancient "godys", are both found in such a region seems more significant than if only one were found. To trace these names it is necessary to turn from *The Times Index-Gazetteer of the World* with its 345,000 place names to Bartholomew's *Gazetteer of the British Isles*, the most complete and accurate of all British gazetteers. Here one finds:

Ogbourne, railway station, four miles north of Marl-borough. (Marlborough is six miles east of Avebury, stand-ing on Marlborough Downs. "All over the downs," states Bartholomew's Gazetteer, "are numerous standing stones, earthworks and other ancient remains.")

*Og*bourne St. Andrew, parish and village, two miles south-west of Ogbourne station.

*Og*bourne St. George, parish and village, one mile south of Ogbourne station.

These Ogbourne villages were listed in the twelfth century Domesday Book, the first English "census," as *Och*bourne. (The 'bourne' element stems from the Bourne river in the vicinity.) During the past eight centuries the first element has been alternately spelled *Og* or *Och*. As is true throughout England, Ireland, Scotland and Wales, in place names Og, Och, Ock, Ok, Oc, etc. are synonymous and interchangeable.[1]

As in the case of the Berwick names some twenty miles west of Avebury (see page 70) it would seem as though these three surviving Og-Bourne place names once embraced a single area of several miles dedicated or named after some one personage or deity. It is amusing to observe again the saintly appendages, which are supplemented close by with two parishes named Marlborough St. Mary the Virgin, and Marlborough St. Peter and St. Paul.

Continuing with the Og/Och place names:

The *Og* river. This is a tributary to the Kennet river at Marlborough. The Kennet flows into the Thames at Reading.

The *Ock* river. Nine miles north of Marlborough at Compton Beauchamps this river, bearing a name synony-mous to the Og river, rises and flows eighteen miles north-east, entering the Thames at Abingdon.

[1] See *The Concise Oxford Dictionary of English Place-Names.*

*Og*bury Camp. Less than three miles south of Stonehenge is one of the oldest and largest prehistoric sites in Britain. It is more than a mile in circuit, covering sixty acres. The ramparts are thirty-three feet high. Its name has disappeared from most standard archaeological works but it is in Bartholomew's Gazetteer. Visiting the site several years ago I found it has blended to such a degree into the surrounding countryside it has been all but forgotten even by the local inhabitants. Its name since the beginning of the historic period has been Ogbury Camp.

Before there was a village, a bury on the site, the name would have been, as in the case of Ave-bury, just plain Og. Or alternately, on the basis of the evidence from the Ogbourne place names, just plain Oc. As one studies the unique region which includes both Stonehenge and Avebury and is encompassed by these Og/Oc names, an area of about twenty-five or thirty miles from the Ock river to Ogbury Camp, it is tempting to speculate that there may be a relationship to "Haue Oc". Havoc.

The temptation increases when one discovers, as I did in the course of this research, that according to Judaeo-Christian mythology and tradition, including related Biblical references, the only other "human" survivor of the Great Deluge besides Noah and his family was named Og. Before examining this legendary creature, today all but obliterated from our collective memories, it might be worthwhile to review some of the names that could serve as connecting links between the above English names and the antediluvian Og. A most intriguing starting place looms on the scene across the Irish Sea.

Chapter 8

Place-names often afford far earlier references
for words than those found in literature.
The Concise Oxford Dictionary
of English Place-Names

IN IRISH MYTHOLOGY the supreme rulership of the universe is
taken over by Oc, the In mac Oc. Oc gains possession of the
whole world from his father and half brother Eochaid Ollathair,
the "All-Father," who is known also as the Dagda. These two
half brothers, Oc and Eochaid Ollathair, have another half
brother, Ogma, who through a somewhat incestuous series of
events is at the same time the grandson of Eochaid Ollathair
and the nephew of Oc. Although the personalities of Oc and
Ogma are frequently interwoven, Ogma is the invincible champion of the children of the goddess Danaan, the Tuatha De
Danaan, and it is he who bestows upon them Ogham, the only
inscribed language known to have existed in prehistoric Great
Britain and Ireland. Although three-quarters of the celebrated
Ogham stones have been found in Munster, the southwestern-
most and earliest inhabited Irish province, others have been
found elsewhere in Ireland, in England, Scotland, and Wales.

These two male deities Oc and Ogma finally stand alone at
the pinnacle of power in Irish mythology, as Eochaid Ollathair,

the Dagda, slowly vanishes from the stage. Oc and Ogma are accompanied by their half sister Brigid. The fact that the Romans during their occupation of Britain (they never reached Ireland) discovered memorials to Brigid in England indicates that in the dim prehistoric past Oc and Ogma must havè been held in high reverence by the Britons also.

On the west coast of Ireland, on the side away from England, are the ruins of two mighty prehistoric forts that in their own way are regarded by archaeologists as being equal in importance to Stonehenge and Avebury. They are both on the largest of the fabled Aran Islands a few miles off the Galway coast, and they too both bear Oc/Og names. One of the two principal sites, named Oghil Fort, is presently in sad need of repair despite a campaign headed by Mr. Ian Blake of Balliol College, Oxford. Within its two sets of ramparts, the inner one terraced, are ruined clochans (beehive-shaped stone cells) and huts, with just outside the ramparts pillar-stones, holy wells, ring forts, chambered mounds, and galley graves. Less than a half mile away, a part of the first site, is Oghil Village, notable for a number of curious stone "beds" that are today ascribed to Christian saints and popular figures from Irish folklore but that actually date back to pagan times.

The second site is even more impressive. It covers eleven acres with three massive sets of walls, the terraced inner set built in three sections over twelve feet thick and still over eighteen feet high. The outer part is higher than the inner, affording protection to the defenders, a remarkable feature for such an early structure, as is a jagged abatis of limestone rock along the top of the middle wall. A century ago there was no record of a name for this site. Finally an old resident of the island was found who remembered. It was Dun (Fort) Aongus. And Aongus is an accepted epithet or synonym for Oc.

Not far north of the Aran Islands, closer to land, is Achill Island, another prehistoric treasure house. The evidence from scores of place-names not only in Ireland but also in Scotland, Wales, and England proves conclusively that Ach and Oc have

PLATE 19. Aran Islands: Oghil Fort on Inishmore, largest of the islands. Interior view of the ramparts, looking out across Galway Bay. In nearby Oghil Village remains of curious stone "beds" exist that figure prominently in the text.

Photo: Irish Tourist Board

PLATE 20. Aran Islands: Dun Aengus, on Inishmore Island, covers over 11 acres, with three sets of massive walls. The terraced inner wall, built in three sections, with a total thickness of 12 feet, today is still more than 18 feet high. Its similarity to Maltese construction (Plate 16) is striking, its origin as much of a mystery.

Photo: Irish Tourist Board

been and still are interchangeable and identical, with both Ach and Oc interchangeable with and identical to Og. This raises the question of the most puzzling sentence in Irish mythology— a statement that predicts that the world will not end, nor will an age end, until "Ogham and Achu mix together and the sun and the moon mix together."

I have discussed this with a number of top Irish-language scholars on both sides of the Atlantic, and while there is no problem as to the Ogham reference, there is not the slightest clue as to what is meant by Achu. Later, in Greece, I came upon evidence that seemed to shed light on this puzzle.

Two of the most celebrated sites in Ireland combine within their own names the same two names originally making up the word "havoc"—Haue and Oc. The first is in the east, where three rivers meet close by the Wicklow gold mines, which were of such immense importance during Europe's Bronze Age. It is the Vale of *Avoca*. No accepted source point for this name has ever been discovered.

In the west, in County Mayo, is the most sacred of all Irish pilgrimage points, visited each year by thousands of devout Catholics who make the ascent to its top, Croagh Patrick. This mountain, the very heart site of St. Patrick's conversion of the Irish to Christianity, still overflowing with pagan ruins, is located within the parish of Aughaval. Since Augh, on the basis of the recorded alternate spellings of scores of place-names, is conclusively interchangeable and identical with Og, one finds here Og and Ava, as at Ogbury and Avebury on the Salisbury Plain, but in the reverse order to Haue (later Hava) and Oc in the earliest form of "havoc."

That a long, concentrated, and most successful effort has been made during the past fifteen hundred years of the Christian era to erase from peoples' minds the memory of Oc/Og is perhaps best illustrated by what has happened to a number of place-names around the coastline of Britain. When the Romans invaded England the stronghold of Druidic power was at Mona in Anglesey. It was centuries after Caesar's first invasion before

PLATE 21. Aran Islands: northwest fortifications of Dun Aengus (or Oengus). The author believes that the two names Oghil and Dun Aengus, or Dun Oc, provide a key link between Stonehenge and the Mediterranean, featuring a Semitic name that was taken across the entire surface of the globe in prehistoric times.

Photo: Irish Tourist Board

PLATE 22. Aran Islands: view of Dun Aengus on the ocean side, with a sheer drop of 300 feet to the water below. Its location, plus architectural sophistications unique at the time (circa 2000-2500 B.C.), including a stone cheval-de-frise, point toward a Mediterranean origin.

Photo: Irish Tourist Board

PLATES 23 and 24. Ireland: Croagh Patrick, most sacred of all Irish points of pilgrimage. Located in Aughaval Parish, County Mayo, the ruins indicate that it was equally venerated in pagan times. The earlier mythological name Cruachan Oigle is extremely pertinent to

the theme of *The Key*. On the left is the narrow, tortuous path to the summit, looking out across Clew Bay, an ascent made by thousands each year. On the right are pilgrims returning to the starting point by Aghower Church, with Croagh Patrick in the background.

Photos: Irish Tourist Board

the legions of Claudius in bloody hand-to-hand battle finally
smashed Mona and set it to the torch. Mona was situated on
the Menai Straits, and today the Ogwen River still flows swiftly
from Llyn Ogwen over the Falls of Ogwen into the Menai
Straits. Since Roman times, however, four of the most important
landmarks in Great Britain have been given respectable Christian
names. In each case the earlier names were recorded by the
Romans:

> Octapitarum, a promontory in Wales, has become St.
> David's Land.
> Ocrinum in Cornwall is today St. Michael's Mount.
> Octopitarum in Pembrokeshire is also now known as St.
> David's Land.
> And the large peninsular area in Yorkshire, which we call
> Holderness, two thousand years ago was Ocellum.

Surveying the overall place-name situation as it still exists, it
would seem that in pagan times Oc/Og must have been as
popular a place-name element in England, Ireland, Scotland, and
Wales as St. and San are today in some Roman Catholic countries. There are also three major words still in the Irish language
which cannot be overlooked:

Oc—Youth
Eag—Death
Aegean—the Ocean

The last two are standard variations in the place-name spellings of Og/Oc. Aegean looks suspiciously like a Greek transplant from the Aegean Sea, but I believe it will turn out to be
otherwise. Looking back at the sentence that begins this chapter,
"Place-names often afford far earlier references for words than
those found in literature," there are several cornerstone English
words that seem to be pertinent:

"oak":

Oakham was Ochham in 1067.

Oakford was Ocford in 1224.

Great and Little Oak were Ocle in 1038.

Hucclecote in Gloucestershire was Hochilicote in the Domesday Book.

Okeford: its various spellings over the centuries—Acford, Acheford, Ocford—illustrate the interchangeable nature of these spellings.

Those Oc place-names in England are ascribed variously to such unknown persons as Occa, Hoca, Aki ("Aki is a common old Scandinavian name"), Hucel ("A personal name Hucel or Hucela must be assumed"); and in many instances the presence of oak trees is noted.[1] And yet the presence of Oc in Haue Oc ("havoc"), the predominance of the Oc/Og names around Stonehenge and in the two great forts on the Aran Islands, Oghil Fort and Dun Aongus, or Oc, the unique status of Aughaval Parish in Ireland as a pagan and Christian religious center, the unrivaled position of Oc, the supreme ruler of the universe, in Irish mythology—the combined weight of all these factors inclines me to the opinion that the sacred oak tree, the age-old symbol of fertility with its acorn, whose leaves today are still worn in memory of the past on the British officer's uniform, took its name from a deity, rather than emerging magically out of a mass of unknown and inconsequential elements.

"egg" (once *aeg* and *aig*):

Egg Buckland in Devon was first recorded in 1221 as Eckebokeland. The fact that Eckington in Sussex was spelled Achintone in the Domesday Book and that Ach is synonymous with Oc (see Okeford above) means that Egg in Egg Buckland evolved from an Oc/Og beginning.

Egbrough in Yorkshire was Acheburg in the Domesday Book.

Aighton, Lancashire, was Acton (see Okeford above) in

---

[1] Both quotations are from *The Concise Oxford Dictionary of English Place-Names*.

the Domesday Book, *aig* being an earlier form of "egg," as from the chicken.

Eccles in Kent was Aiglessa in the Domesday Book.

Here again, if Aeg/Aig/Egg place-names have evolved from Oc/Og place-names, then it would seem logical that the word "egg" (earlier *aeg* and *aig*) for the most fundamental of all fertility symbols may well have evolved from the name of the Irish pagan deity or deities, for the personage honored at Stonehenge—Oc/Og. The presence of similar place-names in Ireland, Scotland, and Wales, outside the Anglo-Saxon orbit—note among others Eigg Island and Eigg Sound in Scotland—would strengthen the possibility of such an origin.

"ox":

Ocstead. In 1225 there was an Ocstead in Surrey. Today it is spelled Oxted. Which came first, the name of the deity, Oc, or the name of the most powerful of farm animals, the ox? The Ox Mountains in Mayo are most pertinent here, remote from Anglo-Saxon influence.

Ockeschete. Over seven hundred years ago, Ockeschete in Surrey was a small village. It is now Oxshott. Along the way it was also Oggesett, a switch from Oc to Og, confirming the dual identity of the two names, which leads to the next basic English word:

"hog":

Ockeschete many centuries ago was also spelled Hoggesete.

Ogle in Northumberland was spelled Hoggel in 1170. Seventy-two years later it was Ogghill. The dropping and adding of *h*'s will turn out to be a timeless global habit not confined to the English lower classes.

Such Irish place-names as Hog Head, Hog Island, the Seven Hogs heighten speculation as to whether this sacred animal, the hog, synonymous with the *bar*, derived its name from the deified Oc/Og source.

Perhaps most significant of all, the earliest form of "hog"

is found in the Welsh language. It was *hwch*. Here, by adding vowels that are notoriously absent from Welsh names and words, one ends up with *hawach*, *hawock*, an etymological combination identical to the Haue Oc in "havoc." Over the centuries the preceding *haw* was lost, ending up with the *hog* or *hoc* sound alone.

There is one additional major facet of the Oc/Og picture in Great Britain and Ireland that by its conspicuous absence from our history books throws the spotlight once more on the question of whether or not there has been a long-term, concentrated, highly successful campaign to blot out from peoples' minds all memory of Oc/Og.

Chapter 9

An *Oc!* and a *Wah!* to you.

STANDING STRAIGHT UP against the ice-cold blue horizon above the Isle of Skye is a ninety-foot-high natural pillar of solid stone. Its phallic symbolism is immediately apparent even to the purest mind. Ever since man has kept records or passed names down from generation to generation this upright rock has been called

Uig.

Since the beginning of recorded Christian time and events, wild, maudlin, drunken rituals and festivals were celebrated on Christmas Night throughout England, Ireland, Scotland, and Wales. They were finally stamped out by the clergy, but in outlying rural districts they persisted until the closing years of the last century. County Galway, the portion of Ireland that has persistently clung to the old traditional ways and beliefs more than any other, was the setting until recently of many of these pagan activities. Huge bonfires were set ablaze in the village streets. Wearing animal skins and other bizarre, once symbolic outfits, grotesque masks covering familiar faces, whole communities, men, women, and children, would wind in torchlit, noisy processions from house to house.

As to what took place in the shadowy depths of the woods and fields surrounding the villages on those bacchanalian nights can best be judged by the number of eighteenth- and nineteenth-century writers whose books and pamphlets consisted of lectures on the evils that would befall anyone indulging in such debauched, heathen practices. The high ratio of these volumes emanating from London confirms that at least until the end of the eighteenth century such conduct was not unique to Galloway, as it was then known.

From the recorded beginning this night was called

Og Night.

Among the less spirited traditions, the first person who arrived at a house on Og Night was assured of good luck for the coming year by taking the cream off a pitcher of fresh milk. In another etymologically identical word to Haue Oc, the Irish word for cream is

uach.

The same name or word appears as the first element in the Irish word for the chief of a clan or the king of a people—*uachtarain*. Visitors to President de Valera at his residence in Phoenix Park, Dublin, are ushered into Aras an *Uach*tarain, literally, "House of the Chief."

Other annual events featuring the name Oc or Hock, Oke or Hoke, were celebrated in the spring, at the time of bringing in the harvest in the autumn and on the second Monday and Tuesday after Easter, all times of great fertility significance. *Ock*tide or *Hock*tide is still listed in a few English dictionaries. *The Concise Oxford Dictionary* states that it was "an old festival kept on second Monday and Tuesday after Easter," and gives the etymology of the first element as dubious. In *Kenilworth* Sir Walter Scott writes, "Hock-tide was the time of paying church dues" (Chapter 39).

The second Monday after Easter, Ock/Hock Monday, was reserved for the men; the following day, Ock/Hock Tuesday, for the women. It may be more than a coincidence that the first savage revolt of the early Britons against their new masters, the Saxons, countrywide and for a time successful, took place on an Ock Tuesday. Women were in the forefront of the hand-to-hand fighting. Another occasion of ritual and festivity occurred when the last cart bringing in the harvest from the fields, the Ock/Hock cart, arrived in the village.

Until the early eighteenth century a huge stuffed effigy of a giant was carried in the annual May Day processions, along with the often lasciviously painted phallic symbol of the Maypole. The name of this giant is listed in a dictionary published at Cambridge University in 1676 as

> Eug.

A towering Welsh goblin or giant was named Hough or Ough, and the term eventually became generic to all goblins. As Christianity took over and the once-revered Oc/Og pagan figures became blurred and finally obliterated, superstitious feelings of fear and revulsion must have been prevalent in the transition stage; it is tempting to believe that at that point such words as "*ug*ly" and "*U*gsome" (now obsolete) came into the language. Such place-name transitions as *Og*geberg, Devon (1263), into present-day *Ug*borough; *Og*eford (Domesday Book) into *Ug*ford; and *Og*hill, Yorkshire, into modern *Ug*hill indicate that Ug and Og are synonymous.

Before passing on to the Ava/Haue/Hawa situation in Great Britain and Ireland, there are two ancient Og/Oc expressions that still persist in those islands. The first is an expression of disgust or distaste:

> Ugh!

As in *U*ghill, Yorkshire. One has only to examine the shifting meanings of many modern words over the past hundred years or so to appreciate how readily, during a period of changing centuries, deep awe and reverence laden with fear can change into disgust or distaste.

The second expletive is one of surprise or consternation, less frequently of resignation:

Oc! (in Ireland).

Och! (in Scotland).

Oc! once the supreme ruler of the universe in the minds and hearts of our ancestors.

*   *   *

In considering the Ava/Haue/Hawa names and words, there is one mythical place name that commanded the highest respect among the early Britons. According to Welsh mythology, King Arthur and his knights, as well as earlier heroes, were transported to a blessed island off the western coast. Its name was *Ava*lon. On one hand it is related to the Welsh word for apple, *aballon*, but on the other hand *Ava*lon, the resting place of the immortals, would appear to be a fitting companion name to Ava, the name of the incredible prehistoric circle of upright stones at *Ave*bury.

If Ava or Haue/Hawa were the names of an earlier goddess of fertility who was superseded by a younger God, Oc/Og, then the evidence today is about what one would expect to find. There is no Ava/Awa figure in Irish mythology, nor have I been able to find one in Britain. There are, however, a large number of place-names in Ireland that feature this element. *Knock* in Irish means "hill" and *kill* means "church" or "wood." Separating this generic beginning from the rest of the following names, one arrives at:

Knock *Awa*ddra (four widely separated towns)
Knock *Ava*ddra
Kill *Awa*ha
Kill *Ava*lla (three such: reminiscent of Avalon)
Kill *Ava*lly (ten: again Avalon)
Kill *Ava*rrig
Kill *Awa*rdy

There are scores of others where the element is featured, but if it were not for its association with Oc/Og, as covered above, and what happens in other parts of the world, there is nothing of great moment in the Ava/Awa Irish place-name setup. The situation in England is a bit more interesting. Here is a group of most un-English-looking English place-names:

*Hwa*tele
*Hwa*etincgle
*Hwa*teaker
*Hwa*rrum
*Hwa*elleage
*Hwa*etedenu
*Hawa*ro

Which have become:

Wheatley
Watchingwell
Wheatacre
Wharrum
Whalley
Whaddon
Hawerby

The first and third place-names point up the fact that the earliest known word for "wheat," again intimately associated with the concept of fertility, was

*hwa*et.

The earliest name for the wheel, which was *hweol*, and the earliest name for the largest of all mammals, the whale, which was *hwa*le (believed related to the Icelandic word for the sea, *hava*), also appear most provocative. At the top of the list, however, is the name for the oldest known implement used by man in tilling the earth. Could anything be more appropriate than that such a primitive instrument would bear a name etymologically identical to the Haue in haue and Oc ("*havoc*") and the Ava at *Ave*bury:

hoe, once *howe*, related to *houwa* on the Continent, is our word "hoe."

There is one expletive still used in England that looks like a worthy companion to Oc! In order to explain where this may have come from, I am going to have to explain how the words "what," "when," "where," and "who" came into being.

hwa has become "what";
hwa has also become "*who*";
hwan has become "when";
hwaer has become "where."

These four evolutions, or corruptions, are known to have taken place. In addition, at an early date I believe *hwah* became *wah*. The reason I believe this is that in the back country of Yorkshire today, when two people meet and want to say to each other "God bless you!" they still say

Wah!

Which in my opinion was originally *hwah* or *hawwah*, and once again identical phonetically to the Haue in Haue Oc, "havoc," and Ava at *Ave*bury.

The reason I believe this is that the name of the oldest fertility goddess in the world, known to the Semites as the "mother of all living," the name out of which evolved Eve, our name for the first woman, was

Hawwah.

Chapter 10

Of arms and the man I sing who first
from the shores of Troy . . .
                VERGIL, *The Aeneid*

IN ATTEMPTING TO forge a chain between the British Isles and the Mediterranean, in particular a strong bond between the Stonehenge/Avebury complex and the golden culture of Mycenae and Crete, there are two potentially vital links to examine. If you take the two separated words or names originally in "havoc," Haue and Oc, the same names that predominate at Stonehenge and Avebury, and reverse them, you have

Ochaue, pronounced *Oc-ha-wa.*

The name of the mysterious "Sea People" who invaded the Mediterranean in the thirteenth century B.C. has been preserved in an extant letter and in several inscriptions. The letter was sent by the King of the Hittites, whose empire was later smashed into bits by the "Sea People," to their ruler, whom he addressed on equal terms and affectionately as "brother." The name he wrote as the name of the country inhabited by the "Sea People"

PLATE 25. Mycenae, Greece: Lion Gate and Cyclopean Wall. Except for the relief above the gate, oldest piece of monumental sculpture in Europe, the construction is the same as that of the Postern Gate and Stonehenge. Note the wheel ruts in the threshold of the gate.

Photo: the Mansell Collection

was

Akhaiwa, or Akhhiyawa.

This name has now been generally accepted as directly related to

Akhaioi, or Akhaiowi.

Akhaioi, or Akhaiowi, was the name in Greek for those whom
we call the Achaeans, the race of people who traditionally once
occupied Cyprus, Phoenicia, and Egypt; who created the My-
cenaean/Cretan culture; who, as described in Homer's *Iliad*,
laid siege to and destroyed Troy; whose own fabulous center at
Cnossus on Crete vanished in rubble along with Mycenae; and
whose wanderings were immortalized by Homer in the *Odyssey*.

In a thirteenth-century Egyptian hieroglyphic inscription, the
name of one of the tribes among the "Sea People" was recorded
as

Akhaiwasha

Akhaiwa with an *asha* ending, possibly as a tribal identification?
Thus one finds:

Haue Oc—as in "havoc," as in *Oc*, the supreme god of the
ancient Irish, as at Avebury and Stonehenge.

Akhaiwa and Akhaiwasha—the "Sea People."

Akhaioi—the Achaeans of Mycenae and Crete.

The carved Achaean hilt dagger discovered in 1953 by Professor R. J. C. Atkinson looms up in the center of the stage at
Stonehenge, surrounded by conceivably related Ach (Oc/Og)
place-names.

When the Romans first ventured outside the Mediterranean,
they discovered that a large region bordering on what is now
the west coast, the Atlantic coast, of France was a convenient
stepping-stone along the route taken by the faïence beads. The
region bore a name that appears to fit into the picture. Augustus
incorporated the territory as a province within the Roman
Empire. Its name was, and much of the area still is, called *Acqui-*
taine, pronounced *Akhawa*taine.

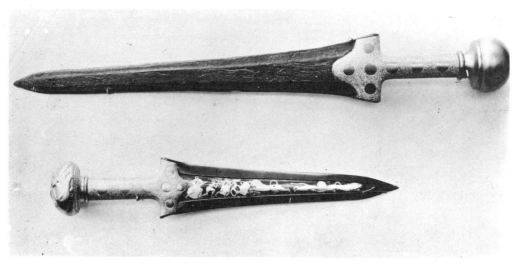

PLATE 26. Mycenae, Greece: bronze hilt dagger dating to about 1550 B.C. This is comparable to the carved "Mycenaean" hilt dagger discovered by Professor R. J. C. Atkinson at Stonehenge in 1953.

Photo: the Mansell Collection

PLATE 27. Ireland: bronze hilt daggers dating to the same period as the Grecian daggers in Plate 26. Note the holes and in one case the intricate construction for securing hilts to the daggers.

Photo: National Museum of Ireland

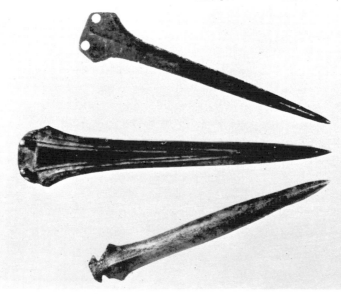

One finds two other pairs of parallel names, one in Ireland, the other in the Mediterranean. In Irish mythology, Oc and Ogma reign over the Tuatha De *Dan*aan, the "Children of the goddess *Dan*aan." Throughout the *Iliad* and the *Odyssey* Homer uses interchangeably the two terms *Ach*aean and *Dan*aean as names for the early Greeks. Only once throughout both epics does he refer to them as Hellenes. In each case the names Oc/Og and Dan/Don are closely identified with one another.

There is another name that shows that the name Og stood unchallenged at the very pinnacle of mythology and worship in the ancient Mediterranean. The name is

*Aeg*ipan.

Aegipan was the name of "the earliest figure signifying the sign of Capricorn, the Goat, in the Zodiac." The fact that the name Aeg, etymologically identical to Og, precedes the name of Pan, the half-man, half-goat god of fertility who was worshiped in Egypt and throughout the eastern Mediterranean, and who was worshiped by the pre-Christian Greeks but was so ancient that even they regarded him as a "pagan" god, would indicate that earlier there had been an even more powerful god of fertility named Og. Or, if you prefer, one that had risen in power and surpassed Pan.

There are in Egypt the almost obliterated and forgotten ruins of a prehistoric city that has often been ascribed as a center of worship to Pan. Its name, however, suggests that the deity who was actually worshiped there bore an Oc/Og name. Achmim, or Akhmim, was located on the Upper Nile. In the early eighteenth century it was still full of architectural wonders that recalled the glories of what Strabo referred to as Panopolis, the sacred city of the god Pan. Under the rule of the Turks the site was sacked, and many treasures were carted off to museums and private locations. There were, however, massive monumental stones too large and heavy for the Turks to move; these were covered with great concentric circles identical to those at New Grange and other sites in Ireland.

In searching for a point of origin from which might have

PLATE 28. Cnossus, Crete: Palace of Minos, West Magazines. The scorched stone in the foreground indicates damage by fire in the final destruction of the palace between 1400 and 1300 B.C.

Photo: the Mansell Collection

105

stemmed the names Oegyptus and Oegypt (Egypt), Acheans, Aegipan, and Achmim, the essential clues are to be found in my opinion in Greek mythology. A unique and absorbing situation develops. The personalities and characteristics, as well as the major events, in the lives of two shadowy but all-important early Greek personages eventually join together to form a single earlier mythological figure, an acknowledged god of fertility, who lay outside the classical Greek orbit. Although the two Greek personages are credited in legends with the founding of practically every region of ancient Greece, they—as well as the fountainhead from which they sprang—have been forgotten or are ignored. During the past one hundred years they have all but disappeared from standard works of mythology, from encyclopedias and dictionaries.

Ogygios of Oguges

From this somewhat ridiculous name comes the English word Ogygian, "of obscure antiquity, prehistoric." But there was nothing ridiculous about Ogygios. He was a legendary figure of enormous stature, the founder of Attica, earlier Actae, in which Athens is situated. Ogygios was also the mythical founder and first king of Boeotia, another large area of Greece north of Attica. In some of the earliest Greek legends Boeotia is called Ogygia. The capital of Boeotia, ancient Thebes, was built by Ogygios, and it too at times is referred to as Ogygia. Elsewhere he is described as the founder of Thrace.

Most important of all, Ogygios was the founder of the Achaean League in the Peloponnesus, a gigantic step toward the Golden Age of Greece. So here we find a mythological Og figure in intimate relationship with the Akhaioi, and Og and Oc forms as in Ireland and England. Three of the most important cities of the league, Aegium, the capital; Aegae, and Aegira, bore Og names. When Ogygios died, the Achaean League changed from a kingship to a democracy, and remained as such in historic times, a shift that is perhaps pertinent to the statement in Irish mythology that the world will not end, *nor an era end*, until Ogham and Achu mix together and the sun and the moon mix together. There are also three words in Greek that appear to bear on this:

ochlokratia—literally "mob rule"; from ochlos, "mob."

hagiokratia—"government by a body of persons esteemed holy"; from *hagios*, "holy, sacred."

ockhumenos—"universal, of the whole world"; hence, "ecumenical." This would appear to be a later, more sympathetic development out of *ochlokratia*, one that runs parallel to the emergence of Oc as the supreme ruler of the universe in Ireland.

In view of what follows, the most significant aspect of the legends concerning Ogygios is that he is closely identified with a great flood or series of floods in Boeotia and elsewhere. In one legend he is said to have perished in a flood. Later, Ogygios and Noah were often confused in peoples' minds. Varro states that in the time of Ogygios the planet Venus went through a marked change in color and shape, a phenomenon related to the floods.

Aigeus/Aegeus

Much of what is covered on Aigeus or Aegeus comes from the fifth of five *Archeological Papers* written by the distinguished antiquarian George V. Elderkin, published in Springfield, Massachusetts, thirty-nine years ago through the Martha Kilbourne Fund. Since Elderkin calls him Aigeus, I shall do the same. It was he who brought Aigeus into the sharp focus that fitted him into a key role in this book.

As a second founding father, Aigeus rounded out what little was left in Greece after Ogygios had completed his work. Aigeus founded Athens, and from him stemmed the names of the Aegean Sea and the island of Aegina. Through his son Medus, by Medea, he was regarded as the ancestor of the ancient Medes. Aigeus arrived in Greece from Asia Minor by way of Cyprus and Crete, a route pregnant with implications. Even more significant, he brought with him the cult of Aphrodite Ourania, an offshoot from the fertility cult of Astarte that had originated at Ashteroth. The cult of Ishtar evolved from the same beginning, and many authorities claim this is the source of the word "Easter."

Tying in with the name Aegipan, Aigeus brought with him to Greece the oldest living symbol of fertility, the goat. He was known as the "Goat King," and his name is related directly to the Greek word for goat, *aig*. There is an older form of the word for goat which is a reversal of Akhaiwa, an apparent combination of Hawa and Og. It is Aiyog, a conceivable blending of an earlier goddess of fertility, Hawwah, with a later Og/Oc god of fertility.

Elderkin states: "The fact that the Dorian Greeks called waves 'goats' may identify Aigeus as a god of the sea like Poseidon. Both were established on the Athenian acropolis and both claimed to be the father of Thesueus, closely identified with Crete. The comparison of the waves of the sea to goats is probably very old. The coins of Karian Aphrodisias represent Aphrodite riding on a sea-goat."

At this point we are faced with two legendary figures, Ogygios and Aigeus, who are credited with founding most of Greece. In one instance there is an intimate connection with floods and confusion and with Noah. In another an association with fertility, with the cult of Aphrodite, related to the cult of Astrate, or Ashtaroth, at the city of Ashteroth.

As mentioned on page 80, there is in rabbinical mythology and the Old Testament a legendary figure who might have served as an origin for the two Greek figures. In this instance we encounter one of the most colorful, flamboyant, unquestionably the earthiest of all mythological figures, and yet at the same time the most sadly neglected. A king and a god in his own right, he was the "last of the giants", which as interpreted in Genesis (6:1–4) would make him the only post-diluvian creature who was "born to the gods" after "intercourse with the daughters of men". His name, short and pertinent in my opinion, was Og.

Since the greatest of all Og figures has, wittingly or unwittingly, been obscured over the centuries, and since some

PLATE 29. Cnossus, Crete: Palace of Minos, Monolithic Pillar Base-
ment, circa 1950 B.C. Two upright stones are the earliest known
examples of pillars, which in rounded and fluted forms became
characteristic of the later Classical Period throughout the Mediterranean.

Photo: the Mansell Collection

American reviewers and readers wrote for source information, I will give two in toto here. In the 1962 edition of E. Cobham Brewer's *A Dictionary of Phrase and Fable* Og has been dropped, but in the 1895 edition of this popular work one finds:

"Og, King of Bashan, according to Rabbinical mythology, was an antediluvian giant, saved from the flood by climbing on the roof of the ark. After the passage of the Red Sea, Moses first conquered Sihon, and then advanced against the giant Og (whose bedstead, made of iron, was above fifteen feet long and nearly seven feet broad, Deut. 3:11). The Rabbins say that Og plucked up a mountain to hurl at the Israelites, but he got so entangled with his burden, that Moses was able to kill him without much difficulty."

And in William S. Walsh's *Heroes and Heroines of Fiction* (Lippincott, Philadelphia, 1915): "Og, King of Bashan, according to Rabbinical legend, was a giant nearly six miles high or, to be exact, 23,033 cubits. He drank water from the clouds, and toasted fish by holding them before the orb of the sun. When the waters of the Deluge were at their height they reached only up to his knees. Noah refused to admit him into the Ark, but allowed him to sit on its roof and handed him out every day a dole of food. In return Og promised that he and his descendants would serve him as his slaves in perpetuity."

Og obviously, in spite of Moses, did not stay dead. As head of the fertility cult founded at his capital of Ashteroth, he was worshipped throughout the Mediterranean area and, if the data herein is valid, his memory was preserved in place-names all across the face of the earth. As one takes a brief look at some of the names around the Mediterranean and in the parts of the world accessible from the Mediterranean, it would appear that rather than regarding themselves as the slaves of Noah's descendants, or as Noah's descendants, many of this earth's inhabitants in earlier times regarded themselves as springing from Og, born of the gods and of women.

Chapter 11

What's in a name? That which we call a rose
By any other name would smell as sweet.
SHAKESPEARE, Romeo and Juliet

SINCE THE MOST conclusive evidence as to the universality of these key names is where they have been carried across long stretches of open ocean, only highlights will be covered in the Mediterranean and on adjacent land masses:

Achisarmi was the name used by Pliny for "the ancient inhabitants of Africa."

Ogliostra is the name for one of the largest regions in Sardinia. Hence the word for Agate.

Acherini was the name of the earliest inhabitants of Sicily. The earliest name for Syracuse was Achradina, a name still preserved in the city's oldest quarter.

Achamantis was at one time the name for Cyprus.

Achaea was the name of the oldest city on Rhodes.

Oceanus, whom Homer looked on as the beginning and end of all things, the creator of the gods themselves, was the father of three thousand sons, the most famous Achelous, preserved in many areas and said to be the source for the word *aqua*. Europe still teems with Oc/Og river names. To mention a few:

Belgium—The Ogy and Okegem.

France—The Ognon and Oger.

Germany and Austria—the Oker and a number of Ach,
Ache, and other such names.

Italy—the Oglio, Occhiobello, Oggiono, Oggebio.

Spain—the Oca, Ocaña, and Ocaña Plateau.

Sweden—the Ocke and Ockelbo.

The Acholi tribe in North Africa is not only reminiscent of
some of the Irish and English place-names; one of the major
passes between Pakistan and Afghanistan is named the Ochili.
The name Achilles stemmed from his grandfather, Aeacus, King
of Aegina.

India is full of such Og/Oc names as Ogna, Achad, Ugu.
Three of the oldest and most important archaeological sites in
Afghanistan are Aghao Jan, Agha Dosti, and Aghangai. The
Turkish words for "master" and "commander," *agha* and *aga*,
should not be overlooked.

Further on the mythological front:

Aegir, Swedish God of the Ocean, with his nine veiled
daughters, the Aegids, or waves, appears directly related
to Greek mythology.

Aegicorus was the son of Ion, legendary ruler of the Ionian
Greeks.

Aegimius was the mythical king of the Dorian Greeks.

The island of Ogygia, where Ulysses was entertained by
Calypso for seven years, was placed in five or six Mediterranean
locations by classical writers, but more than one antiquarian in
the past three centuries have claimed it was Ireland. Ogylus, an
island in a highly strategic location between Crete and the
Peloponnesus, and Ogyrus, an island off northern Arabia, have
disappeared from modern maps.

Further on the folklore front:

Hugun was the king of the French goblins. See the word
"huge," etymology "dubious." And in view of Og's

amorous propensities, note "hug," originally a Cornish word.

Hagan, or Haco, was a legendary giant in Norwegian and German mythology. "Long were his legs and sinewy . . . deep and broad his chest . . . terrible his visage."

Ogier was a mighty warrior in Danish mythology.

Last, on the metaphysical front:

Achar, in Hindu philosophy, personifies the All-in-All in the same sense as Oecumenicus. The whole world is pictured as being spun out from within Achar and will eventually return inside Achar, who is conceivably a fertility symbol. In Persian mythology, Zrvan Acharan represents Boundless Time, the creator of all things, beyond the concept of man.

In order to examine combinations of Oc/Og and Hawwah/Avvah in the Mediterranean and to trace the two names into Africa, it will be necessary to look at Hawwah/Avvah for a moment alone in the Mediterranean. If Hawa, to use the simplified form, preceded Og/Oc, then the picture in the Mediterranean is exactly what one would expect it to be. Hawa plays no active role in Mediterranean mythologies, except as the Semitic "mother of all living," but she is featured in an immense number of place-names, notably.

Haua or Hava Fteah

Still bearing the two forms Hawwah/Avvah found in Haue/Havoc, this immense stratified area contains evidence of a stone-ax "industry." It is one of the oldest archaeological sites ever excavated, carbon testing to approximately 29,000 B.C. It is located in North Africa, in Cyrenaica, itself one of the earliest settled parts of the world.

Kaubab el Hawa

This is one of the earliest occupied sites excavated in Israel.

Unfortunately, its name has recently been changed to, of all things, Belvoir!

Avvah

Mentioned once as Ava, thrice as Ivah, in the Old Testament, this ancient city's location is today unknown. It was one of the cities whose inhabitants colonized Samaria after the deportation. (See II Kings 17:24.) See also "river of Ahava" in Ezra 8:21, 31. The Ivah spelling follows the same form as the Ive River in England, which is related to the Avon and other Av rivers.

Avasis

One of Egypt's oldest cities, again an extremely important archaeological site, Avasis was also called Oasis, Oa being a frequently encountered variant spelling of Hawa. Others that occur in numerous recorded instances are: Ua . . . Awa . . . Huwa . . . Uwa . . . and as mentioned in connection with the Ouar Ouadi watercourse (recently changed to the Wa'r Wadi watercourse), Oua.

Lastly, Aya, which in certain Hindu dialects means "wet nurse," and is directly related to the Italian *ava*, "grandmother," and Ava, the forerunner of our word Eve. For example, the Al Hawaya Area, Al Hawiya, and the Hawiyah Khabrat Salt Marsh, all in Arabia, are each composed merely of Hawa Hawa.

The landscape in the Old Testament part of the world is still overflowing with Hawa place-names, and it is one of the most common elements in Hamito-Semitic tribal names. Pulling out a handful at random from hundreds: Hawa and the Awai River in Syria; Hawaiah Jebel Mountain in Libya—Jebel, a common personal name and the name of one of Noah's uncles; the Ouahila tribe in Algeria; the Hawashiya watercourse in Egypt, reminiscent of the Akhaiwasha tribal name preserved from the "Sea People," with a second Hawa(iya) at the end; the Awal watercourse in Libya; the Huwa River in Arabia; the Awamir tribe and region in southern Arabia; the Awata River in Ethiopia—and so on, ad infinitum. Massawa or Massaua, the major Ethiopian seaport on the Red Sea is an excellent example of the Awa/ Ua alternate spellings. *The Random House Dictionary of the English Language* lists it as Massawa in the dictionary section, as Massaua in the gazetteer section.

The names fan out into Europe, including Russia—the sprawling Bratislava region in Czechoslovakia is typical of hundreds of *ava* endings, while in Poland and elsewhere the *awa* ending has been retained in such names as Warszawa, the correct spelling for the Polish capital. Throughout the Indo-European portion of the world, Awa/Ava is one of the two or three most frequently encountered place-names, many of which were there when history began. Ava alone is a common place-name in Greece and is featured prominently in Italy. The ancient Romans believed the small round lake of Averno (Avernus) was the entrance to the other world.

Note also Awah Island in Kuwait, Huwaila on the Persian Gulf, and the priceless Awali oil fields in Bahrein where Scandinavian archaeologists have recently unearthed a magnificent prehistoric center that has long been associated in local myth and legend with Noah. The equally priceless Avanah oil field in Iraq is one of scores of Avana and Havana names in the Indo-European area, ranging from a number of Havana city mountain and river names in Iceland to identical names in the island of Ceylon.

Such names as 'Uwanah in Syria and Uva Province, Uva, and the Uvagal River in Ceylon bring up the question of two Indo-European words that are perfect symbols of fertility:

uova—Italian for "grape," from the Latin and Greek.

ova and *ovum*—"egg" and "ovary," from the same source.

Pushing cautiously out of the Indo-European area, we come to Burma, whose ancient capital, the beginnings of which are lost in the mists of prehistory but which was controlled by an alien Ari priesthood until the eleventh century, is named Avvah.

In India we encounter one of the cornerstone names in this book:

Avalokitesvara,

which, if your education and training followed the same lines as mine, you are probably seeing as

Avalo-kitesvara,

reminiscent of Avalon, the blessed island of the immortals in Welsh mythology.

Now, for a few moments, I am going to explain what has been going on inside my mind for the last eight years. At the same time I shall lay the third of the six key names from the first, the world-wide, key group on the table. This will also involve telling you why *The Key* is dedicated to the five people listed in the front of the book.

The first person who gave me a tremendous leg up on this project was Herman W. Liebert, the librarian of the Beinecke Rare Book and Manuscript Library at Yale University, a good friend since we were undergraduates at New Haven. Originally an outstanding authority on the Age of Johnson, Liebert, through his years spent among the great manuscripts and rare books from all periods and countries, has become one of the finest general scholars in the world.

Although not a professional etymologist, Liebert liked the sound of what I was doing and passed me on to Dr. Professor Johannes Rahder, a seventy-year-old Dutchman with a charming Japanese wife. After many years in the Orient, Dr. Rahder spent an equally long time in the Hall of Graduate Studies at Yale and, although now retired, with Dr. Morris Swadesh gone, he is regarded by many as the outstanding authority in the field of comparative etymology. It was Dr. Rahder who, among many other invaluable suggestions, urged me to start looking east and southeast of Asia Minor, rather than spending all my time in Europe and the Mediterranean, which I had been doing.

Dr. Frederick L. Santee, whom I met through David Mc-Dowell of Crown Publishers, was the youngest man ever to graduate from Harvard University. After taking degrees at Oxford, and further studies at the Sorbonne and the American Academy in Rome, Dr. Santee taught classics at Lehigh, Vanderbilt, and later at Kenyon College, where he was the colleague and/or teacher of such outstanding writers as John Crowe Ransom, Allen Tate, Robert Penn Warren, Robert Lowell, and David McDowell, my American editor, a scholar in his own right.

During several intensive weekends at his home in Wapwallopen, Pennsylvania, Dr. Santee, an authority on Sanskrit, Greek, Latin, as well as half a dozen modern languages, not only gave me a multitude of splendid suggestions on specific names and words but also put his finger squarely on what I was doing. "I didn't think anyone could change a lifetime habit, formed after fifty years of study," he remarked, "but you have me looking at names and words from a completely different angle."

And that is all I have been doing. I have tried to isolate prehistoric names and words from historic ones, and then have tried to observe whether or not any recognizable, intelligent, and intelligible pattern ran through them, disregarding present-day geographic and nationalistic boundaries. I have undoubtedly rushed in where many wiser men have feared to tread, but I have encountered this group of scholars who have encouraged me to keep on searching. The fifth person, my close friend and agent, Rosalind Cole, who seemed to understand from the beginning what I was up to, and who on innumerable occasions kept me from abandoning the project, was the one who brought me into contact with David McDowell and Dr. Santee.

Keeping in mind this question of looking at names and words from a fresh, objective viewpoint, and holding Avalokitesvara aside as an ideal case in point, here is the third key name:

> Eloah—the Semitic name for God. From it stemmed the
> Moslem name for God, Allah. There is a name in Greek
> that is phonetically identical:
> Haloa—"an annual festival held in ancient Greece in honor
> of Demeter, Persephone and Dionysius."

Such an association with three of the most celebrated Greek deities, Eloah's lofty stature among the Semites, and the transfer into the Arabic word Allah made me take a close look at its position in the place-name structure of the Old Testament world. There is no point in laboring what I found. Such names as Halawa in Jordan and Halawa Jebel Mountain in Sudan are obvious blendings of Hala or Ala with Awa, one of the other two key names, the pair together, in my opinion, lending credibility to the theory that this type of blending of key names was standard practice in prehistoric times. One has only to run back over the Hawa list just presented to see how popular a practice it was:

The Ouahila tribe, the Awal watercourse, Awala, with a final vowel casualty, Huwaila, Awali—these are etymologically all accepted variants of Allah out of Eloah, combined with Hawa. Such other names as Aluakluak in the Sudan (Eloah/Ok/Eloah/Ok) strengthened greatly my feelings about the importance of Oc/Og as a place-name element, sandwiched in, as it is, twice between Eloah, the name of God.

Joining Akhouava (Ok/Hawa/Ava) in Turkey are two mountains each named Allahuëkber—Allah/Hawa/Ok(Ek), an obvious blending of the three key names.

The name of the most "sacred" parish in pagan and Christian Ireland, Aughaval, now became a blend of Og (Augh), Ava, and Ala (with an end-vowel casualty). The nearby parish in western Ireland, Ogulla, appeared as a simple blending of Og and Alla. There are scores of similar instances where variants of Eloah have been blended with Og/Oc or Hawa/Ava, either singly or all three in combination, and many more specific ones will be encountered.

Viewed against this fabric of place-names, the further presence of such place names as Alloa, in Clackmannan, Scotland; Lake Allua in Ireland, Allowan Island off the coast of County Mayo, Aluuarestorp (today Allerthorpe) in the Domesday Book, plus several score more, made me consider seriously for the first time the possibility that Halloa, the earliest form of Hello, had in the beginning been Eloah, phonetically identical, the Semitic name for God.

My feelings about this, as well as the Wah! (once Hawwah?)

greeting, meaning "God bless you!" still prevalent in outlying districts of Yorkshire, were firmed up by the discovery of an early British expletive that has always baffled etymologists. The expletive, which expresses sorrow or despair, still survives in Scotland as Waly! In its earlier form it was

Walawa!

A blending of Ala and Awa, preceded by a *W*. As the number of initial vowel casualties continued to pile up, I returned to Walawa! from time to time, and each time saw it more and more clearly as once having been Awalawa! Awa, "mother of all living"; Ala/God/Awa, "mother of all living." Which brings us back to

Avalokitesvara.

Chapter 12

A lamp to the blind, a sunshade to those consumed
by the heat of the sun, a stream for the thirsty; he
takes away all fear from those who dread a disaster, he is a doctor to the sick, a father and
mother to the unhappy.

Karandavyuha 14, 18

THUS IS THE compassionate, understanding Avalokitesvara depicted to his millions of worshipers in India and Ceylon. *The
Larousse Encyclopedia of Mythology* says of Avalokitesvara:
"Mother! That was the shape in which he conquered the Far
East." This dual male/female personality for the Hindu deity
who has been most often compared to Jesus Christ appears
especially appropriate to the name viewed as Avalok-itesvara,
a blending of Ava/Ala/Ok which I saw only after looking at
the name fifty or a hundred times. Here was one of the most

PLATE 30. India: Avalokitesvara, the understanding, compassionate
Hindu god who is often compared to Christ, as depicted in a copper
statue from Tibet, century A.D. 1600. *The Larousse Encyclopedia
of Mythology* says of this male/female deity: "Mother! That was
the shape in which he conquered the Far East." Avalokitesvara is
one of the cornerstone names in *The Key*.

Photo: Radio Times Hulton Picture Library

significant names in India and the Far East, blending subtly together what I believed to be three key Semitic names.

Moving out of the Indo-European area for the first time, into Africa, one follows the route that Henri Lhote, who led the two French expeditions into this part of the world in the early 1960s, believes was taken by the people who migrated westward into what is now the barren Sahara Desert six thousand years before Christ. The Oc/Og, Hawa/Ava, and Eloah/Ala place-names are encountered in the greatest profusion along this route. And the very heart of the fertile pastureland where those unknown men, women, and children settled down seven or eight thousand years ago is still called the Hoggar region, adjacent to the Tassili-n-*Oua*-A*ha*ggar Mountains. Other important Og/Oc names are in this same area.

There is a color reproduction of a painting on page 49 of *The Concise Encyclopaedia of Archeology.*[1] It is also reproduced in *Vanished Civilizations of the Ancient World,*[2] one of the most provocative books published on archaeology in this century, to which Lhote and Gale Sieveking both contributed chapters that have greatly influenced the views expressed herein. The reproduction is of the most famous of the many rock paintings discovered in the Hoggar region. There are actually two scenes depicted, one upon the other. I am looking at them at this moment, and studying the main personage featured, who also appears in a number of the other rock paintings. In view of the name Hoggar, and other, similar, ones in this area, I believe I am gazing upon Og, the "last of the giants," the sole survivors of the Great Deluge except for Noah and his group, Og, mighty symbol of fertility.

The main figure is indeed a giant, towering over the supplicating women who surround him. One woman at the right is giving birth to a child. Both the giant and the women are white, unlike the smaller figures in the other, imposed, scene, who are

[1] London: Hutchinson & Co., 1960. A black-and-white reproduction of this painting is included herein. See Plate 31.
[2] London: Thames & Hudson, 1963.

PLATE 31. Africa: a rock painting from the Hoggar region in the mid-Sahara. This 6,000 to 7,000-year-old portrayal of naked women before a monstrous male white deity is, in the author's opinion, the only known depiction of Og, "the last of the giants," mentioned in Deuteronomy and five other books in the Old Testament. Og survived the flood by riding on the roof of Noah's Ark, and founded the fertility cult of Ashtaroth. The gridwork over the face of the principal figure assumes a special significance in text.

Photo: Henri Lhote Mission

123

dark-skinned. The giant is endowed with an enormous penis, but the most curious thing about him is that there are no features to his face. Instead, it is crossed by what looks like a gridwork, a series of horizontal, parallel, brownish-black bars. The symbolism of this gridwork will in the end I believe be understandable.

Surveying the Oc/Og and Hawa names in Africa today, it would appear that those prehistoric adventurers and explorers, traders and settlers, who took the trail up the Nile marked by the faïence beads fanned out through one vast expanse of the "Dark" Continent, while, again as held by Lhote, the people from the Hoggar region were driven south and, from the evidence, west. Settlements from the sea are also indicated. Touching only the highlights, from the starting point in Ethiopia, whose largest region, the southernmost, is called Ogaden:

> In Uganda: Achwa (Ok Awa) and three Og/Oc/Ala blendings: Mount Ogili, Okollo, and the familiar-looking Acholi tribe.
>
> In Bechuanaland (Botswana): Okwa. Okawa? (as in Akhaiwa). Two hundred years ago, when the first European explorers arrived, it was called Oegwa, an Og/Oc switch, as in England. Oegwa was long the center of the gold trade in this part of Africa. The explorers were fascinated by the exquisitely made, delicately balanced scales manufactured and used by the natives in the weighing of gold dust. They were also astounded by the extraordinary fishing skill of the natives.
>
> In French Equatorial Africa (Gabon): the Ogooué River, again an Og/Hawa blending.
>
> In the Central African Republic: Awalawa. As suggested for Walawa, the early British expression of sorrow and despair. Awa/Ala/Awa.
>
> In Algeria: Ait el Khaoua. If an initial vowel were once here, another Akhaoua (Akhaiwa).
>
> In Tanganyika: Hawha Mountain.

In the Congo: Avakuli as in "havoc." With an *ala* ending
for good measure; the same three elements found in
Avalokitesvara.

In Upper Volta: The capital of this West African republic,
far inland, bears a favorite name: Ouagadougou, or
Hawa(Oua) and Og(Ag), with another blending of the
same at the end. With two *a*'s added, it becomes Ouaga-
douagoua, Hawa/Og/ and Hawa/Og/Hawa.

While Mauritania on the Atlantic coast of Africa, contains
two close seconds:

Nouakchott: the capital. The first part of the name appears
to be similar to that of the Anouak tribe in Ethiopia with
the *A* gone. Ouak: Hawa/Ok.

Oualata: Hawa and Ala.

Also in West Africa, the closest thing to Akhaiwa is Ahkaoua;
and a town named plain Oua.

Next are two place-names, one of which you have seen: Aughaval and Aghouavil.

Aughaval is the name of Ireland's "holy" parish.

The Aghouavil region is in West Africa.

Both are blendings of Og/Hawa/Ala.

Coming last to Nigeria, the area where Lhote believes most of
the people from the Hoggar region were driven, we find the
most important of the Og and Awa names in terms of numbers
and size. Including:

Ogoja Province: Oja is a corruption of Hawa via Aya.

Ogwashi-Uk: a variant of Akhaiwasha, with another Ok
added.

Alawa: identical to Halawa in Jordan and Halawa Jebel in
Sudan.

Awava: the two forms of Awa/Ava.

But the greatest, most exhilarating surprise came in Nigeria
from an unexpected direction when I discovered the two place-
names Adamawa region and Adamawa Mountains. There is an
Adama in Ethiopia honoring the first man, and the other Dam

place-names mentioned earlier, but here is a perfect blending of
Adama (earth, the first man) with Hawwah (the "mother of all
living," hence Eve, the first woman): Adam and Eve.

Ten thousand miles or more to the east of Nigeria, there are
two islands off the coast of Celebes. Their names are Damalawa
Br. Island and Damalawa Kt. Island. Eventually it seemed reasonably safe to assume that these at one time were names made
up of the names of Adama and Hawwah joined together by
Eloah, God.

Before crossing the Atlantic, as the start of a trek around the
world, here are four names of immense stature in the Mediterranean to consider:

> *aquila:* "eagle," the majestic royal bird, a northern constel-
> lation, the name of an Italian city leveled by Attila the
> Hun.
> *aequator:* Latin form of "equator," the great circle around
> the middle of the earth, halfway between the two poles.
> *aqueous:* an epithet for Zeus, with a "water" connotation.
> *aqua/agua:* "water."

All these are conceivably blends of Oc/Og and Hawwah/
Avvah. The *aqua/agua* name for "water" is said to come from
Achelous, the river god, but an Ua/Hawa element is also present. The shift from the name El Ouar Ouadi watercourse to the
Wa'r Wadi watercourse makes plausible the possibility that the
Egyptian word *wah,* meaning "oasis," was once *hawah;* and that
the Arabic word for water hole, *wahat,* was once *hawahat.* For
the Semites to bestow the name "mother of all living" on the
substance water seems logical. At any rate, I decided to try to
find out, among other things, whether the name or word *aqua/
agua* was in the Americas before the historic explorers arrived.
It turned out to be, in my opinion, a fruitful thought. But it was
three and a half years before the fruit ripened. I shall speed up
the process for you.

Chapter 13

There is no sure beginning. At the opening of
history many and various tribes already held the
land, and had given it a thin scattering of names.
The names themselves can be made to reveal the
manner of the giving.
    GEORGE R. STEWART, *Names on the Land*

WHEN CORTEZ BURNED his ships on the shore and led his handful of men and horses upward toward the Halls of Montezuma,
the great Empire of Mexico stretched out before him was called
    Anahuac: Huac, as in Haue Oc—"havoc."
    The oldest cultivated part of the equally great Empire of the
Incas in what is now Peru, the lush flatlands at the mouth of the
Chicama Valley in the northern part of the country, first inhabited by prehistoric people who tilled the soil and fished the
waters of the Pacific, is still called
    Huaca Prieta: Huac, as in Haue Oc—"havoc."
    In between these two countries, Mexico and Peru, lies a third
with a name that appears provocative, *Ecua*dor. It was, however, apparently coined in modern times because Ecuador lies
on the Equator.
    In Mexico there is a native word, and in Peru another, that

127

both reflect in profound though different ways man's deepest "religious" feelings. In Peru there is

> Huaca: "a general term for objects connected with the religious worship of the Incas, as idols, temples, mounds and graves."

José de Acosta's *Historia Natural ey Moral de las Indias* states: "In every province of Peru there was one particular Huaca or House of Adoration." The word also applied to "mounds or sepulchres, usually full of gold."[1]

In Mexico the native word for "testicle" is

> *ahuactl*, as in Haue Oc. Because of an obvious visual symbolism, the native Mexicans applied the same name to a delicious vegetable. The Europeans took the name and did to it exactly what they did to Havoc and the Vale of Avoca. They turned it into "avocado."

There is another native Mexican word that bears directly on the question of the relationship of the name Hawwah to the substance water. The word is

> *ahue*, pronounced Hawwah. Its meaning is "all water."

A native Mexican word signifying "of great antiquity" is pronounced Hawwah/Hawwah, and it is spelled

> *ahuehue*.

The Pawnee Indians in the Midwest of North America have a name for the "Abode of all Spiritual Power" that is a startling blend of Hawwah and Ok to find on this far side of the Atlantic:

> Awahoksu.

When the English first moved in along the mideastern coast of North America they found the powerful Delaware Indians in control. A majestic mountain range and a broad, winding river each bore the same name, a name that had no relationship to the name Delaware. When the white men asked where the name came from, the Indians replied that it was the name of an ancient people who, according to legend, had once lived on the

---

[1] London, 1604. Translated by "E.G."

banks of the river and in the mountains. Their tribal name had been

> Allegawa, or Alla/Og/Awa. As in Avalokitesvara, but in a different sequence. If we take the exact same three elements in the exact same order, but with an Ock form rather than Og, and blend them together, we get Ala/Ock/Awa, or Alackawa.

And if the initial vowel is lost, one ends up with

> Lackawanna, a city on the shore of Lake Erie, built upon an Indian village that once too must have fallen within the territory of the Allegawa people. There are also Lackawanna place-names in Pennsylvania.

Differing sharply from the overall picture in the Mediterranean, in Europe—including Great Britain and Ireland—and in Africa, Hawa maintained a position throughout the Americas that in sheer weight dominates Oc/Og, except in Alaska. Oc/Og is very much in evidence, and the two names are frequently blended together, but the balance favors Hawa. The name holds undisputed sway in personal and tribal names, and in North America is the dominant element in mythical and spiritual personages. The impression grows that Hawa was strongly entrenched in the Americas before Oc/Og grew to full stature. While she shared honors with him, she was never dislodged by him. The third key name, Eloah/Ala, plays a role equal to the one on the other side of the Atlantic. A number of quite extraordinary specific usages emerge. Sifting out the vital information on all three names:

When the conquistadores took over Mexico, the inhabitants did not refer to themselves as Aztecs. The name they used was Huastec, a Hawa beginning with an Oc ending, fitting closely with the name of the country, Anahuac. The loss of the first vowel destroyed the name's original significance. Two of the four kingdoms making up Anahuac also contained the Huac element:

> Acolhuacan: once Oc/Ala/Hua/Oc Ocalahuacon?

Michuacan: today spelled Michoacán, another *hua/hoa* switch.

Indicating the geographic spread of the names *Hua*xotla and Cojo*huac*an were two outlying strongholds that had just been brought under Montezuma's control. Containing the Akhaiwa name within his own name, Tot*oquihua*tzin ruled Tacuba under Montezuma, while Neza*hualc*atohil (with what seems to be Hawa/Ala/Oc in the middle of his name) sat on the throne of Acolhuacan. Ranging through Central America up to Arizona and Texas, where a town still bears the name of the Kingdom of Anahuac, one finds the state of *Oaxac*a, the Acuaca (Oc/ Hawa/Oc) River, Huehuetlán, *Ahuac*a and *Ahuac*atlán, strategically located in the state of Sin*aloa*. There are also the state of Chihuahua, the Hualiajapa River (Hawa/Ala/Hawa), Ahuachapán in El Salvador, the Huahua River in Nicaragua, Huehuetenango in Guatemala.

These are not obscure names. They jump to sight off any reasonably detailed map. Prehistoric Mexico, from the top down, beginning with the names of its kingdoms, its rulers, its principal states, cities, rivers, and mountains, its names for water, testicles, ancient times, was saturated with the two key names Hawa and Oc/Og, with Eloah/Ala, the third key name, woven through the entire fabric of early Mexican nomenclature. These three names are rivaled only by the Christian saints' names, and heaven only knows how many of the old names were displaced by these.

In Peru, when Pizarro brought the mighty Incas to their knees, the three principal rulers were the emperor, Huayna Capac, and his two sons, the half brothers Atahualpa and Huáscar, who, like their subjects high and low, worshiped at their Huacas and were buried in other Huacas, surrounded by their earthly treasures. In Peru, and throughout South America, the Hawa and Oc/Og names were of primary stature, as in Mexico, with Hawa receiving top billing: The Huallaga River (again the same three key elements found in Allegawa), the Huaillilas

Mountain (Hawa followed by two Ala's), Huaco, Huacho, and scores of others in Peru.

"The mightiest ruins in South America," to quote Thor Heyerdahl, are high up in the Peruvian Andes, near Lake Titicaca, and are named Tiahuanaco. From clues which will be submitted shortly, I suspect that in the very beginning the name was Tiahuanacoa, *acoa* as in Akhaiwa, not even the Incas themselves suspecting what a difference that final vowel meant to the meaning.[2]

The Incas knew little about the builders of the stepped pyramid, constructed of gigantic stone blocks, expertly finished and grooved together, surrounded by huge statues of human beings. Pedro de Cieza de León, the Spanish chronicler, was with the first band of conquistadores to see the ruins. He was told by native guides at the site that legends maintained they had been built centuries before the Incas by white-skinned, bearded strangers.

Close by, on the shore of Lake Titicaca, is the highest city in South America. Its name, in an appropriate gesture of reverence and awe, is

Ach/Ac/Ach: Achacachi
Oc/Oc/Oc.

It is a name repeated in one of the tallest mountains in the world, at the exact opposite corner of the New World, in the Canadian Northwest:

Akiachak Mountain.

In Brazil there is a river whose name is identical to Akhaiwa. It is called the

Acua: hardly distinguishable from the Latin word for water, *aqua*.

And the Brazilian city of Uaua (Hawa/Hawa) is situated on the Uauaris River. Another ancient center of humanity is called

---

[2] Note the similarity between the two names Tiahuanaco and Teotihuacán, the Pyramid of the Sun in Mexico, built by an unknown pre-Aztec (Huaztec) people. See Plate 46.

PLATE 32. Peru: Inca fortifications featuring cut and grooved stones highly characteristic of native megalithic construction. Inca architecture was apparently the renaissance of an earlier, unknown, civilization that flourished in the uplands of Peru and Bolivia, and subsequently spread westward across the Pacific.

Photo: Paul Popper, Ltd.

PLATE 33. Peru: celebrated "Stone of the Twelve Angels" in Inca wall at Haton Rumyoc, an ancient site near Cuzco. Such expertly cut and fitted stones, with terraces, arches, and other details common to prehistoric native architecture, lend physical support to Inca legends that their earliest civilization was founded by white-skinned strangers who arrived across the sea from the east.

Photo: Paul Popper, Ltd.

133

Uaca: reversing Acua.

The Guarani Indians in central South America call their short-tailed monkeys

  uakari: Hawa/Ok.

The natives of northern South America call their howling red monkeys

  alouatta (Eloah).

There are three rich hauls in Chile out of many that feature the three key names:

Ulloa: the Peninsula.

Achacala: Oc/Oc/Ala.

Achecalane Mountains: again Oc/Oc/Ala.

Achecalane is matched by the towering peaks of Huachama-cari Mountains in Venezuela and lofty Lake Huachi in Bolivia.

Ending this first cursory swing around Central and South America, when the Christian explorers and priests, the soldiers, adventurers, and seekers after gold and plunder poured into the West Indies in the wake of Columbus, they found living there in peace and fruitful plenty over a million pagans. At the end of the first century of exposure to European culture and the blessings of civilization, the million had been reduced to a few thousands. Some fled to smaller islands and along the gulf coast, mainly in the Bahamas and Guiana. Most of them disappeared forever into the mines or were buried under waves of black slaves imported from Africa.

The name by which these people called, and still call, themselves, a blending of the same two names that reigned supreme in England and Ireland, across Europe, and around the Mediterranean, in Asia and Africa, and in South America, was

Arawak: Awak, or Awa and Ok.

Chapter 14

THE MOST SIGNIFICANT place-names in the world in terms of
solving the mystery of mankind's prehistory are, in my opinion,
a small handful clustered along the coast of New England. It
took me four years and ten months to find them. I never would
have discovered them if twenty-six years ago George R.
Stewart had not written his great classic, *Names on the Land*.
I shall try to condense my search into the next three chapters.

The name Hawa or Hawwah stands unchallenged in the
panoply of North American Indian deities and legendary figures.
The names that follow were not dug out. They appear on any
popular list, the best-known ones, and there are probably others
that I have missed. Hawa, Oc/Og, and Eloah/Ala names are
included. In addition to Awahoksu, the Pawnee name for the
"Abode of all Spiritual Power" already mentioned, one finds in
the Southeast:

> Awahili: the Sacred Great Eagle of the Cherokees. Awahili
> is identical phonetically with a name already presented as
> a blending of Hawa and Ala, the Ouahili tribe of Algeria,
> North Africa.

> Heloha: the Great Thunder Bird of the Choctaw tribe,
> who, like the Cherokees, originally lived in the Southeast.
> Heloha, a female deity, bore a name phonetically iden-
> tical with Eloah.

135

Oklatabashih: This was the name the Choctaw had for the "Survivor of the Great Flood": on one side of the Atlantic, Og, the only "outside" survivor of the Deluge in Semitic mythology. On the other, Oklatabashih, with a second key element, Ala, indicated. Okalata, as in Ocala, Florida.

Nanih Waiya: the Choctaw name for the Great Creator. Either as one name, Nanihwaiya, or with a vowel added to the second part, Nanih Awaiya, this looks like a reasonably certain double Hawwah ending.

This is an astounding trio of key names to find in one tribe for three major deities on the western side of the Atlantic, in close geographical association with Awahili.

These four mythological names in the Southeast are accompanied by a large number of place-names made up of the same key elements, including four especially pertinent ones:

Okaloacoochee Swamp in Florida: appropriately featuring an Ok followed by Aloa followed by two more Ok's.

Oklawha River and the town of Oklawha, both in Florida. As in Okalawha River, again Oc and Hawwah joined by Ala (Eloah).

Alachua: another town in Florida. The same three key words. Ala preceding Oc/Hawa: Akhaiwa. This name has an Og counterpart in the name of the Alaguilac tribe (Ala/Og/Hawa/Ala/Oc). And featuring the same elements, but with switches in spelling, the Alikwa tribe (Ala/Ok/Awa).

Dramatically pointing up the sweep of these names in North America, at the exact opposite corner of the continent, one finds in Alaska the identical trio of elements in:

Avalik River (Ava/Ala/Ok).

Ogalvik: a town (Og/Ala/Ava/Ok).

While in the northeast corner of the United States, in New York State, one finds the same three elements hidden away in:

Amawalk.

PLATE 34. North America: Choctaw squaws with children. Originally from the Southeast, the Choctaws were pushed westward into Montana, where they now reside. Their mythological and place-names, on the basis of evidence presented in the text, are threaded together, as are those of a number of North American tribes, out of key Semitic words and names that were dispersed from the Mediterranean during prehistoric times.

Photo: Paul Popper, Ltd.

Am followed by Awa/Ala/Ok (Awalak-Walk).

Amawalk is in the area that once belonged to the Allegawa tribe featuring the same three names.

A simple blending of Oc and Ala in Ocala, Florida, leads to such variations on the same theme as: Ocilla, Georgia . . . Acala in Texas and Mexico . . . Akela, Texas . . . Oglala, South Dakota . . . Ogallala, Nebraska . . . Ogallah, Kansas . . . Ogahalla, Ontario . . . to a stirring double-headed finish at: Achille, in the state of Oklahoma. Achille, reminiscent both of the immortal Grecian hero and of prehistoric Achill Island off the west coast of Ireland. The word *ogallah* was used by a number of North American Indian tribes to describe their ancestral records and accomplishments.

The name of the Ochlockonee river in Florida, with a town in Georgia bearing the same name, consists of Ock/Ala/Ock, as is true of the Ekalluk River and Lake Ekallulik (which receives two Ala's) in Canada. One can spend many hours on a number of these combinations.

As one moves out of the Southeast, Hawwah continues to dominate both place-names and legendary names. The Ouachita River and Ouachita Mountains have already been mentioned (now Washita and Wichita); also, the Awabasha, presently the Wabash River. But most revealing of all is the name Iowa, as first recorded by Spanish explorers:

Ouaouaia: pronounced Hawwah/Hawwah, with conceivably a third Hawwah indicated in the *ia(aya)* ending.

On the mythological front one finds:

Wonawilona: the First Cause, the creator of all things, among the Pueblo Indians. By changing all the vowels to *a* (it should be remembered that these vowels were written in arbitrarily by the first white missionaries), and putting an *A* in front, the result is Awanawalana (Awa/ Ana/Awa/Ala/Ana), with an *awala* in the center.

Moving through the Americas, a number of *ana* and *ata* elements begin to emerge. The same elements were also observed in other parts of the world. They never assumed top stature but were apparently used as fillers. Eventually I discovered abstract Semitic meanings as follows:

ana/anna: "blessed" or "favored."

ata/atta: "greatness."

These meanings gave additional significance to such names as Anahuac, the name for the ancient Kingdom of Mexico, and to Atahualpa, the heir to the Inca throne. *Ana* and *ata* will continue to appear in other names.

The Pueblo name for First Cause, Wonawilona, affords an opportunity to introduce one of the most remarkable place-names in America—Walla Walla in the state of Washington. The nearby place-names of Lake Wallowa, the Wallowa River, and the Wallowa Mountains suggest that the name was originally

Wallawalla. *W* followed by Alla/Awa/Alla. Initial vowel
casualties suggest that the name was even earlier
Awallawalla
Awa! Alla! Awa! Alla!

A voice crying out in the primitive wilderness: "Mother of all living! God! Mother of all living! God!" thus echoing the early English cry of anguish and despair: Walawa!

The change by white men of the name of the Chacahuala, the Shoshone Indian name for the Iguana lizard, to Chuckwalla (IIawala to 'Walla) strengthens the suspicion that the name Walla Walla was once Awallawalla.

Buried within another mythological North American Indian name is the same Awa/Ok blending featured in Awahoksu, the Pawnee name for the "Abode of all Spiritual Power":

Tarhuhy*iawahku:* The giant in Iroquois legends who holds
up the heavens on his shoulders. A vowel mortality at the
end may have obliterated an original Awahkua (Awa/
Ok/Awa) blending. The similarity between Iroquois and
the Akhaioi, Greek for the Achaeans, is worth noting.

There are three place-names between what are today the states of Kentucky and Ohio that suggest that the name Ohio, like the name Iowa, owes its origin to Hawwah:

Kanawha Forest.

PLATE 35. Mexico: Temple of the Mayan god, Kukulcan, located at the center of the ruined capital of the second Mayan empire, ninety miles east of Mérida. Two smaller, older pyramids are contained within this 200-foot-high edifice. The author sees the name Kukulcan as composed of the same key elements found in such far-off names as Cuchulainn—pronounced Coo-Coo-Lane—mighty legendary Irish champion, and Aku-Aku the Polynesian god.

Photo: Ewing Galloway

140

Kanawha River.

Little Kanawha River.

The two rivers are tributaries of the majestic Ohio, like the Iowa, a tributary to the Mississippi. Since the Kan element appears to be related to the Indian name Kantuck, then the *awha* element appears to be an earlier form of Ohio, comparable to Ouaouaia, today Iowa.

Other *awa* endings in place-names pop up everywhere: fifteen or twenty Ottawa and Attawa names, found also in Peru as Atahua names, and in Ethiopia, with the elements reversed, as the *Awa*ta River; in Chipp*ewa*, Et*owah* in the South, and scores of others that will come into the picture again.

Further on the mythological front:

Tawa was the all-powerful sun-god of the Pueblos. Once *A*tawa?

In addition to Tawa and Wonawilona, the First Cause (once *A*wanawalana?), the Pueblos worshiped:

Yanauluha, the "High Priest first sent down to earth by the Creator." The *uluha* ending appears to be a corruption of Eloah. If there had once been an initial vowel here, as *A*yanauluha, it becomes a blending of Aya/Ana/Eloah.

These three mighty Pueblo deity names become key names only through the simple process of adding and changing vowels.

Ha Wenneyu, the "Great Spirit" of the Iroquois, bore a name conceivably formed from the same elements. As one name, Hawenneyu, vowel switches produce Hawannaya, or Hawa/Anna/Aya.

The name of the most famous of all legendary Indian figures, in its true native form, gives prominent billing to Hawa:

Hiawatha is a corruption of Haio *Hwa* Tha.

As Haiohwatha, a combination of Hawa/Hawa/Ata?

Looking at the tribal name Mohawk, I saw for the first time that the Hawk element could be a Hawa/Ok blending similar to "havoc." This prompted me to check the early spellings of the name for the bird of prey, the hawk. To my delight I discovered that the same earlier forms as in Haue Oc/"havoc" did

PLATE 36. Peru: "Palace of the Inca" at Colcancha, another well-known example of the building skills of ancient Peruvians. Each year new excavations reveal that early civilizations in this part of the world were directly related to those that evolved in the Mediterranean area.

Photo: Paul Popper, Ltd.

PLATE 37. Peru: Doorway with lintel stone at upland Inca site. Its resemblance to innumerable ruins on the other side of the Atlantic is striking. This photograph, when shown unidentified to fifteen residents of western rural Ireland, was unanimously identified as of local origin.

Photo: Paul Popper, Ltd.

143

exist: *havok, hafok, hawok* were all precedents in English for the present name "hawk."

Before pursuing this further in North America, it is necessary to lay on the table another, the fourth, of the six key names in the first, worldwide group. The name is

Mana, or Manna.

Chapter 15

WHEN THE CHRISTIAN missionaries first came among the North American Indians, they were astounded to discover the reverence with which the pagans regarded the name Mana, or Manna —the same name the Christians had adopted from the ancient Hebrews, meaning "spiritual nourishment." They were even more startled when they heard the legends and saw the ritual associated with the name Manna among the Indians. These were recorded by a number of missionaries and explorers, but in the rush to take over the New World they were soon ignored or forgotten.

Manido universally was regarded by the North American tribes as the Great Spirit who had sent to earth Manabozho, the "God of Dawn and the East," the "Great White One." When the winds were invoked in the medicine lodges, the Indians faced to the east and invoked them in Manabozho's name. Manabozho was regarded throughout the continent as the common ancestor of all the tribes. He was "the founder of their religious rites, the inventor of picture writing, the creator and preserver of earth and heaven." Manabozho had traveled all over the face of the globe, and it was he who generations earlier had taught the Indians how to perform the Midewiwin Ceremony.

In the Midewiwin Ceremony, a small white shell was placed in the mouth of a young brave who was about to be initiated into manhood. Having swallowed the shell, the brave then be-

145

came the center of an elaborate ritual and incantation during which he either feigned or actually went into a state of unconsciousness. At the end of the ceremony he was brought back to his senses, rose to his feet, and regurgitated the shell, having partaken of the Spirit of Manido through the intermediary, Manabozho. The word the Indians used to describe the small white shell was

> Manna: the same word used by the ancient Semites to describe what Christians call Holy Communion or the Holy Eucharist; the same name that appears in Assyrian manuscripts dating back to 700 B.C. for the district in Armenia embracing Mount Ararat, one of the oldest place-names on earth.

Manna among the Hebrews and Manna in North America are only segments of a spiritual and mythological concept that encircled the globe:

> Manda: Aramean for "knowledge" and "fire."
>
> Mana: "a spiritual force or power which may be concentrated in objects or people"; it is a term common among the Polynesian and Melanesian tribes of the South Pacific.
>
> Manas: In Hinduism and Buddhism, "the rational faculty of the mind."
>
> Min: the Chinese word for "humanity," with a number of other related Min/Man names and words.
>
> Manassa: literally, in Hebrew, "oblivion. He shall forget his home." A wanderer.
>
> Manannan mac Lir: Manannan, the mighty "God of the Sea" in Irish mythology. In Welsh legends he was called Manawydan a Lyr, and he was also looked on by the Scots and the British as the son or god of the sea. The Irish called him "the Outer High King of Ireland," for he dwelt in his palace far across the sea to the east, but for convenience he also used the Isle of Man as a residence. He is described as "the best pilot in the west of Europe," as "a renowned trader" in another legend. He

is the only figure in Irish mythology who continues to appear in human form throughout all the cycles from beginning to end, helping the people of Ireland in crucial battles and in moments of great decision. As a worldwide wanderer and as a helper to his people, the comparison to Manabozho's role in North American mythology could not be closer.

The fact that Mycenae was situated in the Kingdom of Mani on the Peloponnesian Peninsula, with their king at the time of the siege of Troy named Menelaus, plus the Min element in the legendary Minos, founder of Cnossus on Crete, appears like another Mana chain of clues linking the Mediterranean civilization to Ireland and Great Britain.

It would take a separate book to do justice to the worldwide role of the name Mana. There are certain North American tribal and place-names of great pertinence, blending with the other key names:

Manahoac tribe: like the Manhuac River and the town Manhuac in Brazil, a blending of Mana/Hawa/Oc.

Mangoac tribe: Mana/Og/Hawa/Oc.

Manicouagan Lake, Manicouagan River, and Manicouagan Peninsula, all in Quebec. Mana/Oc/Hawa/Og/Ana.

Monaca, Pennsylvania, on the Ohio River, like Monach Island in the Hebrides, is a Mana/Oc blending that I discovered while cruising around Sardinia and Sicily several summers ago. It exists in enormous profusion along the coastal stretches and along the rivers of the entire earth, with the most famous, Monaco, principality of Monte Carlo, in the Mediterranean.

On the Little Colorado River there is a name reminiscent of the Adamawa region in Nigeria (see p. 125). It is Adamana, which looks like a blending of Adama and Mana. Like Ecuador, however, it is modern, a blending of Adam and Hanna, the first and last names of an early cattle rancher (see Stewart's *American Place-Names*).

PLATE 38. Ireland: tumulus at Knowth under excavation in 1967, a year prior to discovery of the passage. Sections cut into the side of the mound indicate previous unsuccessful attempts to locate the passage. Note the similarity to the view of the "Treasury of Atreus" at Mycenae in Plate 40.

Photo: Irish National Monuments Branch

PLATE 39. Cnossus, Crete: Palace of Minos, entrance ramp into the Central Court from the north. Note the megalithic stones characteristic of those found in prehistoric Britain, Ireland, South America, and elsewhere in the Mediterranean.

Photo: the Mansell Collection

PLATE 40. Mycenae, Greece: tholos, or beehive tomb, the so-called "Treasury of Atreus," 1400–1500 B.C. The view is from the east of the unroofed passage and mound covering the grave. Related structures exist in Spain, Portugal, and Ireland, notably at New Grange and Knowth.

Photo: the Mansell Collection

Mana: spiritual nourishment, the Eucharist.

There are a number of place-names that point up the interchangeable nature of Minna and Manna, including Manahawkin, New Jersey, and Minnewaukan, North Dakota, both variants of Mana/Hawa/Ok/Ana. The most famous Mana name in America was originally a blend of Mana/Atta/and Ana. When Henry Hudson arrived at the mouth of the river now bearing his name, there were two small Indian villages, one on either bank:

Manahata and Manahattana. The latter survived as Manhattan. There are a hundred or so such Manna/Atta combinations from coast to coast and throughout the world.

The interchangeable nature of Mona, Mana, and other variants is vividly pointed up by the following:

Old English—Mona
Icelandic—Mani
Gothic—Mena
Greek—Mene

All are words for the moon.

Mona Lake in Canada is one of hundreds of such names that dot the surface of the earth. Others more famous are:

Mona, the heart center of religion in Angelsey, Wales, when the Romans first invaded England.

Mona Straits, the gateway to the West Indies, approaching from the east.

Mane Lud, on the coast of Brittany, is an archaeological site where the most famous of the carved stones depicting prehistoric sailing ships with thirty or forty men aboard has been found.

The Mana River in Ethiopia finds its identical, unadorned counterpart in *Mana* in Guiana, Greece, the Hawaiian Islands, Iceland, Liberia, Sumatra, Uttar Pradesh, Venezuela; in the Mana River in Guiana, Mana Bay in Chile, Mana Island in the Fijis, Mana Island off New Zealand, Mana Pass in Tibet, the

PLATE 41. Peru: fortress of Sacsahumán, ancient Inca citadel in the hills above Cuzco. Both architecturally and in nomenclature, Sacsahuamán provides an interhemispheric link, along with other Peruvian sites, to Mediterranean, Great Britain, and Ireland.

Photo: Paul Popper, Ltd.

Mana Oya River in Ceylon; and, in slightly different forms: Manah in Muscat and Oman, Mannah Point in Sierra Leone, Manna'ah in Aden, Manna'ah Mountain in Arabia, the last two apparently once Manna Hawah.

*Mana*ssa: "Oblivion. He shall forget his home."

And his homeland shall forget him.

And now a name, a Mana blending, that led to two major developments. For over a year and a half I had been working in the wrong group of names, or rather the second group of key names, those that did not play any significant role in North America, Mexico, Peru, China, or in the Pacific east of and including Hawaii. Then, while on that same cruise in the Mediterranean, I became fascinated by the number of coastal places in the British Admiralty series Pilot Books of the World that bore names like Man of War.

I first began to run into these in the West Indian pilot books— bays, points, islands, channels, cays, and so on. At first I thought they must have to do with battleships, but they continued to pile up, and some of the places were pretty small. So I checked further and found them in Africa, in Sierra Leone and Liberia, then in India, including Manawar, which is more than a thousand miles from the sea.

And the Manwar River in India, a long, long way from Manawar. And El Manwar in Jordan. Three Manuwuri islands in the Maldives, famous for its skilled fishermen and navigators. Manawaru and Manawoara in New Zealand. Manoerwar and Maniwori in West Irian, Dutch New Guinea, a thousand miles from New Zealand. And, of all places, Menéwéré in Central Africa.

Then I came upon something most provocative. Until then I had not suspected that key names might have been blended during prehistoric times to form single names. But I found what looked like an obvious instance where this had happened. In Aden, in southern Arabia, there are two large adjacent regions called the Awamir area and the Manahil area. They are inhabited by the Awamir and Manahil tribes. Just to the west,

near the Yemen border, strategically positioned near the Red
Sea, across from Ethiopia, in what was once a fruitful land but
is now a desert, is a town or village named
        Manawa: *Mana*hil/*Awa*mir/*Manawa*.

It certainly looked as though someone at some time had
blended the two tribal and territorial names together. I decided
to look further. In Sudan, across the Red Sea, was *Manawa*shi.
Which led me to the *Manawa*li River in Ceylon, *Maniwa*li in
the state of Punjab, India, to *Manawa* in the Solomon Islands,
and finally to Manawa, Wisconsin.

Before too long I had come upon Lake Manawa and Lake
Manawa State Park in Iowa, Lake Manawan (Mana/Awa/Ana)
in Saskatchewan, Maniwaki (Mana/Awa/Ok) in Quebec. Starting with the Manawa blending in Aden, my eyes were suddenly
opened to scores of similar combinations that I had been passing
by unnoticed for many months.

Searching under other spellings, I came upon the age-old
Manoah watercourse in what is now Israel, which led me to
Manoa, Venezuela, the Manoa River in Hawaii, to Manoa,
Pennsylvania, and to another town in the same state that blends
Mana/Og/Awa: *Managua*. A name that later sharpened my
interest in the Aqua and Agua place-names I was beginning to
pick up all through North, Central, and South America.

The name Manoa, Pennsylvania, tied into one of the most
exciting single pieces of research during the entire project.
Thirty-one years ago, back in 1938, I had come across eye-
witness reports of two expeditions from Europe that in the
eighteenth century had reached a fabulous "City of Gold"
buried deep in the Brazilian jungles. Both expeditions had
ended in bloody carnage, and there were only a few survivors,
but in one of the museums of Europe there is today a small solid-
gold statue that came from this city. A few months ago I pulled
the notes about it out of a file of old papers. You can imagine
my feelings when I read, thirty-one years later, that the survivors
stated that the natives of the lost city called it Manoa.

I determined then that once this book was finished I would,

with the help of several friends, try to find this long-forgotten Manoa.[1] Having amassed a huge number of place-names in which Mana was obviously blended with Hawa and with Og/Oc, occasionally with both, I next examined blendings of Mana with Eloah and variants such as Ala. Here there was, if anything, an even larger number of pertinent names.

Beginning with *Manala*pan in New Jersey, there are scores of Manelas, Manillas, Manallas, and other variants scattered throughout North America, the West Indies, Africa, the Mediterranean area, and in Europe and Asia. Mineola, which turns up time and again, is another variant. It is the sort of picture that could only result from a blending of two prehistoric key names, each of great significance. Yet the most significant, or most revealing, of all the Mana blendings in North America, as it so happened, did not contain an Eloah or Ala element.

If you take an accepted etymological variation of:

Manna—Munna
Hawwah—Awha
Atta—Atte
Og—Aug

and line them in a row, you get:

Munnawhatteaug.

When the early Pilgrim fathers explored along the rugged New England coastline, shortly after landing at Plymouth Rock, they discovered that among the most daring and skillful of the native fishermen were the Narragansetts, an Algonquin tribe now listed as officially extinct but whose blood is intermingled with that of many "white" people living in the vicinity. Their tribal name is perpetuated in the name Narragansett (Rhode Island). This was the center of their activities in prehistoric days.

The new New Englanders soon learned that the Narragansetts not only went far offshore in all sorts of weather at all times

---

[1] Note, too, the ruins of *Mnaji*dra on Malta, Plate 7, a conceivable blending of Mana (Mna) and Hawwah (aji).

of the year but also that they had learned how to net a species of shad in great numbers, and through an intricate pressing process turned the crushed flesh and small bones of the shad into a highly beneficial fertilizer. The white men learned where the schools of fish ran and also learned the process, which had obviously been handed down from generation to generation, for making the fertilizer. Today it is a multimillion-dollar-a-year business, wtih fleets of deep-sea fishing boats operating all up and down the East Coast. It is still one of the best of all fertilizers, and the oil squeezed out of the fish is also sold commercially.

Aside from their fishing craft, this fertilizer must have been the most precious commodity in the lives of the Narragansetts, something they must have regarded as the chief gift bestowed on them by their benevolent Creator. At great personal risk, often in the face of death, they lifted this gift out of the depths of the sea and laid it on the face of the earth, and God miraculously helped them to reap ever more fruitful harvests.

It is difficult to imagine anything that would have been looked upon with more profound reverence by the Narragansetts. I believe you will agree that in the beginning, though the original meaning was forgotten by the time the Europeans settled in, this fertilizer must have received a proper name in every way worthy of its role. At least that is the line of reasoning I have taken and that is why I was so encouraged to read that the name of the fertilizer, the native name, was

Munnawhatteaug.

Which I do not believe happened by accident or through some million-to-one chance of a group of four "sound-alikes" ending up together in the same name. Rather I believe that the name was a blend of Manna (spiritual nourishment), Hawwah (mother of all living), Atta (greatness), and Og (ancient symbol of fertility).

My convictions on this point became even stronger in view

of two additional North American mythological names, one of which is

> Ketchimanetowa: the Great Spirit, the Creator, of the Fox Indians, whose earthly hunting grounds were once the verdant, river-fed country now called Wisconsin. By replacing a hypothetical lost vowel, one arrives at

Oketchimanetowa.

And the same four names found in *munnawhatteaug* are magically reassembled:

OKETCHIMANETOWA	MUNNAWHATTEAUG	KEY NAME
Ok	Aug	Oc/Og
Owa	Awha	Hawwah
Mane	Munna	Manna
Eto/Et	Atte	Ata/Atta

The same thing holds true of:

> Keckamanetowa, the Gentle Manitou of the Fox Indians, a less awesome, more humanistic concept of God, Manitou being a "spirit or deity," a "supernatural creature that controls nature." Manitou was a name used all through the North American Indian world above the tribal level, a name perpetuated in scores of place-names from coast to coast. In Keckamanetowa there was once conceivable Ock (Eck), already visible. By restoring an initial *O*, one has Ok twice and the same three other names once each: Manna, Hawa, Atta, in Okeckamanetowa.

An interesting cross-check developed out of this. By following the same sequence of elements in Munnawhatteaug and (O)Ketchimanetowa, one arrives at

> Munnawhatteaug

and

> Manewatok.

Which brings them much closer together in looks and even more so in sound. While Manewatok helps immeasurably to unlock the true elements in the name of a city in Wisconsin on the shores of Lake Michigan:

Manitowoc.

Here the Hawwah and Oc names stand clear at the end. Owoc, as in our starting place, Haue Oc, "havoc," as in Oconomowoc, Wisconsin, and as in the name of the bustling Wisconsin metropolis near Manetowoc and Oconomowoc:

Mil*wauk*ee.

Hawk as Hawa/Ok in the tribal name Mohawk seems like a more reasonable speculation. And one wonders as to the true origin of the name of the fierce bird of prey the hawk, which in Old English was the *hafoc*. As in Haue Oc, "havoc."

The dimensions of the earth, the differences between the peoples of the world, do they seem to be rapidly shrinking? Such Manitouwa place-names as Lake Manitouwadge suggest that the all-powerful name Manitou was once

Manitouwa: Manna/Ata/Hawa.

Note also Owachomo, Utah, which appears to blend Hawa/Oc at the beginning. This Owa prefix is one of a number of what I believe are Hawwah place-names that the white men wrote down as Owa, some already encountered, some like Owatona, Owasa, and many others, as well as in endings like Ketchimanitowa.

I previously suggested that the greeting still extant in Yorkshire, meaning "God bless you!" Wah! was once upon a time Hawwah. The English took another of the most common words in our language and did the opposite with it. Whereas the words "what," "where," "when," and "why" all originally had hwa beginnings, which were lost, they took:

hwah

and turned it into

"how."

They knocked off the back end of *hwah*, the earliest recorded spelling of "how," leaving only the front end.

As the Europeans fanned out across North America, the Indians apparently extended to them what must have been an all-important, highly significant greeting, one the white men jotted down as

How![2]

But which I strongly suspect was the same name found in their most profound mythological names and key place-names:

*Haw*wah!

[2] According to Mrs. Ruth Wilcox, Librarian at the Museum of the American Indian Heye Foundation, New York City, the evidence indicates that this greeting sounded like "How!" Some writers claim that the Indians picked this up from the white man's "How are you?" There are greetings in at least four recorded dialects that sound like "How!" notably "Hau!" in Ute-Paiute.

Chapter 16

THE ROLE PLAYED by the Manna/Mana key name in prehistory will take on added stature with the other key names as we move on geographically, but now the time has come to concentrate in the Americas on the question of Aqua/Agua names and their significance in the pre-Columbian Americas.

Concentrating on Aqua/Agua names means looking only at those that begin with Oc or Og. In this group it is worth noting that a large number of Hog/Hogg and Egg names turn up everywhere: Ege, Indiana; Egavik (Og/Ava/Ok) and Egegik (Og/Og/Ok) in Alaska; Egg Harbor in New Jersey and Wisconsin; Egg Island, Alaska; Egg Island Point, New Jersey; Hogg Lake, Canada; the Hog river in Alaska; Hog Island, in Maine and Michigan and eastern Virginia.

Such names as Lake Ogoki and Ogoki River in Ontario, Canada; Lake Ochek in Canada, Ekwok (Ok/Hawa/Ok), which is an Aqua beginning, as well as a "havoc" ending, and Ugak Island and Ugak Bay, all in Alaska, strengthen the conviction that the Egg/Hog names were originally in honor of Og, "the last of the giants." (As mentioned earlier, Oc/Og overshadows Hawwah in the Northwest.) These names lead smoothly into such Aqua/Akhaiwa names as: Lake Echouani in Quebec, Akwatuk Bay in Alaska (Ok/Hawa/Ata/Ok), Okawville, Illinois; Lake Ahquabi State Park, Iowa; the Aguanus

River, Quebec; and Oquawka, Illinois, on the bank of the Mississippi opposite Iowa, where Oquawka = Akhaiwa followed by the reverse Hawa/Ok.

Keokuk, Iowa, at the confluence of the Des Moines and Mississippi rivers, rises up as a mighty Okeokuk. Farther upstream there are some celebrated caves that are billed in Iowa tourist literature as the home of prehistoric Indians:

Maquoketa Caves State Scientific Preserve: Aqua or Akhaiwa followed by another Ok. Aquok, as in Oquawka, Illinois, a few miles away.

Note also Chautauqua, Iowa, as in Lake Chautauqua and Chautauqua, New York, scene of the celebrated outdoor meetings, lectures, and concerts which attained such popularity in the late nineteenth century and early twentieth.[1] There are also Chappaqua, New York; the Metakawa Trail in Canada, and the Agawa River and Agawa Bay in Canada. And in the vast, fortunately for this study, relatively untouched stretches of the same fantastic country: Lake Aquatuk and the Aquatuk River, identical etymologically to Akwatuk Bay above, with Aqua or Akhaiwa, followed by Ata and Ok. There are also Aquanish, Canada, and Aigle Lake and the Aigle River, with Og and Ala, taking a spelling identical to the earlier form of the majestic royal bird the eagle.

Contributed by one of my dedicatees, Dr. Frederick L. Santee of Wapwallopen, Pennsylvania, in his home state, is Mocanaqua, according to the map but billed in the Berwick newspaper as Mocanagua: Aqua and Agua, the two classical forms of "water." There are also the Conococheague Creek, and the peacefully English-sounding Aughwick River (Og/Hawa/Ock).

In New York State, one of the loveliest sounding of all the Oc/Og/Hawa names blends Ouaquaga, Aqua/Akhaiwa, preceded by an Hawa, followed by an Og: Massapequa and Massa-

[1] As the fame of Chautauqua, New York, spread throughout the land, the name was frequently transplanted by white men. But the name was originally an Indian name.

pequa State Park on Long Island, which are near Aquebogue, Long Island, with Aqua and Agua in the same name. And far upstate in New York is the city of Canandaigua.

There is a group of Akhaiwa names that remained hidden for a long time. I should have found them when I got on to Keokuk. One of the most romantic-sounding names is of the hard-riding tribe from the Southwest Plains of North America, the tribe whose name is

Kiowa.

Since Ouaouaia became Iowa, it would seem that the "Iowa" in Kiowa was also once Hawa, particularly since the Kiowa Indians came from this region. Which would leave the *K* as a logical Ok: Okhaiwa or Okihawa.

And the Kaw (Kansas) River, which flows through Kansas City, Missouri, would have once been

Akawa (Akhaiwa) River.

The name Kiowa led me far up to the headquarters of another river, perhaps the most famous in the world, the Nile, into the heart of Uganda, to one of the largest lakes on the continent of Africa, one thousand square miles in area, most suitably named

Lake Kioga (or Kyoga): again, as Okioga, the duel Ok/Og form.

Which in turn led me in a great sweep across Africa to the Kwango River, and to the people I had overlooked before, the tribes who live along the coast of West Africa and who, befitting such a maritime location, bear the name

Kwa: once Okawa? Oc/Haiwah? Akhaiwa?

Strengthening this origin point of Okawa, one group of the Kwa people speaks a language that is spelled Ewe but is pronounced

Ava or Awa.

These names led me back again many thousands of miles to the rugged country of the American Northwest, to

Kwethluk, and the Kwethluk River: Alaska: Akhaiwa (Ata/Ala/Ok);

And to another place in Alaska that must either be extraordinarily beautiful or awe-inspiring, or else in some faraway century some momentous event happened there. For the Indians called it

Kwigillingok: Aqua or Akhaiwa (Og/Alla/Ana/Og/Ok).

The original Indian name of the Yukon River was recorded by Russian explorers as

Kwik-Pak, meaning "river big." With a vowel in front and one added internally this becomes Okawik: Ok/Awa/Ok. Note also the Kokwok River in Alaska. As Okoka-wok: Ok/Ok/Awa/Ok.

The Indians who bestowed these "names on the land"—and I can understand now why George Stewart in his book states that Alaska and Hawaii, the last two states to join the Union, are the two parts of the world where place-names have been tampered with the least—these Indians were undoubtedly those whose tribal name is

Kwakvatl, which with four vowel additions or replacements becomes:

Ok/Awa/Ok/Ava/Ata/Ala: Okawakavatala.

Akhaiwa, Akhaiwa, Ata, Ala.

Ata/Atta appears so often you might wonder why it is not classified with the other key names in the first group. The fact, however, that it was an abstraction, Greatness, just as Ana or Anna meant Favored or Blessed, indicates in my opinion a filler role, compared to Oc/Og, Hawwah/Avvah, Eloah/Ala, and Mana/Manna.

The Kwakvatl Indians, who have been the subject of much research by anthropologists and etymologists, live on Vancouver Island and along the coast of British Columbia, again befitting their Akhaiwa sea name. They speak a language that is one of a group identified by the name

Waukashan: the reverse sequence of Ok/Hawa, Hawa/Ok, as in Haue Oc, "havoc." This is almost identical to the name of another Wisconsin city, Waukesha. And in the same category, there are Waukegan, Illinois; Wauchula, Florida; and, last, the theatrical-sounding name Waukon, found in both Iowa and Washington.

This collection of Aqua (Ok/Awa), and Agua (Og/Hawa)

place-names far out of the orbit of Spanish exploration and colonization, convinced me I should go back to Central and South America and take a closer look at the Agua/Aqua place-names in that area. I had been passing over many of them for several years, figuring they were names brought in by the Spaniards, and in a number of instances they are direct transplants. It soon became obvious, however, that the majority had been there long before the Iberians. There are at least two Mexican Indian tribes whose names begin with Agua:

Agualulco tribe and Aguatecan tribe. The other elements also look familiar.

The capital of Nicaragua (a native name itself) is

Managua: a key blend of Mana/Og/Hawa. Mañagua is on one of the largest lakes in Central America, Lake Managua, in the district of Managua. It is far and away the most prominent place-name in Nicaragua. It was soon joined by Masagua in neighboring Guatemala, another important native name. In Mexico is Agualeguas, river and city, a name composed of Og/Hawa/(Akhaiwa) Ala/Og/Hawa/(Akhaiwa). Two Akhaiwas joined together by Eloah/Ala, a powerful name.[2]

Another one, just as powerful in its own way, is the highest mountain in South America, in Argentina:

Aconcagua, again a native name, originally Ocanocogua: Oc/Ana/Oc/Oc/Hawa.

My thoughts returned to Achacachi, the highest city in South America, close to the great ruins of Tiahuanaco. To Akiachak, the thirteenth tallest mountain in the world, in British Columbia, the home of the Kwakvatl people. Were these towering Oc names purely coincidental? Certainly they were not imported by Europeans.

Elsewhere one finds: the thousand-mile-long Araguaia River

[2] Note also Gualaguala Pta., Chile, and three Gualilagua names in Ecuador.

in Brazil: Og/Hawa/Hawa. And the even more famous Para-
gua(y) and Uragua(y) rivers, native Og/Hawa names that have
each been given to a country. Note Aiguá, an intriguing spelling
in Uruguay; Aricagua in Venezuela; Aconcagua Province in
Chile, similar to the tallest mountain in South America; Aragua
Straits off the coast of Chile.

These names, plus scores more like them, convinced me of
two things: First, North, Central, and South America had been
overflowing with major Aqua/Agua place-names, and some
tribal names, long before "Columbus discovered America."
Second, in view of this, taken in the context of the parts of the
world so far covered, it looked extremely logical that the Latin
word for water, *aqua*, and its Spanish variant, *agua*, had both
come from the same source as these other Aqua/Agua place-
names in North, Central, and South America.

At this point I began to experiment by putting vowels in
front of names starting with Gua and Qua. I had done it with
many other names and words before, but I had never thought
of doing it with these. The first name I took was the name of
the capital of a country. It had fascinated me for a long time
because of some internal elements and because of the name of
the country. I took the capital of Ecuador on the northwest
coast of South America, lying between ancient Anahuac and
ancient Huaca Prieta. The capital's name and the name of the
bay on which it is situated is

Guayaquil.

Simply by putting an *O* at the beginning, and an *A* at the
end, I came up with

Oguayaquila: Og/Hawa/Hawa/Oc/Hawa/(Akhaiwa)/
Ala. The name contains two Akhaiwa elements, and has
an ending comparable to Aquila, the same name as that
of the northern constellation—Aquila; the same name as
the northern Italian city destroyed by Attila the Hun in
the fifth century A.D., a great citadel whose founding is
lost in the unrecorded past—Aquila; the same name as the

Latin word for "eagle"—symbol of kingship since time began, down to the standards of Napoleon and the seal of the United States—*aquila.*

The discovery of this name in association with Ecuador, half-way between Huaca Prieta and Anahuac, encouraged me to go on, and the result with the Aqui part of the name decided me to go north as soon as I had finished with one other name of high rank in the south. It had slowly penetrated my consciousness that whether or not these various names had or had not once had an initial vowel, the elements within the names were made up primarily, about 85 percent, of the key names, preceded by a consonant that did not make much sense without a vowel. For example, the present spelling Guayaquil = G + Hawa(ua), Hawa (Aya), Oc (Aq), Hawa(ui), Ala(il).

Turning to the "other name of high rank in the south," if you blend Og, and the Ua form of Hawa, and the Blessed or Favored word Ana, you get

Oguaana.

Remove the *O,* change one internal *a* to an *i,* and you get

Guiana, the gateway to South America from the Caribbean.

After this, I headed up the coast of North America to the eastern shore of Canada. The entire portion of the country from the Atlantic west to Toronto and Cleveland, an immense trackless region extending up to Hudson Strait and Baffin Bay, into which you could comfortably fit New England, New York State, and the Middle Atlantic states, bears a single name. The land is crammed with Aqua place-names—towns, lakes, and rivers—and the region itself bears a name beginning with Que. It also ends with Oc (Ec). The name is

Quebec. Once Ocua (Akhaiwa) (b) Oc?

From here I moved down the coast to New England, back to the coastal region where the Narragansett Indians for unknown centuries netted fish out of the depths of the sea, changed it into what they called Munnawhattaug, and laid it on the soil as fertilizer. The town of Narragansett is located in what is today the state of Rhode Island. Here I found five names that

not only firmed up my convictions about the ancient name
Quebec, and most of what has gone before in these pages, but
which also shortly unlocked a number of mammoth doorways
leading into prehistory.

Rhode Island wasn't always called that. The natives called it
   Aquethneck (Aquidneck): Oc Hawa (Akhaiwa), with an
   Oc ending.

On March 13, 1644, the Court of Providence Plantation ruled
that the name Aquethneck should be changed to Rhode Island.
And so it has remained. Aquethneck disappeared, but two Indian names remain in the vicinity to this day. One is called
   Agawam.

The other is the name of a village that is so small it doesn't even
have its own post office; and it is so close to the boundary between Massachusetts and Rhode Island that while it is itself in
Massachusetts, its mail goes to the post office in Little Compton,
Rhode Island. Ever since history began in this part of the world,
the name of this village has been, and still is,
   Acoaxtet: Acoa = Oc Hawa? Akhaiwa? An unfamiliar
   form. Acoaxtet on the island of Aquethneck where the
   Indians used to spread the fertilizer, Munnawhattaug, on
   their fields.

Also on Narragansett Bay, only three miles across the boundary from what was once Aquethneck, and within a few miles
of Acoaxtet, is the seaport of Fall River. Like Rhode Island, the
name was not always Fall River. The name was changed at
some time during the eighteenth century. Until then the Indians
had always called it
   Quequeteant.

Aquethneck and Quequeteant, only a few miles apart, a large
island and the largest center in that area at the mouth of the
biggest river. Was Quequeteant once
   Aquequeteant? Oc/Hawa/Oc/Hawa? Akhaiwa/Akhaiwa?

This is of great import, because Quequeteant meant to the
Indians "Place of the falling water":
   aqua (Latin) = water.

Akhaiwa = the name by which the "Sea People" called themselves.

(A)quequeteant in Narragansett = "Place of the falling water."

Armed with what appeared to be a new variant, Acoa, I headed back down the coast to Central and South America, pausing only to note that the name of one of the greatest beaches in the world, a strange, haunting name known to everyone who has ever been to the Hamptons at the far end of Long Island, New York, now had come into the light:

Quoque. Once Oquoque: Oc/Hawa/Oc/Hawa? Akhaiwa/ Akhaiwa?

In *The Random House Dictionary of the English Language,* which has been a steadfast companion because it contains the etymology of so many Indian names and words, the next entry after Quebec, in the Gazetteer section, is a Mexican city:

Quecholac. Once Oquechoalac? Oc/Hawa/Oc/Hawa/ Ala/Oc? Akhaiwa/Akhaiwa/Ala/Oc?

The name Quecholac led to one of the most important names in prehistoric South America, a name still very much on the scene. It is the name of a people and of their language. About 4,000,000 of these people live on the Andean plateaus, a mountain people stretched out from Ecuador in the northwest to Argentina in the southeast. Their language was once "an official language" of the Incas, and the territory where they live encompasses the ruins of Tiahuanaco and the cloud-encircled town of Achacachi. The name of the people and their language is

Quechua. In the days of their splendor, Oquechua? Ochua/ Ochua? Akhaiwa/Akhaiwa?

PLATE 42. Maya: stele from Quiriguá, one of a number of such intricately carved monolithic stone monuments discovered at the site. As with many widely scattered names today beginning with Qui, Que, and so on, the author believes the name was once *A*quiragua, featuring twice in combination two most important prehistoric names discussed in *The Key*.

Photo: the British Museum

Looking back at a name I had jotted down weeks before, I now saw that Oc/Ata/Oc/Hawa/Ala blend into
Ocataquala.
With the mortality of the vowels at either end, the name becomes
Cataqual
and hence
Catequil, the dreaded thunder god of the Incas.
Near the city of Tlalpan in southern Mexico is a huge oval mound erected by an unknown prehistoric people. The site is so old that when the Spaniards came to the New World, the Aztecs had no records or any legendary explanation as to who had built it.
If you take Oc/Awa, Oc/Awa, Ala, and Ok/Awa, the same two names found clustered around Stonehenge and at Avebury, the same two names featured in Haue Oc and in Akhaiwa, but with three Akhaiwa's, and if you blend these together with an Ala, you get
Ocawaocawalokawa.
By changing the Awa's into more familiar Mexican forms, you get
Ocuacualocoa.
Then, by dropping the hypothetical vowel at the beginning and end and between the *l* and *c*, you get
Cuacualco.
And last, by substituting two *i*'s for the two *a*'s, you get
Cuicuilco.
And that is the name of the huge prehistoric mound near Tlalpan:
Cuicuilco. Once Akhaiwa/Akhaiwa/Ala/Akhaiwa?
Most significantly, the name is still broken up into three parts when pronounced, with the phonetic sounds much more readily identifiable:
Kwé-kwé-lko.
The name Tlalpan led by association to an unexpected bonus, to the name
Tlaloc, conceivably a combination of Ata/Ala/Ala/Oc?
*Ata*laloc, *Ata*laloc, Tlaloc.

PLATE 43. Mexico: Tlaloc, Azetec God of Rain. According to the basic premise of the text, Tlaloc was formerly *Ata*laloc, a blending of Ata/Ala/Ala/Oc, all familiar Semitic name elements.

Photo: Museo de Antropología, Mexico City

And Tlaloc is the name of the Aztec God of Rain.[3]

On the Acoa front, I experimented with names of high standing. First, Coahuila, the name of a Mexican state that has been there since the recorded period commenced. If, like *Acoa*xtet in *Aque*thneck (presently Rhode Island), Coahuila originally had an initial vowel, then

> *O*coahu*a*la = Ocoahu*i*la = Øcoahuila = Coahuila. Oc/ Hawa/Ala. Avalok in a different sequence. Akhaiwa/ Eloah.

Next two tongue twisters, one beginning with the same Coa element, the other with Que. The first is on the Gulf of Mexico, just where the Yucatán Peninsula begins to curve out from Mexico proper:

> Coatzacoalcos, a key site, one of the fabled Mayan ruined complexes. In this name one *acoa* is already visible: Coatz-*acoa*lcos. By adding three *a*'s, Acoa appears twice again: *Acoa*tazacoa*lacoa*s. Three Akhaiwa's? Three couplings of Oc/Hawa?

. [3] TLaLoC appears to have highly significant interhemispheric relationships. T*L in Hebrew means "moisture, dew." An earlier T*L word with the same meaning exists in Ugaritic. The name aTLantic, its origin lost in prehistory, provides an etymological "water" link between "moisture, dew" in the eastern Mediterranean, and "rain" in Central America. While in Ireland TuLCa means "a large wave, a flood, *a heavy fall of rain*." See also TuLCaighil, "the act of raining."

The name of the ancient, mystery-shrouded Irish goddess TLaChtga is one to conjure with. "Silent" Tlachtga died giving birth to triplet sons sired by three legendary brothers of Asia Minor. She conceived her offspring while traveling in the Mediterranean region with her "giant" father, Mug, "master of thousands." (In Christian times the three brothers were updated to the role of sons of Simon Magus, the Samarian sorcerer reputedly converted by Philip the Apostle, but the myth of Tlachtga and her eastern lovers predated Christ by many centuries in Ireland.)

Miss Margaret Murphy of the Dublin Institute for Advanced Studies advises that the "Palace of Tlachtga" above the Boyne River outside Athboy, today unromantically called the "Hill of Ward," a 390-foot-high, unexcavated mound with four rings of ramparts, was in earliest pagan times held sacred even above the nearby Hill of Tara. Tlachtga's name appears to be reflected in Tlacht, "mourning dress." Note *Tlacht na neamh marbhtachta*, "the garment of immortality."

The second name is another well-known archaeological site, this one in Guatemala:

> Quezaltenago. By adding a vowel in front and one in back, the name becomes:
>
> *Aque*alten*agoa*.

Another Akhaiwa beginning with an Og/Hawwah ending.[4]

The elements in these two names point the way toward a similar interpretation of the name of the best-known mythological figure in the Western Hemisphere. There is only one element, a z, in this name, for which no explanation has been offered in these pages (but this will have to wait until a later chapter):

> Oc/Awa/Ata/Z/Ala/Oc/Awa/Ata/Ala
> Ocawatazalacawatala
> Øcawatazalacawatala
> Cawatzalcawatl

If you pronounce this name aloud, Cawatzalcawatl, I believe you will agree it is phonetically identical to Quetzalcoatl, who was the dreaded plumed serpent god of the Huaztecs and the Toltecs but who in other legends was a "white-skinned" stranger who "came across the sea, from the east, in a great winged ship." See Plates 44 and 45.

It seems significant that the same elements suggested for the name Quetzalcoatl are the same elements found in the names of the two ancient peoples who worshiped him:

> Hua (Awa)/Z/Ata/Oc
> Huazatoc
> Huazatoc
> Huaztoc—Huaztec

And

> Ata/Ala/Ata/Oc
> Atalatoc
> Atalatoc

---

[4] Note also the name of the Mayan site Quiriguá, Plate 42. Once *Aquirigua?*

PLATES 44 and 45. Mexico: two interpretations of Quetzalcoatl, most dreaded, most widely worshipped god in Central America. On the right, one sees the deity as the great plumed serpent. On the left, a statue from the Musée Nationale d'Anthropologie, Paris, blends the early mythological concept of Quetzalcoatl as a white-skinned benevolent stranger from the east, who brought wisdom and knowledge of the arts and sciences to Mexicans, with the majestic plumed serpent god.

Photos: Plate 44, Museo de Antropología, Mexico City; Plate 45, Giraudon

Taltoc

Toltec

At the end of Chapter 6 I stated, "While the temptation to insert, remove, and change vowels indiscriminately in names and words has been at times overwhelming, I have tried to hold the process within bounds." In connection with this last group of names, beginning with Guayaquil and ending with Quetzalcoatl, I must confess that the temptation has been irresistible. Faced, however, with a large number of key place-names and mythological names that still today contain within them, featured prominently, what in my opinion are recognizable Oc and Hawwah elements, the experiment appeared to be worth making with other equally important names that conceivably once featured these same elements.

Throughout, the only process followed has been to delete, add, and change vowels, and here, as stated before, one is dealing with an ephemeral process that during the historical period has provably altered and obliterated the original forms of innumerable names. This simple process alone, using the cluster of place-names on the coast of Rhode Island as the formula or code, has produced what is at least a consistent rationalization of the following "prehistoric" names:

> Guayaquil . . . Guiana . . . Quebec . . . Quequeteant (Fall River) . . . Quoque . . . Quecholac . . . Quechua . . . Catequil (the Peruvian Thunder God) . . . Cuicuilco . . . Tlaloc (the Aztec Rain God) . . . Coatzacoalcos . . . Quetzalcoatl . . . Huaztec and Toltec.

Other comparable names, which contain additional elements not yet presented, will be discussed in subsequent chapters, both in the Americas and elsewhere. The place of honor at the end of this chapter is reserved for my home state of Connecticut. In its first recorded form it was spelled

Quinetucquet.

In the far-off past, *Oquanatocoquata*? Oc/Awa/Ana/Ata/ Oc/Oc/Awa/Ata? Another Akhaiwa coastal region?

Chapter 17

I BELIEVE YOU will agree that to cross the Atlantic Ocean and to find in the Americas what appear to be the same key names playing the same key roles in mythological and place-names as were found in the Mediterranean basin and the surrounding land masses bolsters up one's overall faith in the names. If one did not find them in the Western Hemisphere, I think it would shake one's morale pretty badly. And the whole premise is so contrary to what we have been taught, every bit of evidence that strengthens conviction is more than welcome.

Moving westward across the Pacific Ocean from the Peruvian coast, hopping from island to island all the way to and including China and the rest of the Asian mainland, the impact of the same key names is overwhelming, far greater than it has been anywhere else. The four key names covered to date, Hawwah/ Avvah, Og/Ok, Eloah/Ala, and Manna/Mana, dominate the scene. The identical combinations appear again and again on islands separated from one another by thousands of miles of open ocean.

In Hawaii one finds:

Hawaii: the native name for the islands, identical to Hawwah.

Aloha: the word or name extended both as a welcome and a farewell, identical phonetically to Eloah, the Semitic name for God. With a global relationship growing

PLATE 46. Mexico: Pyramid of the Sun at Teotihuacán. Built in the same manner as Egyptian pyramids by unknown pre-Aztec people, this most imposing of all Mexican monuments is 216 feet high, and measures 721 feet and 761 feet at its irregularly shaped base. The name Teotihuacán, closely resembling Tiahuanaco, "mightiest ruins in South America," is interpreted by the author as a blending of Ata/Ata/Hua/Oc/Ana, elements that appear over and over again in prehistoric place-names, mythological names, and tribal names across the whole face of the globe.

Photo: Ewing Galloway

stronger, Alloa, the oldest recorded greeting in the British Isles, the forerunner of Hello, commands more attention.

"hula": the name of the celebrated native dance, accepted as coming from a religious origin with strong fertility overtones, is a common variant of Eloah/Allah/Ala in place-names. In addition to a number of Ula names, some already mentioned, note Hula in Ethiopia, El Hula in Lebanon, Lake Hula in Israel, the Hulahula River in Alaska, Hulah and Hulah Reservoir in Oklahoma, as well as Mount Huila and Huila Division in Colombia, a name which appears twice in Angola, Africa.

Ua: a common variant of Hawa in place-names, Ua is the Hawaiian word for Life. A direct relationship in meaning to Hawwah, the Semitic name for "mother of all living."

wai: with a striking resemblance to the Semitic words *wâh*, meaning "oasis," and *wâhat*, meaning "water hole," *wai* is the Polynesian word for "water." It appears to fit into a worldwide "Hawwah" picture:

Egyptian—wâh (oasis) wâhat (water hole)

Hawaiian—wai

Mexican—ahue (pronounced Hawwah)

Latin—aq*ua*

English—*water*

Narragansett Indian—*queque*

All these "water" words contain at least part of a Hawwah element. Recent changes in North African "water" place-names have been from Hawa (Oua) to Wa, a process that goes on constantly in place-names all over the world. There is no prior form of the English word for "water" that indicates a *Hawa* origin, although one does find *hwaet* for "wheat," and so on. The Latin *aqua* is said to come from Achelous and is related to Oceanus, which does not account for the *ua* element in *aqua*.

There are three important native Hawaiian words that appear to be related, in two cases to Hawwah, in one to both Og/Oc and Hawwah:

ahu: "a stone heap or platform used by the Polynesians as a marker or memorial; once *ahua*?

> *ahupuaa*: the basic land unit or plot into which Hawaii was
> divided among families.
>
> *kahuna*: once *Okahuana*? Ok/Hawa/Ana. *Kahuna* is the
> Polynesian name for medicine man or priest.

One thing is true about the place-names in Hawaii and throughout the Pacific, as well as in China. If I had written the pages already written and then had "invented" another part of the world, and had given you a list of the place-names I claimed to have found there, I could not have made up a list that dovetailed more perfectly with what had gone before. What is so fascinating is that with thousands of miles between many of the islands, and apparently for centuries with no communication back and forth, although the languages differ to an incredible degree (there are in the neighborhood of two thousand dialects in that part of the world), the same blended place-names, containing the same four key names, turn up over and over and over again in the most remote, miniscule corners of the Pacific.

The only logical explanation I can think of is that the same names were taken in prehistoric times from one common source, and then, through lack of communication, and with people remembering less from generation to generation, they took on a wide assortment of local meanings that had nothing to do with the original ones. Being ancient, however, they were regarded with reverence and tampered with as little as possible.

In his chapter on Hawaii in *Names on the Land*, George Stewart registers a basic point that applies not only to the Pacific but to place-names everywhere. He states that "one might venture to apply a principle so nearly universal that it has even been called a law, that is, that unintelligible but repeated elements in names are to be referred back to some generic term in an earlier language." Which in my opinion is a law or principle that my collective evidence is supporting in each part of the world covered.

Of the name Hawaii, Stewart explains that it is "of such ancient origin as to defy attempts at translation." Some scholars believe it "echoes the name of an ancient homeland." Stewart also mentions an alternate name found elsewhere in the Pacific, one that I couldn't have topped on my "made-up" list:

Hawaik: Hawa/Ok.

Hawaik could well be a transitory form between Haue Oc and "havoc," complete to internal vowels. Other place-names Stewart mentions as being difficult or impossible to find satisfactory meanings for are:

Alalakeiki: Ala/Ala/Ok/Ok.

Kahoolawe: Ok/Hawa (Akhaiwa), Ala/Awa.

Kaiwi: As Okaiwi, again Akhaiwa; an ancient name for a channel between two of the islands, and "dubiously translated as 'the bone.' "

Kealaikahiki: With an initial *O*, Ok/Ala/Ok/Hawa/Ok— the name of a sea passage the natives say means "the way to Tahiti."

Waiwa, Waiaka, Waikoko, Wailuku, four names of places by water, were once Hawa names. In each case blends of Ok and/or Ala are involved. (Waiakoa is another particulary pertinent Hawaiian place-name.)

The name Hawaiians use when they refer to the people who traditionally were already there when their own ancestors first came on the scene is one to conjure with. Blending Mana/Hua/Ana into Manahuana leads with vowel switches to Menehuane, and then dropping the *a* results in Menehune. This is the name of the legendary first inhabitants, Menehune, an especially significant Manawa combination, as in southern Arabia, Wisconsin, Iowa, and elsewhere throughout the world.

In order to show the universality of names throughout this immense stretch of ocean, and not only their similarity to each other but also to those that have gone before, I am going to choose among different islands and from the Asian mainland. There are so many pertinent ones that it is hard to choose.

Halawa Cape and Walawa Heights above Pearl Harbor are identical to a number of names, already encountered, which blend Ala with Hawa. Walawa Heights is identical to Walawa, the early English expression signifying sorrow or despair.

The name of the Walla Walla River in New South Wales is identical to Walla Walla, Washington.

Ua Huka Island, in the Marquesas, is another Hawa/Ok blending.

Kuala begins hundreds of names, especially in Indonesia and Malaya: once an Akhaiwa name? Ok/Ua/Ala/Okuala. At least we know we have here Hawa and Ala blended together preceded by a *K*. Such names as Kualakapuas in Borneo contain in them Hawa/Ala/Ok/Hawa, regardless of whether or not the first *K* was or wasn't an Ok in the past.

The Akimanawa mountain range in New Zealand is made up of Ok plus the same *manawa* found in southern Arabia, Iowa, Wisconsin, and many other places. The Awakino River (repeated as a town name) is one of a number of Hawa/Ok names in New Zealand.

The name of the Arawak Indians in the West Indies, the Awak of which was proposed as a Hawwah/Ok blending of the Haue Oc/Havok/"havoc" category, is balanced off in Borneo, on the opposite side of the planet, by the name of one of its principal regions, for some generations a separate kingdom under the "White rajahs" of the English Brook family:

Sarawak: Arawak.

Uwekuana (Uwekahuna) Park in Hawaii is a magnificent example of a Havok (Uwek) and an Akhaiwa (Akua) blended within the same name.[1]

And now I see that if you take two Akua's and put them together into

Akuakua (Akhaiwa-Akhaiwa),

and then take them apart a little differently:

Aku-Akua,

and knock another of those fickle vowels off the end, you have

Aku-Aku,

---

[1] In this category are such names as Uakaku, Borneo; El Uach and El Ualac (Hawa/Ala/Oc), Somalia; Uala (Hawa/Ala) Bay and Ualik (Hawa/Ala/Oc), USSR; repeated in Lake Ualik, Alaska. Uala also is a town name in New Caledonia.

the mighty Polynesian god whose name is perpetuated in Thor Heyerdahl's great book *Aku-Aku*.

The islands of Samoa—and Samoa itself boasts an Awa ending—offer a number of key blendings that are near-pristine, including

Avalua Island: the Ava form of Hawwah and Eloah (Alua).

Iva, the largest town on Avalua Island, is identical phonetically to the ancient city of Ivvah in the Old Testament, and to a number of small towns named Iva that are scattered throughout the United States.

A channel that cuts past Avalua Island is named

Oagava: Hawa/Og/Ava.

And elsewhere in Samoa are a bay, a channel, and a passage all called

Avatele, with three familiar elements: Ava/Ata/Ala.

Another fascinating concentration of key names is found on the third largest of the Hawaiian Islands, the island on which Honolulu is situated. The island is named Oahu. Once Oahua? Hawwah/Hawwah? Reminiscent of the Mull of Oa in Scotland, the Oahe Dam in South Dakota, and other such Oa place-names. On the island is Waiakoa. Originally *Ha*waiakoa? Hawa/Ok/Hawa. An Akhaiwa ending. And Wailuku. Once H*a*wailuku*a*? Hawa/Ala/Ok/Hawa. Another Akhaiwa ending.

The "mother of all living," and Og, the fertility-cult founder, joined together by Eloah, the Lord, as in *Avalok*itesvara.

The name of Waialeale Park and Peak on the same island—Hawa/Ala/Ala—is very much like

Awaila (Hawa/Ala) in Singkiang,

and, in New Zealand,

(11a) Waikawa: Hawa/Ok/Hawa.

The most famous surfing beach in the world appropriately honors the once most famous male deity with two mentions, while the "mother of all living" gets one:

Hawa/Ok/Ok/Hawokok

Wokok: Wakik

Waikiki.

Key names are also prominent in the renowned volcanoes of Hawaii, and here a pattern seems apparent. There is a dormant one with a nineteen-mile-square crater. The area around it has been made into a United States National Park. The name Ok appears to be enshrined between two Eloah's:

Hala/Ok/Ala

Haleakala.

There is another, equally famous, one where Hawwah is honored with two Eloah's:

Hua/Ala/Ala

Hualalai.

And one where both deities are featured:

Ok/Ala/Hawa

Okalawa/Økalawa/Kalawa

Kilauea.

Elsewhere in the Pacific, in Indonesia, there is a volcano, again among the largest in the world, whose name is plain:

Awu: pronounced Hawwah.

On Hokkaido Island in the Japanese islands, where the last of the "white" Ainu people are herded, there is another gigantic crater whose name is familiar to every Japanese child. It contains two Ok's:

Ata/Ok/Och

Atokoch = Tokach: today, Tokachi.

The largest volcano in the world, in northern Chile, bears an Og/Hawwah/Eloah name, if the dropping of an initial vowel took place at some forgotten date. Today it is Guallatiri. A long time ago it was Oguallatiri? Og/Hawa/Alla.

Two more volcano names are worth a glance, both in Iceland: Okala, which today is Hekla; and Okatala, today Katla.

This seems like a good moment to introduce four of the world's great waterfalls, whose names, at widely separated points in the world, attest to Og's international reputation. The second highest in the world, in South Africa, with Og's name enshrined between Ata and Ala:

Tugela: once Atogala, Atugela. Ug and Ela, preceded by *T*.

The fourth largest in the world, on the British Guiana–Venezuela border, taking a by now familiar form:

Cuquenán: once Ocuqenan? Oc/Oc/Ana/Ana.

The thirteenth largest in the world is in British Columbia, but the Indians who named it must have thought it was the largest, for they gave it three Ok's, an Hawa, and an Ata:

Takakkaw: Ata/Ok/Ok/Ok/Hawa.

And the highest waterfall in the eastern portion of the United States, in New York State:

Taughannock: Ata/Og/Anna/Ock.

The key names in the Hawaiian Islands have only been touched on. They are woven into the fabric of place-names at all levels, the most important and the most humble. A name, for example, like Kahakuloa already ending in Ok (Ak) and Eloah (Uloa), but which, as Okah*w*aakuloa becomes a blending of Ok/Hawa/Ok/Eloah.

Ataahua, reminiscent of Mexico and Peru, but located in New Zealand, is the only place-name observed where two internal *a*'s have been preserved in a combination of Ata and Hua or Ahua.

It would be worth taking a look at the place-names in the Aiwa Islands in the Fijis, a name repeated over a thousand miles away in Aiwa Island, or to examine the situation in some of the Mana-named islands. All through the South Pacific there are scores of Mana names that, in their blendings, are more revealing than the straight Mana names. In Samoa there are three Manua (Manawa) Islands, several thousand miles across open ocean from Manuae Island in the Cook Islands, as well as the *Manawa*tu River in New Zealand.

Mantuan Downs in Australia, like Mantua in New Jersey, the Mantua River and Mantua in Cuba and Mantua in Ohio and Utah, is much more significant, as far as this particular study is concerned, than Mantua (Mantova) in Italy. George Stewart, when he was writing *Names on the Land*, was surprised to learn that Mantua, New Jersey, a small coastal town, was not an Italian transplant, but a native Indian name that had come from

a "local tribal name meaning 'frog.' " Perhaps the explanation is
that groups of the same Semitic people headed in different directions several thousand years ago, bearing with them, along with
a few other "sacred" names, Mana, Ata, and Hawwah. And each
group took those three very meaningful names and blended
them together, as was their habit, and bestowed it as a name in
their new homeland, those in Australia adding an Ana at the end
for good measure. Then, as the centuries rolled by and generations were born and died, each group slowly forgot the original
meanings of the three names, just as we, in a few short centuries,
have completely forgotten there were ever two pagan personages named Haue and Oc who were worshiped in England—or
in Ireland or in Africa or wherever your particular ancestors
came from. So that Mantua on the coast of New Jersey came
to be related to the word "frog." And Vergil, who was born in
Mantua and invented such immortal fables as the founding of
Rome by Aeneas, undoubtedly made up equally charming fables
about how his hometown got its name. And in Mantua, Cuba,
they will probably tell you the name means "place where pig
got hind foot stuck in mud."

There is scarcely a Mana place-name to be found anywhere
in the Pacific that does not constitute a significant blending of
key names, and there are scores of them, everywhere:

    Manua River (Mana and Awa)
    Manila and Manilla, etc. (Mana and Ala)
    Manuk Island (Mana and Ok)
    Manawak (Mana/Awa/Ok)
    Manacnac (Mana/Oc/Ana/Oc)
    Managuak (Mana/Og/Hawa/Ok)
    Manakaua (Mana/Ok/Hawa)
    Maninoa (Mana/Ana/Hawa)

And Manuwalkaninna (which with one vowel added between
the *l* and the *k* becomes Mana/Awa/Ala/Ok/Ana/Anna) which
is reminiscent of Amawalk, New York.

There is a large category of Eloah/Aloha place-names in the
Pacific where an initial vowel would appear to have been lost

over the centuries, as in Loaloa, once Aloaloa (Eloah-Eloah)?
These Loa names continue in an unbroken chain back to the
Mediterranean, and they turn up everywhere in the world.
There are seventeen important rivers in Africa that begin today
with Loa; but, judging by their other elements, they were first
named Aloa—in honor of Eloah, the Semitic name for God.

In Utah, the town of Loa (once Aloa?) is close to the Wah
Wah Mountains (once the Hawwah Hawwah Mountains?). In
the islands of the Pacific, especially in Hawaii, over a third of
the prominent place-names contain a recognizable Eloah/Aloha
element, and as one digs slightly below the surface, in almost
any direction in the world, others emerge:

Calôa in Angola. Once Ocaloa? Oc and Eloah.

The Calue River and Kaluata in the same African state.
Calue is identical to Calôa, and Kaluata is the same, with
an Ata ending.

Kologha mountain range in South Africa. Once Okolog-
hawa? (Ok/Ala/Og/Hawa).

Koluahi in India (Ok/Eloah)

Kelouamene in Tunisia (Ok/Eloah/Mana)

These names find their counterparts throughout the Pacific,
as in the town of Koloa in the Hawaiian Islands (once Okoloa,
Ok, and Eloah?).[2]

There is scarcely a place-name in the Pacific that is not pertinent to the theme of this book. Continuing on to the Asian mainland, the same picture continues to unfold.

---

[2] The loveliest Ala mountain name in the world is in the Andes: today
Llullaillaco Mountain, but once *Ala*lullaillocoa Mountain? (Ala/Ala/
Alla/Alla/Oc/Hawa).

Chapter 18

THEY CALLED HIM Huang-Ti. They pronounced his name Hawang-Ti. And they still do so today. Hua, Hoa, Hue, Hawa, Hw, and other variations switch back and forth indiscriminatingly in Chinese place-names more than anywhere else on earth. *The* (London) *Times Gazetteer* in many cases gives alternate spellings, and records a number of recent changes.

Huang-Ti was the mighty legendary hero who founded the ancient Empire of China. He first brought wisdom and a knowledge of the crafts and sciences to the Chinese. His name from time immemorial has been associated with the sea. From it stemmed:

Hwang Hai, the ancient Chinese name for the Yellow Sea.

Hwang Ho, the ancient Chinese name for the Yellow River.

Two riddles come into the light if one pursues the name "Yellow" a bit further. The names Yellow River and Yellow Sea are conceivably related to the name of another great Chinese river, the Yalu. If these names once began with *A*yal, then everything comes closer together, for we have seen elsewhere that Aya and Hawa are variants of the same name. Thus the beginnings of Hwang Hai and Hwang Ho are identical with Ayala.

Carrying this a step further, there are scores of place-names all over the world, especially of rivers, that have been corrupted into "Yellow" but that have nothing to do with the color yellow.

188

PLATE 47. China: Huang Ti, or Hwang Ti, legendary founder of the Chinese Empire. The Yellow Sea and Yellow River are named after him. Said to have been the first to build houses and cities, Huang-Ti's consort is credited with the invention of silk making.
Print: Radio Times Hulton Picture Library

It would seem logical that in their original, "prehistoric," forms these names were formed from the same elements as the Yalu. One Yellow River is located in a particularly strategic area, a branch of the Mississippi flowing through Iowa and surrounded by some of the most fascinating place-names in the world. In the triangular section between the two rivers is located Effigy Mounds National Monument, containing huge mounds, earthworks, and fortifications, built in the shapes of various animals, some of them over three hundred feet long. Where the two rivers meet is Waukon Junction, and farther up the Yellow River is Waukon, already suggested as a Hawa/Ok ("havoc") blending.

On the other side of the Mississippi is another Yellow River, in Indiana, and in Wisconsin there are three Yellow rivers, as well as Yellow Lake. Another Yellow River flows through Florida and Alabama, and there are a number of comparable Yellow bays, creeks, and so on, throughout North America, including the Yellow-Water River in Canada. Surveying the world picture, one finds the Yellow River in New Guinea, the Yala River in Turkey, and the Yala River in Kenya; Yala in the Congo, in Ceylon, and in Thailand; also Yalalag (Aya/Ala/Ala/Og?) in Mexico; the Yalak (Aya/Ala/Ok?) River in Turkey; Yallock (again Aya/Ala/Ok?) in Australia, to mention three of many. Did this network of phonetically similar place-names evolve during prehistoric times by accident or were the same elements taken out from one common point of origin? Some of the earlier forms of the English word "yellow" for the color—*yelwe, yolwe, youlowe*—appear to bring this into the global pattern.

The second puzzle has to do with the Ch'u Silk Manuscript, mentioned in Chapter 4, which experts believe may establish an earlier relationship between the "high cultures and civilizations" of South America and China. Press reports describing the manuscript state that "among twelve creatures pictured along the borders . . . are what appear to be deities with antlers and long, protruding tongues." They are almost identical to "symbolic creatures which are featured in South American art from the same period."

Among the favorite animals of the Incas was a species of deer from the high mountain regions. Some people call them "Andean" deer. The Incas must have regarded them with deep veneration, for they bestowed upon them their most "sacred" name, the one featured in the names of their emperor and his two sons. The name was

Huemul.

This is a name that is also featured in the name of the legendary founder of the Chinese Empire, Huang-Ti, whose name is synonymous with the word "yellow." And the Huemul is "yellow-brownish." Which may be one reason why the Incas regarded this deer as sacred?

There is another legendary or mythological Chinese name that occupies a lofty pedestal comparable to the one on which Huang-Ti is enshrined. The name is

Kuanyin or Kwanyin. Once Okuanayana? Ok/Awa/Ana/ Aya/Ana.

Kuanyin/Kwanyin is the name of the gentle goddess beloved throughout the Orient for her understanding and tenderness toward humanity. A male (Ok) and female (Hawa) blending fits in with the fact that Kuanyin is usually portrayed carrying an infant son, which in turn explains why she is often compared to the Virgin and Jesus. Kuanyin is also frequently compared to Avalokitesvara, the Indian god whose name has been presented as a blend of Hawa (Ava), Ala, and Ok. A "mother" god whose name contains the same two names proposed for Kuanyin/Kwanyin, plus Eloah, God.

As one looks down the list of the prominent place-names in China, it is apparent that an extremely high percentage of them owe their origins to the same elements featured in the names Huang-Ti and Kuanyin/Kwanyin. Aside from the fact that Huang-Ti was the founder of the prehistoric empire, the place-names indicate that Hawwah preceded Oc/Og into this part of the world. Huang-Ti gets the great sea and river that were

named after him, and another of the largest of the rivers, the Huai, phonetically identical to Hawaii.

Tihwa, the age-old name of the capital of Sinkiang Province, now Urumchi, is a name phonetically identical to the first two elements in the great Peruvian ruins of Tiahuanaco. Once *At*aahuanaco*a*?

There are numerous other Hawwah names in China: Hawa, Hua Muong, Hu He Hot (much like the Mexican word for "old," *huehuete*), Hualyin (Hawa/Ala/Aya/Ana), Hweilli (Hawa/Alla), the Huai-yang Mountains and the Hwaishan Mountains, Hwaan, and many more.

The bulk of the sprawling land regions were apparently named in honor of Ok/Hawa:

Kwangtung Province, in southeastern China

Kwantung Territory, in northeastern China

Kwangchowan Territory, on the southwestern coast of Kwangtung Province

Kwangsi Chuang, Autonymous Region

Kweichow Province, in southwestern China

Kwangchow, the Chinese name for the seaport of Canton

These are only the most important of a great number of Kwa (once Okawa Akhaiwa?) names in China. They are comparable to many others already observed in North America, Africa, and elsewhere, including one important African name that was bypassed—Kwilu, the Democratic Republic of the Congo, named after the Kwilu River, once the Okawala River? (Ok/Awa/Ala).

Mana is another common place-name element in the Orient that etymologically embraces the Chinese name for "humanity" already mentioned—Min.

PLATE 48. Orient: Kuanyin, or Kwanyin, goddess beloved by millions for her active, sympathetic concern for troubled humanity. Frequently depicted with an infant son, Kuanyin has been likened to the Blessed Virgin as well as to Avalokitesvara. The author maintains that her name is composed of identical elements found in the name Hoa-Haka-Nana-Ia, but in different sequences.

Photo: Victoria and Albert Museum

The definitions of another word, the essential element identical with the ancient Semitic word for both knowledge and fire, *manda*, are worth including:

Mandarin: the standard Chinese language; the North Chinese language, especially that of Peking.

Mandarin: in the Chinese Empire, a member of any of the nine ranks of public officials.

Mandarin orange.

Note also "mandala," in Oriental art, "a schematized representation of the cosmos, characterized by a concentric organization of geometric shapes, each of which contains an image of a deity or an attribute of a deity." It is related to the Sanskrit *mandala* (Manda and Ala). This not only helps to bring the Orient into the worldwide philosophical concept of Mana/Manna sketched briefly some pages back, but immeasurably strengthens the overall picture of that concept. The name for the people presently living in the region partly in Siberia, partly inside China, and contiguous to Manchuria, appears to be a blending of the three key names:

Mana/Og/Ala = Manøgalʒ = Mangal = Mongol.

Raising one's sights to cover several other aspects of the Orient, Hoa is listed as an alternate spelling for many Hawa names, and is pronounced Hawa. This is a common place-name element throughout China, Vietnam, Laos, and Korea, but the site of major archaeological interest is

Hoabinh: pronounced Hawa Binh, an excavated area where Stone Age tools have been found, along with skeletal remains. Similar material has been found throughout Indo-China, Thailand, Malaya, and Sumatra. The skeletal remains have been linked to the Melanesian Islands.

While on the subject of the pronunciation of Hawa, although many television announcers pronounce it as though it were Hooey, the proper pronunciation of the Vietnamese seaport that is so much in the news, Hue, is Hawa.

In Japan the reverse situation to China prevails. While Hawwah is very much in evidence, and appears to have got there first, Ok/Og has assumed a dominant position. There is one

Japanese Ok name that fits neatly into the worldwide jigsaw puzzle, of primary significance in the spiritual life of the people. The name is Kokka, meaning "the State." Dr. Johannes Rahder advises that Kokka is a blend of Kok (once Okok?), meaning "the country," and Ka (once Oka?), meaning "the people."

Nine thousand miles due east of the Japanese islands, across open ocean, in the country with the key name Ecuador, the fourth largest volcano in the world has borne since prehistoric times the name

Cotacachi.

Keeping in mind that of all natural phenomena in the world, ancient people looked on volcanoes with the most awe and with the greatest fear, when you put underneath each other the two names

Tokachi, the Japanese volcano whose name has already been suggested as a blend of Ata/Oc/Och,

and

Cotacachi (Ok/Ata/Ok), the Ecuadorian volcano with the same three elements in a different sequence, it would seem likely that the Japanese pottery of 2500 B.C. recently found in Ecuador was not taken there just on a casual visit.

Exploring further in the Japanese islands, one finds more readily discernable Oc/Og and Hawa combinations in those waters than anywhere else. To mention just a few:

Kanagawa Prefect in Japan and Canagua in the nearby Philippines look like Okanagawa and Ocanagua (Ok/Ana/Og/Hawa). Kanagawa was the former name of the important prefect which is now called after the port of Yokohama. As Ayokohama this latter name would be a direct parallel to our Haue/Oc starting point: "havoc."

Okawa and Ogawa both appear at least twice each, as well as Ogawashima Islands. All are Akhaiwa names. Okinawa Island and Okinawa Archipelago is one of the most famous Akhaiwa blendings in the world—Ok and Awa with an Ana in between. Kanawha, in Japan, identical to the Kanawha names between Ohio and Kentucky, as well as in Iowa and Texas, is identical to Okinawa with the initial vowel lost. Kanawalla, Australia, falls into the same category, with an additional *alla* added. Note also Kanava in Russia.

Iwo and Iwa are provable variants of Hawa that appear throughout the world, but there are so many of them in the Japanese islands they have become generic. The most famous is Iwo Jima.

Dozens of familiar combinations turn up everywhere, including the Otawa/Atawa favorite. The key names are in such profusion along the coastal stretches that it confirms the evidence from other waterways of the world that these ancient wanderers traveled primarily by ship. One can understand why the Japanese still rank among the greatest of sailors. And the key names are so universally found throughout the islands that one begins to suspect that all or most of the Japanese people are in fact descended from the ancestors of the Ainu people. But there is space here for only five special names:

1. Tekoa was an ancient city in Judah. The same name turns up near Walla Walla, in Washington, on the Palouse River, and in Tekoa Mountain, New Zealand. It appears with slight variations of spelling in a number of other strategic places, as well as in Minnesota as Toqua Lakes, almost identical to Ta'qua, the present name of Tekoa, the biblical city in Judah.

2. Dongola is a tribal name in the Nubian Valley, North Africa, which is at least seven thousand years old. Dongola is found on opposite banks of the Ohio River in North America. It shows itself in at least four places in the Southwest Pacific, as Donggala Island and Dongkala Island off the Celebes, Dangkala in another remote island, and as Danggala Bay in the island of Palau.

3. Another already "fully fashioned" name in this category is touched on by George Stewart in connection with a Hawaiian place-name, Molokai. Molok is one of the oldest known Semitic names, and was established in the western Mediterranean before history began. Molok, or Moloch, was at first a Semitic word meaning "king," but it became the name of one of the most feared and bloodthirsty of all Semitic gods—Moloch. The terri-

tory called Malacc or Malag or Moloch on the Mediterranean coast was already there when the Carthaginians arrived, and it is still there as the resort center of Málaga in Spain. The name is found along all the coasts of the earth, and it went across North America as a river name, not only as Malaga but also, in thirty or more instances, corrupted into such Irish-sounding names as Mulligan, Milligan, Milliken, and so on. It would appear to have been transplanted across the Atlantic as a Malaga/Malac complete name, originally a blend of Am/Ala/Og.

4. The fourth name is that of a tribe that has lived on the island of Luzon in the Philippines ever since legend can recall, but anthropologists believe their ancestors must have come from the Melanesian Islands. They bear the name

Tagalog. Once Ata/Og/Ala/Og? Atogalog?

5. Lastly, there was once a Tok River in Alaska, surrounded by a multitude of other Ok names—a nice, respectable Ata/Ok river. Then in 1890 one of the early United States expeditions came along and facetiously changed the name to Tokio River, thinking future generations would wonder whether the Japanese might once have been there. Which brings up the question whether Tokyo is derived from Atokaya. Ata preceding Akhaiwa?

*   *   *

And now we come to the fifth of the six key names that I believe were first taken out as a group in prehistoric times to all corners of the earth. Combining history as well as prehistory, encompassing place-names as well as mythological figures, this name has already figured in the monumental work done by Max Förster, the German etymologist, whose years of research won him a permanent niche in *The Concise Oxford Dictionary of English Place-Names*. More than any other, the name pins down the origin point of these worldwide wanderers, and provides the solidest mortar in the edifice that is being erected herein. The name is

Tema.

Chapter 19

MAP 18 in Father L. H. Grollenberg's superb *Atlas of the Bible*,[1] covering the period from the fourteenth century B.C., to the seventh century B.C., includes only *two* place-names in northern Arabia: The District of Tema to the east and the District of Dedan to the west.

On the basis of place-names still in existence, the two districts encompassed the entire region between Egypt and the Red Sea on one side and the Persian Gulf on the other. On the basis of these same existing place-names, Tema extended well down into southern Arabia along the Persian Gulf coast, and eastward into what is now Syria, Turkey, and Iraq. The district lay directly across the great trade routes of the ancient world, a bridgehead leading to the three continents of Europe, Asia, and Africa. Tema had direct access to all the waterways of the world: on the north via the Mediterranean to the Atlantic Ocean; eastward to India, Ceylon, Borneo, China, and the Pacific.

Tema was in the finest strategic position in the world. Today a barren desert, seven thousand years ago it was a flowering paradise, watered by such rivers as the Thamar and the Al Thamalai, the Thamri, Thumrayt, and Thumayl watercourses,

---

[1] London: Thomas Nelson & Sons, 1956.

the Oasis of Teima—names that still exist and that lie halfway between the two "Rivers of Darkness" linked together by Max Förster and so listed today in *The Concise Oxford Dictionary of English Place-Names*, the Tamasa, a tributary of the Ganges in India, and the Thames, once the Temis, Tamesa, Tamensis, in England.

In Father Grollenberg's atlas I not only found the adjacent districts of Tema and Dedan, but also all my other key names: Og, whom I had never heard of; Hawwah, whom I knew only as Eve; Eloah, familiar to me merely as Allah; Manna, which I thought of purely in terms of "bread from heaven." And the sixth name in the first group, which will be presented in due course.

The name of the District of Dedan I believe points the way to the true source of the Danaan legends and names mentioned in Chapter 3. Dedan appears in chapters 10 and 25 of Genesis. Ham, the oldest son of Noah, was his great-great-grandfather. Cush was Dedan's grandfather. He had a brother and uncle both named Sabah (Saba, Seba, Sheba). Historically, Cush was a large district in Ethiopia, and there were apparently two Sabah or Sheba districts, one in southern Arabia, the other across the Red Sea in Africa. It would seem logical that the name for the district of Dedan came from the same biblical family. Unlike the name Tema, however, Dedan seems to have played no significant role as a place-name outside the Indo-European area, but the two names of the Din people in Siberia, and the Dinh people, the legendary ancestors or predecessors of the Navahos, come back to mind.

While I was attempting to discover whether the name Tema was carried outside the Indo-European part of the world, there emerged two place-names in Libya, west of Egypt, which looked startlingly familiar. They are only a few miles apart and near the Mediterranean coast:

Tmassah: identical phonetically to the Tamasā River in India.

Tmessa: the first two elements identical phonetically to early forms of the Thames (Temes, and so on) River in England.[2]

The name of Tamayah Mountain, located in what was once the northern Arabia district of Tema, which I was regarding as a hypothetical home base, provided the next etymological link with Africa. The relationship between *Tema* and *Tama*yah seemed obvious, with Tamayah a conceivable blending of Tema and Hawwah. The trail led first to Tamaya in Egypt, and hence, with three interconnecting links, to

Tamaiya, the principal archaeological site in the mid-Sahara region of Africa.[3] Close by is a second key site bearing a "Tema" name: *Tama*nrasset. Taimaya led to:

Tamaya River, Peru

Tamaya, Chile

Tamaya and Tamayo Island, Cuba

Tamayopo, Bolivia

Temuah Island, Southwest Pacific

Tamayu-wan, Japan. In Japan one also finds the Tama River, the Tama-Gawa River, the Tama-Gaito River, Toma, and others.

In Mexico are the Temoaya Mountains (Tema/Hawwah/ Hawwah), as well as the names that opened my eyes to the fact that Ahua/Hua in Mexico was the same name as Awa/Awha in North America: Tamiahua and Lake Tamiahua on the Gulf of Mexico, another Tamaya (Tema/Hawa) form. Note also the name of the principal mountain range in northeastern South America: the Tumucumaque Mountains, which begins with Tema/Oc and ends with Akhaiwa.

While exploring Tema place-names in this area, I became aware of the Tema in Guatemala, once Oguatemala? (Og/

[2] See "Thames," in *The Concise Oxford Dictionary of English Place-Names*.

[3] For the importance of this Tamaiya, see Chapter 1, "The Fertile Sahara," by Henri Lhote, in *Vanished Civilizations of the Ancient World*, edited by Edward Bacon.

Awa/Tema/Ala?), and of Tamaqua, Pennsylvania (Tema/Ok/Hawwah/Akhaiwa).

The name Guatemala, as Oguatemala (Og/Hawa/Tema/Ala), seemed of special importance. This strife-torn Central American country contains more unexcavated prehistoric sites than any other part of the New World. It is literally a treasure-house of the past that has been only partially explored. Guatemala, and Managua (Mana/Og/Hawa) and Lake Managua in Nicaragua round out, within Central America, in terms of top billing, the five key names covered to date: Oc/Og, Hawwah/Avvah, Eloah/Ala, Mana, and Tema.

Among these New World names featuring Tema, there eventually appeared the name of a Mexican deity second only to that of Quetzalcoatl, and in some ways more revealing in terms of key elements. The name is

    Zoutem-que,

which, if two vowels have been lost over the centuries, was once conceivably

    Zouatemaque (Z/Oua/Tema/Oc/Oua?).

Which looked like a big name, and is.

Among the ancient legends of the Kingdom of Anahuac (Mexico) referred to in Chapter 2 are several that tell of the fall of angels out of heaven, of their being driven down to earth by other, purer, spirits. The legends are regarded as closely related to that of the expulsion of Adam and Eve from the Garden of Eden and to that of the Tower of Babel. In the Mexican myths the name of the leader of the fallen angels is Zoutem-que. In a later chapter the question of the Z at the beginning of the name Zoutem-que will be discussed, as well as the z in the center of the name Quetzalcoatl. The Tema in Zou*tema*que, however, calls for immediate comment.

According to the Old Testament, the District of Tema was inhabited by the thirteen tribes who believed they were descended from Ishmael. And Ishmael, along with his mother, Hagar, the Egyptian handmaiden, was driven into outer darkness by his father, Abraham, who begat his other son, Isaac, by Sara

PLATES 49 and 50. The legends of Hagar and Ishmael. According to Genesis, Hagar (Agar, Akkar) was twice expelled from the household of Abraham. In Rubens' painting (left), the barren Sarah, vexed at Hagar's arrogance at having borne a child to Abraham, persuades her lord to drive Agar into outer darkness. In Rembrandt's painting (right), Sarah, having given birth to Isaac thirteen years

later, induces Abraham to drive Hagar and her son, Ishmael, into exile. The thirteen tribes claiming descent from Hagar settled in the District of Tema, North Africa. The traditional descendants of Sarah are the Hebrews. This early cleavage is still perpetuated in animosity between Arabs (Ismaelites) and Israelites (Hebrews).

Prints: Radio Times Hulton Library

(Sarah). A relationship between the "Angel of *Darkness*," Zoutem-que (Zoua*tema*qua), and the name of the District of Tema in which dwelt those thirteen tribes who believed they had been driven into *darkness* by their ancestor Abraham would seem logical, and the fact that the Thames and other Tema river names have been conclusively proved to be related to each other and to be all "Rivers of *Darkness*" names strengthens this overall picture.

In Africa there is some indication that historic events took place that bear on the subject. The name Hoggar and other contiguous areas already mentioned had placed over them a new name that from then on became dominant, and still remains so. The new name was
    Sahara.
And Sahara is identical to the name of the woman, Sarah, who became the mother of Abraham's son Isaac. After which Hagar and Ishmael were abandoned and settled in Tema.

There are four Tema mythological figures in the Mediterranean part of the world, and the legends concerning them, all featuring dispossession and darkness, clarify the status of Tema as the homeland of those Semites who believed they were descended from Hagar and Ishmael. For the first time I began to see a logical, underlying reason why the five names Hawa, Oc/Og, Eloah, Manna, and Tema were taken as a group all over the face of the earth. When the sixth key name finally emerged, it fitted so perfectly into the group that everything became even more logical and understandable, but I will have to leave this sixth and final name aside for the moment.

Two of these Tema legends are Semitic; one is Greek, and one is Egyptian:

   Tiemat: In the earliest Semitic mythology of Babylonia and
      Assyria, familiar to the Sumerians and Akkadians, tow-
      ered the figure of Tiemat, the maternal element in the
      creation of the earth. Tiemat personified all the waters
      of the globe, the oceans, seas, rivers, and lakes. With the
      development of Babylonian and Assyrian mythology,

Tiemat gradually became an antagonistic force, standing
for blind, unreasonable Chaos, against younger, more
intelligent gods.

In a striking parallel to the traditions attached to the founding
of Tema, the new gods decided they must slay their own mother.
No one had the power or courage until her son Mardok was
born. He then killed her and became the chief Babylonian deity.
Establishing a theme that is repeated in the three other legends,
Tiemat still continued to serve mankind in a universal, immortal
fashion. Marduk carved her into two equal pieces out of which
he created heaven and earth. The tale is of a central beloved
figure who is dispossessed by someone close to her. As is true of
the tale of Abraham, Hagar and her son, Ishmael, and the founding of Tema.

Tammuz/Thammuz: In the immortal legend of Tammuz,
one never learns how he died. We never learn whether
he died of natural causes or was killed. What we do know
is that Tammuz perished because of the overwhelming
love bestowed upon him by the fertility goddess Ishtar.

As in the case of Tiemat, Tammuz was not forgotten, nor did
his usefulness end at his death. Ishtar never recovered from her
passion for him. Her eternal love was a theme sounded in countless legends, echoed in those concerning Venus and Adonis.
Like Tiemat, the bones of Tammuz were ground up and used
to enrich the soil. He represented the fertility and the annual
rebirth of the land. Each year he was mourned in elaborate ceremonies, chants being sung in his honor, and rituals, funeral
services, processions taking place on the last day of the harvest.
The cult of Tammuz paved the way for the cult of Dionysius as
Greek influence spread into Asia Minor, Dionysius in turn helping to condition humanity for the arrival of Christ.

Themis: In spite of the similarity in name to the Themis
"Rivers of Darkness" names, I cannot find that anyone
has ever linked these to Themis, the first wife of Zeus,
replaced by Hera but honored by the Greeks until inspir-
ation died and darkness closed in on their wondrous

mythology. Her dispossession is again comparable to
that of Hagar and Ishmael, the founders of Tema.
Themis, the only one of the twelve Titans who remained
with the later gods and goddesses on Mount Olympus, is
the single figure in Greek mythology who survived from
the legendary creation of the earth right through to the
death of the gods. She predated Zeus himself, Zeus who
bore the now portentous epithet

Aqueous: Oc/Hawa/Akhaiwa.

The names of the two adjacent first regions of northern
Arabia now come into bold relief, for Themis had a beloved
sister, Dione:

Tema and Dedan,
Temis and Dione.

Even after Zeus replaced her with Hera, Themis continued to
sit on his opposite side at the festivities of the Olympians. She
gave him frequent advice, to which Hera never took exception.
It was Themis who offered her the welcoming cup of nectar
when she first arrived on Mount Olympus. In another glimpse of
what the ancient Greeks thought of the role of Tema in the
prehistory of humanity, it was Themis who gave birth to Pro-
manthus, later Prometheus, the first man, who stole fire (*manda*)
from heaven. As the strongest symbolic link to the "Rivers of
Darkness," Themis, in her role of mother by Zeus to the Fates,
personified Darkness and Night. She was the mother of the
Horae and the Hesperides, also referred to as the "Daughters
of Night." Lastly there is

Tem, the first god of the Egyptians, also known as Tum.

If, as put forward by Henri Lhote, the people of northern
Arabia pushed westward across Egypt and Ethiopia into Africa
about 6000 B.C., then they must have been in Egypt and Ethiopia
a thousand years or so earlier, and must have left those lands
peopled with their descendants. What better proof of this than
that the Egyptians themselves named their first god, the father
of all the others, Tem? Tem, in his solitary role of the only
god, with no female counterpart, solved the problem of filling

the world with other gods and goddesses, and eventually people, through masturbation. Then, as the younger gods and goddesses flourished, following the broad pattern of the other legends, he was relegated to the background. But, like the others, Tem was given a permanent role in Egyptian mythology, and became the "sun when it has set," the God of Darkness.

Thus in all the myths one finds darkness and dispossession, plus evidence that the Babylonians and Assyrians, the Greeks and the Egyptians, the first civilizations to come into being in the Mediterranean, associated the name Tema with antiquity, with their own earliest beginnings.

Moving out from the Mediterranean area, one finds in far-off places mythological figures and place-names, besides those already mentioned, that add immeasurably to the Tema stature:

> Tiamuni, who was believed by the Acoma Indians to have been the first man. The Acoma Indians believed their ancestors were white. Tribal names similar to Tiamuni include:
> Timuquana (Tema/Oc/Hawwah/Ana).
> Timucua, as above but without an Ana.
> Timuquanan, the same but with two Anas.

These closely related tribes are from the southeastern United States. The *timucu*, a needlefish who appears to have had his tail bitten off, is found in great profusion in warm western Atlantic waters. Elsewhere are the

> Tamal tribe (Tema/Ala) and
> Tamaleka tribe (Tema/Ala/Ok). And in North America:
> Tehama tribe and
> Tameroi tribe, identical to Tameroi in Japan
> Timogas tribe (Tema/Og).

The name Tamal has extraordinary intercontinental connections. The Tamale, popular favorite food among the Mexicans, comes from the Nahuatl word *tamalli* (Tema/Alla?) Tamale also turns up as the name of the capital of the Northern Territories of the north-central Gold Coast. In southern India, *tamil* is also a name meaning "white" or "stranger." Other native

names for foods that feature Tema are: "tomalley," the liver
of a lobster in the West Indies, from the Carib word *tumali*;
"tomato," from the Mexican Nahuatl, *tomatl* (Tema, Ala, Ala);
"tamara," a mixture of cinnamon, cloves, and other spices used
in Italian cookery. The etymology is questionable.

Filling a role comparable to that of Tiamuni among the
Acoma Indians, the god who first brought knowledge to the
powerful Delaware tribe was the "wise, freedom-loving, and
benevolent" Tammanend, from whose name came the name of
Tammany Hall in New York City. Farther south, in Nicaragua,
Tamagostad was worshiped by all the tribes in that Central
American country as their "principal god and the creator of the
world." He dwelt "in the east where heaven was situated." The
Nicaraguan natives believed that if you lived a good life "you
joined Tamagostad in heaven." Tamendonare was the name of
the "good, wise twin" in Brazilian mythology. He and his evil
twin brother Ariconte, with their wives, were the only survivors
of the great flood.

In Japanese mythology the name of the "Paradise of the Pure
Land," a favorite subject in silk screens, watercolors, and tapes-
tries, is named

> Taema-Mandara, a powerful cross-check between two of
> the five key names, Tema and Mana. It would seem that
> when the early Japanese longed for their original home-
> land they, like the Nicaraguans, thought and prayed in
> terms of Tema.

Among the natives of the New Hebrides in the South Pacific,
and on a number of adjacent islands, all separated by a thousand
miles of open ocean from Australia to the west, the creator of
the world and its supreme ruler is prayed to in the name of

> Tamakaia
> Tema—the beloved homeland
> Ok—who needs no introduction
> Hawwah—whom we all know by now
> Tema and Akhaiwa.

When Captain Cook and his crew dropped anchor at the

largest of the New Hebrides Islands in 1779, on the first English odyssey around the world, they listed its name as

Mallicolli.

Today it is more accurately known as

Malekuala. Am/Ala/Ok/Hawa/Ala?

There is one other mythological name of enormous stature in the South Pacific. In this case it does not have to be broken down into its component parts. It is plain

Taama.

Taama is worshiped on a large number of widely scattered Polynesian islands as the first god who brought earthly joys, fruits and vegetables, flowers and ambrosial drinks, into the .South Pacific. It is easy, reflecting on the beauty of this part of the world, to see why darkness miraculously changes into heavenly light as far as the Tema name was concerned. The gift bestowed by Taama which the natives appreciated most bore a supremely suitable name. It was a blending of

Oc/Oc/Hawwah: Ococoa,

which with an initial vowel casualty becomes

Cocoa.

And Taama traditionally was the god who first brought the cocoanut tree into the South Pacific.

*   *   *

The mythological pattern on the Tema names, ranging from the figures of darkness in the Mediterranean, who are reflected in Zoutem-que, once Zouatemaqua? the fallen angel of the ancient Mexicans, to the supreme god of Nicaragua, to Taema-Mandara, the "Paradise of the Pure Land" in Japan, to several supreme gods in the Pacific, is supported in all parts of the world by a place-name pattern comparable to that of the other key names.

The Tema "Rivers of Darkness" in the Indo-European part of the world can be traced in *The Concise Oxford Dictionary of English Place-Names.* The fact that the principal river in

Tema, northern Arabia, was named the Thamar, may account
for the large number of Temar and Thamar names all over the
earth: the Tamar "River of Darkness" in Cornwall; several
widely separated Tamarack (Tema/Ock) names in North America; the island of Timor and the Sea of Timor in the Pacific; the
huge undeciphered inscribed stones in the back jungles of Surinam
that are called by the natives Timeri; Teamair, a place-name
element in Ireland that will be touched on again. It would be
tedious for you to examine too many more Tema names. Here
are just a few pertinent ones:

> Ponto Tema, Ghana
> Tama, Iowa[4]
> Tima watercourse in Scotland, identical to Tima (Tema)
>   in Egypt and Time in Tanganyika, where one also finds
>   the Themi River
> Tema in the Gold Coast Republic
> Mount Tama, Angola
> Tamgak (Tema/Og/Ok) Mountains, southern Algeria
> The Thamalakane (Tema/Ala/Ok/Ana) River in Bech-
>   uanaland
> Tamatave (Tema/Ata/Ava), the principal seaport of
>   Madagascar
> Tamala, USSR (Tema/Ala), as in Tamale, the capital of
>   the Northern Territories
> Toma tribe, French Guiana
> Temecula, California (Tema/Oc/Ala)
> Tumacacori National Monument, Arizona (Tema/Oc/Oc/
>   Ara)
> The Tamok River, Malaysia (Tema/Ok)
> Lake Temae, Society Islands
> Temaketa Channel, Samoa (Tema/Ok/Ata)

---

[4] Joseph C. Chervenka, postmaster of Tama, Iowa, contributed many
valuable names from his part of the world, as did W. C. Todd, the
postmaster in Attalla, Georgia, an Indian name reminiscent of Atta Alla
Jebel mountain in Egypt.

Tamaha, Oklahoma
Lake Temiscouata, Quebec, Canada (Temis/Oc/Awa/Ata)
Tuma Island, Papua
Tematahoa Island, New Britain Islands (Tema/Ata/Hawa)
Tomahawk, Wisconsin, Lake Tomahawk, New Zealand,
    and Tomahawk Creek, Australia, Tema/Awa/Ok)

All of which leads us to the etymology of the word "tomahawk."

In the pursuit of the name and word "tomahawk," Dr. Frederick Santee, whose keenness has contributed immeasurably to these pages, played a starring role. For some time I had been ascribing the *hawk* part of "tomahawk" to the word Ak or Ok, the origin point for the word "ax" in the Indo-European languages. The fact that John Smith had brought back the Indian name for "tomahawk" from Virginia in the sixteenth century as "tomahack" had pushed me in that direction, since *hack* is also an earlier form of the Indo-European word for "ax." I was moving ahead on that front because I felt that the ax heads carved on the inner stones at Stonehenge, along with the Mycenaean dagger, were a form of trademark, a symbol showing that Oc had invented this ancient weapon. But Dr. Santee, with a far greater understanding of the Indo-European languages, felt it was unlikely that the word *hack* had arrived in prehistoric America. I would have compromised, but he refused to do so.

It was only while considering the *hawk* part of the Indian name Mohawk, and going back to discover that the English word for the ferocious bird of prey the hawk had once been *hafoc*, identical to "havoc," that I realized that the name or word "tomahawk" had been formed from Tema/Awa/Ok. Investigating further into the North American Indian names for "tomahawk" confirmed this. They were recorded as *tomahauke, tommahauk, tommyhawk*, and so on.

This led into a realm that is properly reserved for the etymologist. If one reads the data listed under the word "tomahawk" in *The Oxford English Dictionary*, the evidence indicates that "tomahawk" had entered the English language only when John Smith brought it back from America. Spurred on by Dr. Santee, in the end I found evidence that "tomahawk" had been in Great Britain and Ireland hundreds of years earlier and that the name "tomahawk" indicates

    Toma—made in *Tema*

in honor of the deities

    Hawk—Hawwah and Ok.

The tomahawk was used in North America for the chase, and served as a primary daily tool and agricultural implement. The classic model had a wooden handle two and a half feet long, with a stone sharpened at one end as a head. Sometimes copper or deer horn was used.

In 1670 an explorer named Narborough, writing of a voyage to Surinam in Guiana, South America, tells of "an Indian club called by the Carribbee-Indians a Tomahauke." In 1681 a book entitled *Grew Musaeum* contained the definition "a Tamahauke or Brazilian fighting club." In a book, *Austral English*, published in London in 1898, E. E. Morris states: "In Australia the word Hatchet has practically disappeared and the word Tomahawk to describe it is in every day use. It is also applied to the stone hatchet of the Aborigines." Morris makes it clear that the word was a native Australian word, which is also confirmed by native Tomahawk place-names, also found in North America.

In New Guinea, the tomahawk was used to shear sheep. What makes this already intercontinental pattern for the tomahawk a far more revealing one is that buried in the back districts of Britain the same name has for an undetermined length of time been in common use. Its antiquity is indicated by the wide variants in the local spellings, many comparable to those in North America, as well as the number of products the name has been applied to.

The following paragraph appeared in an agricultural journal of 1830: "Mortises made by a center-bit leave an intermediate piece between the apertures. This is taken out by the tomahawk, a tool made for the purpose. One end is a sharp, stout, pointed

knife, the other end hooks the piece not dislodged by the knife."
Miss Jackson's *Shropshire Word Book*, published in 1881, includes the following definition: "Tummy-awk—a dung fork,
carried at the back of the cart, and used to scrape out the manure
on the land as it is required." *The Wiltshire Glossary* in 1893
lists: "Tommy-hawk—a potato hacker"; and the *Northumberland Glossary* for 1893 includes: "Hawk—an implement or hand
tool for filling manure."

The inference, however, is that these provincial names all
arrived in Great Britain after John Smith brought *tomahack*
back from Virginia. I was mulling over this situation, which
seemed etymologically impossible, when it occurred to me that
if such a *hauck hawk* name existed where I live, in the west of
Ireland, far outside the Anglo-Saxon orbit, it would be conclusive evidence that the name had arrived by a far older and completely different channel than that of a transfer from colonial
America.

It so happened that two young neighbors of mine, Johnny
Mann and Jacky Burke, both from farming families, were doing
some plastering in our house. On an off-chance I went upstairs
and asked Jacky Burke whether he had ever heard of a *hauck*,
used in either building or farming. "Why, sure," replied Jacky,
who had already been a great help on a number of Irish words
and names, "Johnny's using a *hauck* upstairs right now."

So we went upstairs, and there was Johnny Mann holding a
small flat square board by a round handle that stuck out of the
middle of the bottom side of the board. The other side of the
board was piled high with wet plaster, which Johnny was apply-
ing to the wall.

"That," explained Jacky, pointing at the board, "is a *hauck*!"

Now, this may sound very undramatic to you, but I felt as
Keats felt when he first looked into Chapman's Homer. For this
transfer of the name *hauck* from the knife used to clear mortise
from between stones in England to the board used to hold wet
plaster in Ireland is a process that any etymologist will tell you
could have taken place only over a period of many hundreds of

years. I returned downstairs full of elation, and a few moments later Jacky burst into the room. "I've thought of another one!" he exclaimed. "It's used in thatching."

Thatching happens to be one of the oldest crafts in the world. It is dying even in the west of Ireland. Specialists have written of similarities in the art that exist all the way from the thatched huts of the Polynesians to the thatched cottages in Ireland. Jacky drew me a sketch of the device used in thatching to hold the thatch between the crosspieces of the roof. In this case it becomes a permanent part of the roof, placed into the cracks or apertures, an even more extraordinary transfer of the name. The device is called a

hauk or *hogg.*

Which brought back to mind that the dwelling in which Navaho Indians live, sleep, eat, drink, beget children, and park their highly prized tomahawks, a dwelling made of earth, mud, and thatchwork, is called a

"*ho*gan."

The next day I was discussing this whole question with a gifted Irish scholar, Tom Pierce, the guiding spirit of the Munster Archaeological Society. I had been talking about the two-handled tomahawk used in England as late as the nineteenth century, with a knife at one end and a hook at the other. There were other comparable two-ended tomahawks in other parts of the world, including one common in Cuba and Haiti where the knife was used to cut roots and the hook to pull the roots out of the earth. In fact, the general design of the tomahawk suggests a double-ended purpose.

After some time Tom Pierce said, "I think I can show you a tomahawk that was made in Ireland several thousand years ago." He disappeared into his mountainous piles of books and returned with a photograph of an instrument found at Scariff, County Clare, in 1890. One end of the implement is a knife blade, 2⅝ inches long; the other end is a curved hook or tang, 2½ inches

PLATE 51. Ireland: a Bronze Age cutting implement with a hooked handle, found near Scariff, County Clare, in the 1890's. Its present whereabouts is unknown. The photograph was taken at the time of discovery. The purpose of the implement has never been established, particularly because of the hooked handle.

Photo: Journal of the Limerick Field Club

long. Made of "bright, golden-colored bronze," the weight is just under one ounce. The blade is "not unlike that of a skinning knife . . . the edges are still quite sharp but not the point. The rib running down the center of the blade continues to the point itself, and is not fined off there" (from a report by R. F. Hibbert, Member of the Limerick Field Club, 1892). The photograph could not match up more exactly with the tomahawk described in the English agricultural journal of 1830.

Some time ago I suggested that when the Indians greeted the white settlers in North America by raising their right hands and exclaiming, "How!" they were in fact offering peace and friendship in the name of their principal deity, Hawwah. Now, if you would like to see and hear how they invoked the same deity when they rode headlong into battle, simply stand in front of a mirror, or, better yet, in front of your wife, husband, brother, sister, or best friend. Brandish in your right hand the nearest thing you can find to a tomahawk, give the imaginary pony between your legs a sharp kick with your heels, and clap your left hand as rapidly as possible over your open mouth, shouting:

haWAHhaWAHhaWAHhaWAHhaWAHhaWAHha-WAHhaWAHhaWAH.

Chapter 20

Let us make us a name, lest we be scattered
abroad upon the face of the whole earth.
                              Genesis 11:4

In the initial stage of this research I found myself concentrating more and more on the staggering number of Ber/Bar/Bor/
Bir, and Bur place-names which are to be found today in the
Mediterranean area, in North Africa, Europe, and in Great
Britain and Ireland. This channel of exploration had begun with
the Berkshire County name mentioned by Michael Harrison in
London Beneath the Pavement, along with the Thames river
name. It was my wife, Heather (who had earlier persuaded me
to live in Ireland and devote my time to writing), who first
suggested that I look in the Book of Genesis for a possible source
for these Ber names. It was a suggestion that in turn led to all
the other names discussed herein.

The above enigmatic sentence, "Let us make us a name, lest
we be scattered abroad upon the face of the whole earth,"
appears in the chapter concerned with the building and destruction of the Tower of Babel. Taken in the context of the surrounding chapters, it would seem most logical that if such a
name *were* "made," taken out and used as an identifying "trademark," it would have borne a relationship to the name Abraham.

217

Some months later, while discussing the name Abraham with Dr. Harry L. Shapiro, Chairman of the Anthropology Department at the New York Museum of Natural History, he suggested that I investigate the etymology of the name Hebrew, the name of the people who believed they were descended from Abraham through Isaac, the son of Sarah, who had succeeded in driving Hagar (or Aggar) and her son, Ishmael, out of Abraham's household. Under the name Hebrew in *The Oxford English Dictionary* are the following earlier forms:

Ebreus, Abar, Eber.

Subsequently, I discovered a most curious fact. Until the eighteenth century it was accepted by the academic world that, just as the name Semitic stemmed from Sem or Shem, one of the three sons of Noah, so the name Hebrew had come from Eber, the great-grandson of Sem. Eber in turn was the direct ancestor of Abraham, five generations before him. In the eighteenth century, Pierre-Daniel Huet (1630-1721), Bishop of Avranches, decreed more or less arbitrarily that the name Hebrew had nothing to do with Eber, the ancestor of Abraham, but meant literally "people from the other side," possibly from the other side of the Euphrates. The academic world has followed Bishop Huet in this decision ever since.

Looking back now on what must have been quite a weighty scholastic question at the time, the only conclusion to be drawn is that the predominance of Eber place-names in the Mediterranean basin and the surrounding parts of the world must have been a source of embarrassment to churchmen and other academicians. For there appears to be no other logical point of origin for these names except Hebrew/Eber/Abar/. At least, no other origin point has ever been suggested. Reviewing the evidence briefly as it stood when the classical Greek and Roman civilizations came into being, one finds three major areas that bore Eber names:

The *Iber*ian Peninsula embraced present-day Spain and Portugal. The Romans changed the name from Iberia to Hispania, but both names have prevailed. The name Iberia stemmed from the *Ebro* River, where the first known inhabitants had established their earliest settlements.

*Hiber*nia was the name by which the classicists called Ireland, so recorded by Ptolemy in the third century A.D., and this name has also prevailed. In Irish mythology, Eber, the brother of Don, was one of the founders of the Irish nation, and he and the "five sons of Eber" traditionally inherited the southern half of the island. The accompanying name, which again goes back to classical times, *Hebr*ides, would appear related, and one can only look questioningly at the name *Bri*tannia, an etymology long disputed, particularly in view of the ancient Greek province *Ebr*itannia.

At the other, eastern, end of the Roman Empire was another large territory that bore from the dawn of recorded time the name *Iber*ia. The Kingdom of Iberia embraced what is now the Georgian Soviet Republic, and extended for an unknown distrance eastward and southward. In this case, Bishop Huet to the contrary, the inhabitants believed they were descended from Eber, the great-grandson of Sem, for legends still state that the kingdom was founded "by the fifth generation after Noah," and this is the generation into which Eber was born.

Starting from these three key areas it is possible to build a powerful case that at one time the name Eber (as well as its variants Abar, Hebri, and so on) was the dominant place-name throughout Europe and Africa, eastward to Japan, Australia, New Zealand, and to the near islands of the South Pacific, westward into the Caribbean and Brazil. The name for "the land that lay across the Western Sea" in ancient Irish mythology, Hi Brasil, looks like a possible *Hibr*asil, separated at some early date by a churchman's pen.

What is particularly intriguing is that these Eber names are accompanied everywhere within this area by a set of key names that would be natural choices for those who regarded themselves as descendants of Abraham:

Sarah, the maternal forebear of these people
Sala, the father of Eber

Terah, or Tarah, the father of Abraham
Shem, or Sem, the direct ancestor of both Eber and Abraham
Sheba, or Sabah, and Dedan, who were in the same genera-
tion as Eber but descended from Ham.

There are others, of lesser weight, but these names along with
the Eber name completely dominate the part of the world outlined above, not—except for the switch from Hoggar/Aggar to
Sahara in Africa—disturbing the earlier set of key names, but
numerically overwhelming them. (There is one other switch, in
Ireland, worth noting. The name of the palace of the Irish high
kings was changed in mythological times from Temair Brega, a
name reminiscent of Tema, the territory inhabited by the descendants of Ishmael, to Tara, or, as recorded in the ancient
Irish manuscripts, to Terah, the name of the father of Abraham.)
    What is even more intriguing, as mentioned in the first chap-
ter, these Eber/Abra names and their companion names, except
for some slight spillovers, are not found to any significant degree
today in the place-name and mythological-name structures of
North America, Mexico, Peru, China, Hawaii, and the islands
between Hawaii and the west coast of South America. Those
descended from Hagar and Ishmael, traditional inhabitants of
Tema, and those descended from Sarah and Isaac, traditionally
the Hebrews, line up as two opposing camps, the first group
worldwide in their earlier explorations and migrations, the
second regional in their scope.
    It would take an entire book to reconstruct the Eber picture,
but some highlights should suffice to show that at one time the
part of the world outlined above was blanketed and saturated
with Eber/Abar place-names and that similar words occupied a
special niche in the hearts and minds of the peoples dwelling
in that part of the world.
    In Great Britain and Ireland, in addition to the Hibernia and
Hebrides names just mentioned, the large area now called Yorkshire, the city of York and the river on which it is situated,
today the Eure, were all recorded as Abor names by the Romans
when they invaded England. The city of York was written

down as Aboricum, a Latin *um* ending added to what looks like a blending of Abor with *ic,* an Oc form frequently encountered in these pages.

The name Aboricum stood intact for a thousand years until the Normans took possession of the land. They rapidly changed it from Abor to Eure, a process that they had already gone through in Normandy, where they had changed the Abor River and surrounding countryside into what is today the Eure River and the Eure District, northwest of Paris. In Caesar's time this territory was inhabited by a powerful tribe called the

Ebores.

The switch from Eure to York in England can be traced step by step in *The Concise Oxford Dictionary of English Place-Names.* In 1910, Edmund McClure, in his *British Place Names in Their Historical Settings,* stated that he believed the ancient name Aboricum was formed from a man's name, and he linked it to seven or eight age-old sites in England and on the Continent. The most famous, the earliest fortified site in western Europe, was called Abaricum, again Abar before *ic,* which the Romans latinized into Avaricum but which today has reemerged in the *B* form as Bourges. (The fact that Bishop Huet's hometown of Avranches was in pre-Roman times *Ab*ranches may have been partially responsible for his desire to muddy up the waters on the Eber/Abar/Hebrew front.)

Several other names in Britain are worth mentioning. The most common place-name element in Scotland, and one prevalent in Wales and Monmouthshire, is Aber, as in Aberdeen. The generic meaning of Aber is a "crossing," particularly of a river, as in the name Hebrew, and such forms as Ober, Uber, and the word "over," are found in hundreds of place-names on the Continent, extending into Russia, the Balkans, and as far as Mongolia.

One of the most provocative words in the English language is the earliest recorded form of brother and brethren. It is

Ebrooru.

Which I find difficult to pronounce any other way than Hebrew.

The recorded versions of the name Berkshire illustrate graphically the interchangeable nature of Ber/Bar/Bor/Bir/Bur in place-names. During the first hundred years after William the Conqueror's victory at Hastings in 1066, the name was written down variously as

*Bar*rac Scire(shire) . . . *Bur*rac . . . *Bir*rac . . . *Ber*rac.

The question that is still with us as to Berkshire versus Barkshire, Berkley versus Barkley, and so on, has obviously been with us for at least a thousand years. The important thing is that in all these spellings of Berkshire, one finds a Bar form preceding an *ac* form, comparable to Aboricum.

Clustered at the very heart of the English language are a number of Bar/Ber words all of which are imbued with a special "sacred" quality: *bar* for "pig," and *bar* for "barley," *bar* as a place where early rituals were performed, including the preparation of beer; "bier," as a funeral couch, earlier also spelled *bar;* "bar" in the legal sense; "bar" at the mouth of a har*bor* or har*bour;* "barrow" for a castrated pig and for a grave; *bour* for cottage, found today in neigh*bour* or neigh*bor;* "bourne" for the next world, that unknown country from which no traveler has yet returned. Viewed in the overall context of the Eber/Abar/Hebri/Hebrew name, it is hard to believe that this identification of *bar* with such keystone aspects of our ancient life happened through accident.

On the question of the relationship of the name Eber to the name Hebrew, St. Jerome in the late fourth or early fifth century A.D. was one who believed Hebrew stemmed from the direct ancestor of Abraham, Eber. He did, however, perpetrate what I believe was a major hoax on those who came after him— a hoax that still is uncorrected. A thousand years after the legendary founding of Rome, St. Jerome arbitrarily decided that the tribal group who had occupied the Campagna Romana on the banks of the Tiber in those earlier days had derived their name from a source that none of the classicists who had preceded Jerome had ever thought of. The name of the tribe was

Aborigines: Abor before *ig* (Og?)

With a bold stroke of his pen, Jerome cut the name into Ab/ Origine, with the Latin meaning "from the origin, from the beginning." And so the name has been interpreted ever since. Latterday scholars can be pardoned for falling into the trap, but St. Jerome and his fellow churchmen must have known that a swindle was involved, for the same legends and records that stated that the Aborigines had been in possession of the land stated very clearly that there had never been any question of their being there "from the origin, from the beginning." The records stated clearly that before the Aborigines, a tribe had been in possession that bore the name

Sicula. *S I C I L Y .*

This name caused endless wrangling as to origin prior to Jerome, but once he had made his famous *ab/origine* decree, the name Sicula was conveniently forgotten. Pulling it out into the light of day after many centuries, it appears to be a blending of:

S-Icula: Oc and Ala. Or possibly as Icuala: Oc/Hawa/Ala.

The preceding *S* will be discussed under the last, the sixth key name from the first group. Digging a bit deeper in Italy, as in all of the countries in the Eber orbit, one can reassemble shattered fragments of what Wilhelm von Humboldt, the older brother of the naturalist, referred to in the early nineteenth century as an Iberian kingdom which he believed flourished in North Africa and Europe prior to the rise of the Greek and Roman civilizations. The name Iberian has been *verboten* in polite academic circles, but the evidence is still there to be put together again.

The entire southern portion of Italy is still today called Calabria, and here it appears as though an *abr* ending had been attached to an earlier Cala, perhaps, once, like the *cula* in Sicula, Ocala or Ocuala. The same sort of grafting is apparent in Calabar, the seaport on the southeastern coast of Africa. Another, more easily recognizable, Abr portion of Italy is the long, narrow territory that runs down the Adriatic coast opposite Rome. It is still called

*A*bruzzi.

In the end, the number of Ber/Bar names which I felt were from an Eber/Abar origin, interlarded as they were with many names where initial vowels were preserved, became so overwhelming that I fortunately put this part of the research aside and started searching for other key names. I did, however, establish one strong chain of Ibar names that ran all the way from Japan to Brazil, and at each end I found unmistakable evidence that initial vowels had suffered serious casualties over the centuries, the first such casualties I had discovered.

Above Tokyo in the Japanese islands is a large district called Ibaraki, which I now see as a grafting on of Ibar before an earlier Ok(Ak), as in the case of Aboricum (York), Abaricum (Bourges), Barrac Scire (Berkshire), and so on. On the Siberian mainland are two towns near Vladivostok, both named Baraki, where it would seem there had once been an initial vowel. These Baraka/Baraki names continue across the USSR, encircle the Mediterranean, and are found in Africa and in southeastern Asia: Baraka in the Sudan, the Baraka watercourse that runs through Ethiopia and the Sudan, Baraka in the Congo, Barika and the Barika River in Algeria. They cross the Atlantic and end up in Brazil, and at that end of the chain I discovered three companion names where in two cases an initial vowel had also been lost.

Iberanhem and Buranhaem, about eighty miles apart, are connected by the Buranhem River. The Iber beginning in the first name would indicate that all three Bur names were once Iber or Eber names. Ibirama in Brazil would also indicate that the same thing was true of a number of Birama names in that part of the world. After all the vowel mortalities observed during the past few years, these instances now seem like old hat, but at the time their discoveries seemed momentous to me.

All the Ibarak/Barak names take on added significance because of the Arabic word or name

> *baraka*: "A quality of holiness, both in people and such things as tombs of saints, bread, trees, wells, springs, rocks and caves."

The oldest of these names would appear to be the Valley of Blessedness, Berachah, mentioned in II Chronicles 20:26, believed by Father Grollenberg to be the modern city of West Berikut. Predating the Arab word *baraka* is an even earlier Semitic one meaning "blessing" or "benediction":
berhech.

One of the most fascinating examples of an early place-name to which Abar was added is the former name for Rio de Janeiro, still the name of the vast state in which the Brazilian capital was once situated. The name is

Guanabara. Once Oguana (Og/Hawa/Ana)? to which later the Abara was added?

In other parts of the world one finds the Abar element first, as in the province of Abaragamuwa in Ceylon, Abar placed ahead of Agamuwa : (Og/Am/Awa). And on the same island, the Habaragala River (Habar preceding Og/Ala). Such names as Abaer, Habaer, and Habarmur Mountain, all in Iceland, indicate where the Icelandic generic use of Baer for "town" came from.

The predominance of these Ber/Bar names, which considerable evidence points toward once being Eber names, can be seen by a quick glance at North Africa, the Mediterranean, and Europe on any modern map: Barcelona, Bordeaux, Brittany, Berea, Burgos, Burgama, Berber, Brussels, Bercy (an earlier name for Paris still preserved in a district name), Burgundy, Bourbonnais, Béarn, Bar, Biarritz, Bristol, Bournemouth, Birmingham—the list is endless, hopping from Barbados to Boriquén, the native name for Puerto Rico, and to a dozen or more other prominent island and seaport names in the West Indies.

If you would like to measure the true saturation of these names, you should spend a few hours looking through the Pilot Books of the World, for the Mediterranean, the coasts of Africa, for the Caribbean, for the Gulf Coast and along the East Coast of North America. These names are accompanied in profusion by the companion names mentioned above: Saba, and its often listed alternate form, Sava. Sara, which figures prominently in such widely scattered names as Saracen, Saragossa, Sarajevo, filters into eastern North America in Sarasota, Florida, in Saranac Lake, the Saranac River, and Saratoga, three Indian names in New York State. Surinam in Guiana, South America, appears to be Sara-inspired, particularly in view of the extraordinary number of Eber/Abar names to be found there.

In another direction, on an island that has been mentioned frequently in these pages, one finds a prominent Bor/Eber, Sara/Saba combination that again, in my opinion, defies all the laws of chance. On the island of *Bor*neo, the traditional island of *bar*ley, still abounding in wild pigs, or *bars*, the two largest districts or provinces are today called *Saba*h, and *Sara*wak, already suggested as a blending of Sara with the older Awak, Hawa and Ok. If you look over the place-names of Borneo, you will find it difficult to pick out a name that does not fall into either the first group of key names or the second group of key names, with a number in which the two groups are blended.

In this same part of the world you will also find three other names: *Tara* and its variants, which I believe, particularly in view of some of the evidence in the Old Testament part of the world, stemmed from Tareh, the father of Abraham; Sala, the father of Eber—and again the evidence from the Middle East supports such an origin; and Sem/Sam/Sim, the direct ancestor of Sala, Eber, Tareh, and Abraham. These names permeate the limited part of the world, along with the Eber names. It is interesting to note that all these names are often blended with the first group of earlier names, but I cannot think of any instances where they are blended with one another. Some may exist, but not one comes to mind.

Again at the risk of being tedious, here is a thumbnail sketch on each of these names, without reaching into perfectly acceptable variants:

SARA

Sara, East Pakistan
Sarai, USSR
Sarai, Afghanistan

SABA

Saba, USSR
Saba watercourse, Sudan
Sabeh, Iran

Sarala, USSR (Sara and Ala)
Sarata, USSR (Sara and Ata)
Sarawa River, Burma (Sara
and Awa)
Sarawak River, Borneo
Saratok, Sarawak (Sara/Ata/
Ok)
Sarah Mountain, South
Australia
Sara (two) and the Sara tribe,
French West Africa
Sera Island, Indonesia
Serua Island, Indonesia
(Sara/Awa)
Sarra, Libya
Seraya Island, Singapore
(Sara/Awa)
Seram and Ceram Sea
Sera, Iran
Seregovo, USSR
(Sara/Og/Ava)

Sabha, Jordan
Sabbah, Arabia
Sabbah Jabal, Arabia
Saba, Honduras
Saba Bank, Leeward Islands
Saba Island, Lesser Antilles
Sabak Cape, the Aleutians
(Saba and Ok)
Sabula, Iowa (Saba and Ala)
Saba Jeb, Yemen
Sabba, Ethiopia
Sabac, Yugoslavia (Saba and
Oc)
Sabaluka, Sudan (Saba/Ala/
Ok)
Saba Saba, Kenya
Sabae, Japan
Sabak, Malaya (Saba Ok)
Sabalana Island, Indonesia
(Saba/Ala/Ana)

SALA[1]

Sala Hill, Arabia
Salala, Sudan (Sala/Ala)
Salah, Arabia
Salah Tell, Jordan
Salalah, Muscat and Oman
(Sala/Allah)
Salaya, Bombay (Sala/Aya
[Hawa])

SEM/SAM[2]

Samuoko, former Belgian
Congo (Sam/Awa/Ok)
Samokov, Bulgaria
(Sem/Ok/Ava)
Semah River, Sarawak
Sama Islands, Bismarck
Archipelago
Samah, Sudan

---

[1] An exceptionally large number of Sala place-names in the *Cele*bes leads me to believe this should be *Sele*bes.

[2] Samoa Islands, the farthest penetration east. The numbers of Semitic names in *Sam*oa (Sam/Awa) indicates that both groups must have overlapped here.

Salwah District, India
  (Sala/Awah)
Salak Mountain, Java
  (Sala/Ok)
Salawati Island, New Guinea
  (Sala/Awa/Ata)
Sala, Czechoslovakia
Sala (two), Kenya
Sala, Somalia
Salamanca Province, Spain
  (Sala/Mana/Oc)

Samal Island, South Pacific
  (Sem/Ala)
Samu, Borneo Once Sam*ua*?
Simalek, Indonesia
  (Sem/Ala/Ok)
Samawa, Iraq (Sem/Awa)
Samawah, Iraq (the same)
Sama, Jordon (two)
Sama, Syria
Sam, India, USSR
Sam Pass, Afghanistan

TAREH/TARA/TERA

There are three or four hundred Tareh place-names in Ireland, besides the royal Tara.

Tara, Bombay
Tara River, USSR
Tara, USSR
Tarak names in Malaya
  (seven) (Tara/Ok)
Tara, Queensland
Tara Island, the Philippines
Tarakan and Tarakan Island,
  Borneo (Tara/Ok/Ana)
Taranaki Province, New
  Zealand (Tara/Ana/Ok)
Tara, Ontario
Tara Lake, Chile
Taracua, Brazil (two)
  (Tara/Oc/Awa)

Taraauaca, Brazil
  (Tara/Awa/Oc)
Tera, French West Africa
Tera River, Portugal
Tera River, Spain
Tara, Northern Rhodesia
  (Zambia)
Tara Mountain, Yugoslavia
Tara River, Yugoslavia
Tarahouahout, Algeria
  (Tara/Hawa/Hawa/Ata)
Taravilla, Spain
  (Tara/Ava/Alla)
Tarawa Atoll, the Gilbert
  Islands (Tara/Awa).

Tarawa Atoll is the farthest penetration east by the Tara names that I have discovered. Examining the Pilot Books of the World, the evidence from some of the place-names in the Mediterranean indicates that the Latin name or word for "earth," *terra*, stemmed from the name of Tareh, the father of Abraham.

If one goes back to the Domesday Book in England, some quite unexpected blendings of names are revealed. For example, Sawley in Derbyshire was Sallawa in 1166 (Sala and Awa?). Savick Brook in Lancashire was Savoch, Safok, and Savok in the thirteenth century, common river names. Saba (Sava) and Ok? There are scores of others.

The above groups are only the bare bones on which the flesh of these names can be hung. Not to be overlooked is the curious evidence regarding the name Peleg, the son of Eber, "in whose time the world was divided," according to Genesis. Peleg starts out as a mighty name that looks as though it will rival Eber, Tara, and the others. There are Greek and Roman Peleg words and names for "bearded," "bronzed," "of Libya," "royal purple," "of the sea," and "of the shore." Then some conflict must have taken place between two groups of people in prehistoric Greece and Italy, possibly between Semites who remained loyal to their ancient gods and those who took up the younger classical gods. There are four legendary battlefields in this part of the world, all beginning with Peleg, where mortal conflicts took place, with the Pelagians being destroyed for not worshiping the true deities. The climax finds Pelegasus, a mythical early Greek king condemned to the underworld for trying to destroy the temple of Delphi, and the name Peleg peters away in the word *peleg* for "wanderer," hence *pellegrino*, the forerunner of the word "pilgrim." There is some indication that Peleg might be the origin point of the name Philistine/Palistine but the clues are too shadowy to do more than conjure with. But Peleg, the son of Eber, does stand as a name apart from the immediate members of his family.

In looking at the two groups of names, the earlier, worldwide ones, and this latter group centered upon the name Eber/Abar/Hebri/Hebrew, a remarkable situation developed. On the one hand, I had considerable evidence concerning a name that cried out for inclusion as a sixth key name in the first, worldwide group. On the other hand, there was one key name strangely missing that was at the very heart of the conflict between Hagar, her son, Ishmael, and their descendants who settled in Tema, and Sarah, the wife of Abraham, and her descendants. It was only when another blind spot disappeared that I realized that the name crying out for inclusion and the missing name were one and the same. The last major piece in the prehistoric puzzle slipped into place.

Chapter 21

And he will be a wild man, his hand will be against
every man, and every man's hand against him; and
he shall dwell in the presence of all his brethren.
Genesis 16:12

It was thus that the angel of the Lord announced to Hagar
that she would have a son by Abraham named Ishmael. Of all
the main characters in the early legendary story of the creation
of the Semitic races, Ishmael's role is the most enigmatic. Examining the legend in some detail, we find that since Sarah, the
wife of Abraham, was barren, it was she who urged him to go
into her Egyptian handmaiden, Hagar, or Aggar, and have a
child by her. Once pregnant, Hagar treated Sarah with such
contempt that Sarah drove her out the first time, but the angel
of the Lord persuaded Hagar to return and bear Ishmael. Which
she did, and Ishmael grew up for thirteen years, with his mother,
in the household of Abraham.

After thirteen years the Lord returned to Abraham, who was
ninety-two years old, announced to him that his name would no
longer be Abram but Abraham, and that he would have a son
by Sarah, whose name at that point was changed from Sarai.
The Lord stated that by this son, Isaac, he would make Abraham
"the father of many nations." That Abraham had no quarrel
with Hagar or Ishmael is indicated by his reactions to this news.

According to Chapter 17 of Genesis, "Then Abraham fell

upon his face, and laughed, and said in his heart, 'Shall a child be born unto him that is an hundred years old? and shall Sarah, that is ninety years old, bear?' And Abraham said unto God, *'O that Ishmael might live before thee!'* [Italics the author's.] And God said, 'Sarah thy wife shall bear thee a son indeed; and thou shalt call his name Isaac: and I will establish my covenant with him for an everlasting covenant, and with his seed after him. And as for Ishmael, I have heard thee: Behold, I have blessed him, and will make him fruitful, and will multiply him exceedingly; twelve princes shall he beget, and I will make him a great nation. But my covenant will I establish with Isaac, which Sarah shall bear unto thee at this set time in the next year.' "

Thus we witness the launching, with God's blessing and Abraham's approval, of two great Semitic races or groups of people, both descended from Abraham. It was not until the following year that Sarah, watching Ishmael playing with Isaac, said to Abraham, "Cast out this bond woman and her son: for the son of this bond woman shall not be heir with my son, even with Isaac." This was "very grievous" to Abraham, but at the Lord's behest he sent her away with Ishmael. Eventually, Ishmael having been provided with an Egyptian wife, we find his descendants settled in Tema in northern Arabia.

My reason for dwelling on this is that I now saw that just as Ashtaroth and Ishtar, the names of the two ancient fertility goddesses, appear related, the name Ishmael emerged as a conceivable point of origin for a group of Ash names that called out for inclusion in the first, worldwide set of key names. The Ishmael legend of expulsion came into clear focus as a possible starting point for the intercontinental superstitions regarding the ash tree and the serpent, an "expulsion" symbol of paramount importance, as, for example, in the legend of Adam and Eve's banishment from the Garden of Eden.

The worldwide custom of putting ashes on one's forehead, as a token of sorrow and repentance, also seemed to fit into the driving out into darkness of Ishmael, with Ash Wednesday the traditional time for such a ritual, five days before the ancient fertility day of Ishtar, now known as Easter. The legend of Tammuz, destroyed by the overpowering love of Ishtar, drew closer to the legend of Ishmael when viewed against the backdrop of the worldwide Ash place-names.

The prehistoric fire-making instrument featuring the wood of the ash tree, the chark, now made more sense as, the Aschark. And the ancient symbol of the mythical founder of the art of medicine, Aesculapius, came to mind, a serpent wound around a staff—made from the sacred ash tree? Irish mythology states that when the founders of that nation came ashore they marched behind a great flowing silken banner on which was emblazoned the same staff with an entwined serpent, a fitting symbol for the descendants of Ishmael. The number of deities throughout the world who were believed to have been born from an ash tree, from Scandinavia to Peru, now also made more sense in terms of Ishmael and the men of Tema. Not to mention the sacred nature of the ash tree and its healing powers, as well as the protection it offered against snakes.

There has been only one name mentioned in these pages that has bothered me for some time. It is Quechua, the language and tribal name of the four million people who live in the Andes highlands, from Ecuador to the Argentine. I had interpreted it as Oqua Ochua (Akhaiwa/Akhaiwa), but on the basis of its pronunciation as Kechewa, it now came into sharper focus as a blending of Oc/Hawa/Ash/Hawa, Akhaiwa/Ashua. At the same time, the name of the most dreaded of all the gods in prehistoric Mexico, except for Quetzalcoatl himself, unveiled itself as

Asch and Oc
Aschoc Aschoc
Choc.

Choc was the ferocious God of Water, to whom human beings were sacrificed, whose silent, sinister companion was the water moccasin, more hated and feared by the American Indians than the rattlesnake.

High in the uplands of Guatemala (once Oguatemala?), a

PLATE 52. Mexico: Choc, the Aztec (once Huaztec) God of Water. Like Quetzalcoatl, Choc evolved into a fearsome deity, to whom human sacrifices were offered. The name Choc is interpreted in the text as a combination of two key names, Ash and Oc, hence Ashoc, Shoc or Choc.

Photo: Museo de Antropología, Mexico City

language closely related to Quechua is spoken by some 350,000 natives. It bears the provocative name Cakchiquel—once Ocokaschoquala? (Oc/Ok/Ash/Oq/Hawa/Ala/?)—which leads to a name of a dance popular among the North American Negroes since the days of slavery, today the cakewalk. But the *walk* names already encountered, and such place-names in Africa as Kakelwe (Ok/Ok/Ala/Awa?), make me wonder if the cakewalk wasn't first performed in honor of Oc/Ok/Awa/Ala/Ok. As for the fabled peninsula adjacent to Guatemala, with an *A* in front and an *a* in back of it, the name becomes Ayucatan— Aya/Oc/Ata/Ana.

A few place-names will suffice to show how Ash blends into the other key names in the first group:

Ashaway, Rhode Island . . . a number of place-names that begin with Ashua, Ash/Hawa, including Ashuanipi River in Labrador, as well as (N)ashua, New Hampshire, Ana/Ash/ Hawa . . . several towns and a river named Asch/Atta/Ana/Og —Chattanooga, and two rivers in the Southeast named Chattooga, Asch/Atta/Og without the Ana, as well as the Chattahoochee River, Asch/Atta/Hawa/Oc. Chacachacare Island in Trinidad, Asch/Oc/Oc/Oc . . . Assateague Island, Maryland, Assa/Ata/Og/Hawa . . . the Shaklolik River in Alaska, Ash/ Ok/Ala/Ala/Ok . . . Shuqualak, Mississippi, Ash/Oc/Hawa/ Ala/Ok . . . Shageluk, Alaska, Ash/Og/Ala/Ok . . . taking an Ishmael form: Ishawooa, Wyoming, Ash/Awa/Awa . . . Oshawa, Ontario, Ash/Awa . . . Oshkosh in Wisconsin and Nebraska, Ash/Ok/Ash . . . Ashikaga, Japan, Ash/Ok/Og . . . Shakikow, China, Ash/Ok/Ok/Awa . . . Shekow, China, Ash/Ok/Awa . . . the Shag River in New Zealand, Ash/Og . . . the Shaw River and Shaw Island in Australia, named after Bernard Shaw? or originally a blending of Ash/Awa . . . a large number of Chalk names widely separated, including several Chalk rivers, Asch/Ala/Ok. The list is endless.

What makes this key name more complicated is that both Ash and Asa appear closely interrelated, and the good symbol ash and the bad symbol snake seem to be written into certain names. Looking at the two names in Mexican mythology, Quetzalcoatl and Zoutem-que, both containing a *z*, may bear some fruit. In Mexican place-names, *s*, *z*, and *x*, are interchangeable, as in Huastec, Huaztec, and Huaxtec. Trying not to enter into a realm of pure speculation, all three of these letters look like snakes, the *s* facing one way, the *z* the other, and the *x* representing two snakes crossed, one above the other.

In the name of the great plumed serpent Quetzalcoatl, we find the *z* in the middle of the name, between two Akhaiwa's, while in the name of the leader of the band of fallen angels, again an "expulsion" symbol, we find the *z* standing in front of Hawa/Tema/Oc/Awa as Azouatemaqua: a "snake" symbol, the Tema name, and the two principal deities Oc and Hawwah. It is curious that in Ireland, where ash were three of the five sacred trees, one finds the name of the great Rock of Cashel, center of worship since prehistoric times, a conceivable blend of Oc/Ash/Ala, and the same thing is true of an equally venerated site in France —Ava/Aza/Alla/Aya, Avazallaya, Avazallayá, Vazallay, Vézelay. I have not experimented further along these lines.

There is a fourth symbol, universally known throughout the prehistoric world, perhaps the forerunner of the letter X, which also looks very much like two snakes crossed one above the other. In ancient times it was a symbol of good luck. But in the twentieth century, it became a symbol of evil and disaster:

In ancient times the swastika (Asa/Awa/Asa/Ata/Ok?) was common to both New and Old worlds, and was used frequently by the Mexicans. Certain place-names and words seem to emphasize the role of the snake in our past. The earlier forms of the word "snake" are worth noting. They all seem to combine Asa/Ana/Ok, whereas the word "serpent" appears to be of a later date, and offers no key-name possibilities. For "snake" there are:

Old English—*snaca*

> Late German—*snaak*
> Swedish—*snok*
> Danish—*snog*

In the last two, OK and Og come clear. It is interesting to note, in *The Oxford English Dictionary*, a sentence written in 1250 that refers to an *"ug*like snake."

Sesha, the great mythological snake in Hindu legends, mentioned in connection with the chark, bears a name that looks like a blend of Asa/Asha. The Shoshone Indian tribe and the Shoshone River and Shoshone Falls in the American Northwest bear a name that literally means "snake." And the name of the Snake River in the same region is an Indian, not a European, name. In his name the dreaded water moccasin appears to blend Am/Oc/Asa/Asa/Ana.

Coming down to our own bodies, there is one word that I have been holding aside because of its first element. It is, I believe, one of the most portentous words in the English language:

> *saiwala.*

The last two elements appear to be a blending of Awa and Ala, with Asa as the first element. *Saiwala* is the oldest recorded form of the word

> "soul."

Here is another clear-cut example of an end vowel that has disappeared with the passage of time. The word *saiwala,* or "soul," is closely related to the word "sea." The similarity between *saiwala* and Walawa! the early English cry of sorrow and despair, seems obvious.

*   *   *

During the past few months, working first with Tom Pierce in Ireland, later with Frederick Santee, Cyrus H. Gordon, Johannes Rahder, and David McDowell in America, as well as reviewing the manuscript with Walter A. Wood, another "splendid Baconian," a number of key names and words were discovered that strengthen the plausibility of what went before.

These names and words come from all corners of the earth, not only emphasizing the universality and interrelationship of prehistoric mankind, but also perhaps, serving as mortar to the work done by the etymologists, archaeologists, anthropologists, and mythologists discussed in the opening chapters of this book. It has been particularly encouraging that these men, each possessing in depth knowledge far surpassing mine, have been contributing supporting evidence to the basic premise, a process that I believe will go on in the years ahead. Taking up various pieces of evidence in what seems like the most logical sequence, including some that take us back to the starting point at Stonehenge and Avebury, let us round out a bit further the worldwide picture of the relationship of the name Hawwah to A*qua*/A*gua*, meaning water. Tom Pierce advises me that there is an early Irish word for water, *oi*, pronounced Hawwah, as is *ahue*, meaning "all water" in native Mexican. *Oi* is retained in such Irish words as:

oitir: a bank or ridge in the sea, a shoal or shallow.

oitir oisiri: an oyster bed.

oitir ghainimh: a sandbank.

It is also found in such a charming name as

Oilioll (Hawa/Ala/Alla), the Irish name for Six Mile Bridge, a quiet little village on a stream in County Clare.

Uallach-: in Irish mythology the chief poetess at one time bore the name Uallach (Hawa/Alla/Oc), the same three key names blended in *Avalok*itesvara, and still found all across the face of the earth.

"yolk":

The universality of these key names is perhaps best exemplified by going inside the egg, once *aeg*, the primary symbol of fertility. Within, one finds, as the fundamental essence of life itself, the same three key names:

Aya (Hawa)

Ala

PLATE 53. Romania: the nomadic Vlach people, whose origins are shrouded in mystery. As *Avalach*, the author sees the name as composed of the same first three elements found in the name *Avalokites-vara*.

Photo: Radio Times Hulton Picture Library

Ok
Ayalok Ayaløk Yalk Yolk.

"Yolk" is in turn closely related to "yoke," meaning the union of two people and the union of body and soul.

"bad"/"bed":

> At one point I asked Tom Pierce if he knew of any old Irish word for "bed." He thought I had said "bad." It was a fortunate error, for he gave me what I felt was a most propitious word for "bad":
> *olc*

If internal vowel casualties took place here, then *oaloc* or *oiloc* would have been the earlier form, again a blending of the three key names Hawwah/Ala/Ok. It is easy to see why with the growth of Christianity such a "pagan" trinity, a fertility goddess and a fertility god, joined together by Eloah, God, would have taken on the meaning "bad."

The etymology of the words "bad" and "bed" in English appear closely related. The Old English form of "bad" was *baedel,* and it signified a hermaphrodite, the blending of male and female into one, which brings the circle around to the Irish word for "bad," *olc,* once *oaloc*?

There is an early Irish word for "bed" that is most pertinent:
fall.

In Irish mythology the high kings were crowned on the Stone of Fal, the great stone penis of Fal. The relationship to phallus, the penis symbol in Egypt, Greece, and Rome, seems obvious. A blending of Afa/Ava with Alla?

There was a mighty god of the East Africans whose name appears similar to the Irish word *olc*. He was called Olakhon, and a photograph of him appears in the 1962 edition of Ignatius Donnelly's *Atlantis*.[1] His face is an extraordinary blending of Caucasian, Negroid, and Semitic characteristics.

---

[1] New York: Bonanza Books.

A brilliant scholar, Philip Baynard, who has been helping in the typing and collating of this manuscript, found a name from Polynesia that constitutes another keystone in this structure. He was stationed in Tahiti during World War II, stayed on for some years afterward, and devoted a considerable amount of time to a study of early Polynesian. He advises me that the original name for Raiatea, in the Society Islands, traditionally the center from which the natives fanned out into all other places and islands, was

Havaiki,

which is identical etymologically to the name Hawaii mentioned by George R. Stewart—Hawaik—and we are once again back at our starting point, Haue Oc/"havoc."

Ogygios of Oguges

During a recent weekend spent with Dr. Santee, he advised me that he had been digging deeper into the question of Ogygios of Oguges. Over and above the facts already presented, Dr. Santee finds that the name and a number of related words carried with them profound meanings of awe and dread, exactly what one would expect to find in connection with a prehistoric god of primary stature. These words run through all classical Greek literature, and appear frequently in the tragedies of Aeschylus and Euripides. They include:

achos: "pain, fear, dread"; hence, via *ege, aghe,* comes the English word "awe."

okualeos: to shrink from doing, through shame or fear; to fill with alarm, fear.

okpudei: "chilling, horrible."

wauk/woc

There was another word besides "tomahawk" that worried Dr. Santee for some months. It was the word "wake," in its earliest English form *woc.* There is a third old and practically forgotten meaning to the word "wake," besides the ceremony performed over a corpse, and the wake of a ship, and it was this meaning that intrigued me most: "A local annual festival in England, formerly held in honor of the patron saint or on the anniversary of the dedication of a church but now having little or no religious significance."

In the earlier form *woc*, one had an *oc* standing clear, preceded by a *W*. It looked like a logical blending of Hawoc, with the same Ha casualty observed in the development of the word "what," once *hwa*. But I was trying to link it to certain Indo-European words that, Dr. Santee warned me, involved complications beyond my ken. Finally an early Scottish form turned up:

wauk.

In one word *W* precedes *oc;* in the other, *Wa* precedes *uk.* It now seemed safe to assume that at one time the word had indeed been formed in honor of Hawa and Oc, Haue and Oc, out of whose names the word "havoc" had been formed. The three meanings, wake, the funeral ceremony; the wake of a ship, seen as the personification of two deities; and wake, the early religious or church festival, all appear worthy of such a high dedication.

Waal and *vala*, the first Old English, the second Icelandic, for the practice indulged in at wakes, to wail, both look like reasonable blendings of Hawwah and Ala, closely akin to Walawa! And the great feasting hall of the Scandinavian immortals, Valhalla, makes sense as Ava/Ala/Alla.

There are two variants, *waught* and *waucht*, of another early Scottish word. It means "a copious drink, a deep draught." At this stage I find it not difficult to conceive of this as a toast to Hawwah and Oc or Og.

wic/weoc

There are two *wick* words that are worth investigation.

The first is *wick*, earlier *wic*, meaning village or farm, especially a dairy farm. The other is "wick," earlier *weoc*, the precious flame or taper part of a candle used to provide light in these early villages and farms. In the second case especially, where an *oc* stands clear in the oldest recorded form, if words and names were blended out of these key names, then what more appropriate again than an Hawwah/Oc, Haue/Oc, origin? Hawa/Oc. The related Greek word for "house," *oikos*, preserves Hawwah (*oi*) intact.

"folk"

The etymology suggests a blending of the three key words Afa (an early form of Ava found in the spelling of Avebury), Ala, and Ok.[2]

* * *

As we have been moving about from country to country, certain pieces of evidence, nebulous clues, have been set aside that, in my opinion, began to fit together into an entity. First, in Deuteronomy, Moses tells us that the prized possession of Og, the last of the giants, founder of the fertility cult of Ashtaroth, was his huge iron bedstead. It measured seventeen feet by seven feet.

Second, in the portrayal of the white fertility god in the rock paintings from the Hoggar region, he has no face. Where his face should be there are instead some parallel brownish-black lines that look like two things, the slats of a bed and the grill or gridwork of a barbecue.

Third, in the West Indies and throughout North America the Indians had as one of their most vital implements a device that served both as a bed and as a cooking utensil. It consisted

[2] The "forbidden" word for sexual intercourse, "fuck," etymology dubious, represents a conceivable blending of the two ancient fertility deities, male and female, Hawwah (again as Afa) and Ock: *afock* (see "havoc") ... *Afock* ... *fock* ... "fuck."

of an oblong-shaped framework, on legs about three feet high, with slats or bars across the framework much like a modern bed. The Indians cooked their meat on this grill over an open fire and then, as the fire died down into glowing embers, they wrapped themselves in their blankets and slept on the grill above the embers. To a nomadic people this was the very center of life. On this device they not only cooked and slept but on it they made love and begot their children. Out of this simple invention came what we call today a "barbecue," still the center for feasting. But the original name, found in the Taino Indian vocabulary was barb*acoa*, the by now familiar Acoa/Oc/Hawa, or Akhaiwa, name preceded by a *bar* element. Was *acoa* formed from the two fertility deities' names, Oc/Og and Hawwah? The grillwork on the face of the giant in the Hoggar rock paintings began to make more sense.

Fourth, in Ireland, at Oghill in the Aran Islands, on Achill Island, and especially at Croagh Patrick in Aughaval Parish, the most distinctive feature in each case is a group of stone ruins that are still referred to as "beds." Today they are called St. Patrick's Bed, or Dermot and Grainnia's Bed, St. Maine's Bed, and so on; but they date back to pagan times, and once they must have been identified as the beds of other personages. On Croagh Patrick there are a number of such beds, and when the faithful make the ascent to the top of the mountain at dawn on Easter Sunday they circle each bed in an elaborate ritual that must also date back to pre-Christian times.

It was in connection with these beds that I asked Tom Pierce if he knew of any early Irish words for "bed," and at the same time I asked him if he knew what Croagh Patrick was called in prehistoric times. The next morning he came over to our house with two small pamphlets with the title *Journal of the Limerick Field Club, Founded 1892, for the Study of Natural Science, Archaeology, and Photography.* In the pamphlets was a two-part article by a Reverend F. J. Lynch, and if I had written the article to substantiate what has been unfolded in these pages I could not have presented stronger supporting evidence. To quote in part:

"The old name of Croagh Patrick was Cruachan Oigle, 'hill of Ocaill,' and the district in which it lay was named Iath Oigle, 'land of Ocaill.' " The *uach* in the middle of Cruachan was worth attention, for Croagh is an extremely common place-name in Ireland; but even more, in Oigle there appeared to be a tightly knit blending of Hawwah (Oi), Og, and Ala, again the same three key names found in conjunction all over the face of the earth. This combination had once provided the name for what is still today in Christian Ireland the most sacred of all points of pilgrimage.

The Reverend Lynch then went on to link the name Oigle to the name Ogaill, to Oc of the Boyne, to "the great Cu" (who will be discussed in a moment), to Ocaill, king of the Connaught fairies, and Dun Ocaill in Aranmore (Irishmore). It now seemed reasonable that these "beds" of St. Patrick and other saints must once have been associated with Oigle/Ogaill/Ocaill. Which threw the spotlight back on Og's great bedstead in Deuteronomy.

In the meantime I had found another word and another name that I thought most provocative. In Italian there is a word for "bed":

> *giaciglio.*

There would seem to be one Oc (Ac) and one Og (Ig) already in this name, and if there were once an initial O, it would have been Og/Oc/Og/Ala, the latter part close to Oigle in Ireland.

The next name is of one of the most famous megalithic sites in the Balkans, a beautifully executed architectural masterpiece called "the Prince's Grave." Its true name, however, is

> Agighiola (Og/Og/Hawa/Ala?).

The name of the ancient nomadic people of Romania who dwell in the area of Agighiola, an ethnic group that has excited the interest of anthropologists and etymologists for the last two centuries, fits into the puzzle:

> Vlach. Again, Ava/Ala/Oc, or Avalach? As in *Avalokitesvara*.

Moving on to Stonehenge, here is a site that has in its immediate vicinity no names of any interest except the Og/Oc names already presented—the Ock and Og rivers, the Ogbourne/Ochbourne villages, and, three miles away, the almost obliterated, ignored, but still mighty ramparts of Ogbury Camp. I have been to Stonehenge three times in the last two years, and in spite of all the sense and nonsense written about it, from a coldly logical viewpoint I see it now as the most ambitious of all the bedsteads of Og created on this earth. The fact that in the earlier circle of holes surrounding the structure have been found deposits of ashes and charred bones indicates that it was a center of worship where not only fertility rituals but human sacrifice may have been the order of the day or night.

*   *   *

The article by the Reverend F. J. Lynch mentions one Irish mythological figure of such stature that we must bring him onstage in this closing scene. He relates the name Cu to Oigle, Ocaill, Oc of the Boyne, as Ocu. This scholar reinstates an initial vowel in front of the name Cu, while for some months I have been trying to add a vowel to his name both in front and back as Ocua/Oc/Hawa, or Akhaiwa.

In Irish mythology Cu Roi was the "King of the World." He was "of Ireland, and yet not of it." He dwelt in the underworld, and the name of his kingdom, to which he escorted the Irish heroes, was the personification of darkness in terms of the Tema material that has been discussed. It was called Temair Luchra. Two Irish words intensify the Tema/darkness relationship:

> *temen*: Old Irish, meaning "darkness."
> *teimme*: modern Irish, meaning "stain" or "obscurity."

Thus one finds *Ocua* (Cu Roi [king]) dwelling in his palace of darkness, Temair Luchra.[3]

*　　*　　*

And now, before we embark on one final journey together, this time up into the limitless expanse of the heavens above us, a few last earthbound names. They illustrate graphically that I have indeed only scraped the surface, that my older and wiser friend was right when he warned me that, if I didn't watch my step, I would be engaged on this project for the rest of my life.

Still cherished in the memories and hearts of the Irish, their greatest champion knew when he took on this role that he was condemning himself to a short life, to an early, violent death. In the end he perished in the midst of heated battle, propped up against, and fastened by his warrior belt to, a highly symbolic, phallic pillar-stone, the ominous bird of doom perched on his shoulder. But until this predestined ending he was invincible against all odds. His name looms up out of the shadowy mists as

Oc/Oc/Hua/Ala/Anna
Ocochualaana
Øcochualaanų
Cochulaann
Cuchulainn.

Cuchulainn, pronounced Coo Coo Lane, as in the name of the sacred cuckoo, ancient symbol of fertility associated since the beginning with the oak tree. When President Kennedy, himself weighed down with a foreboding of impending disaster, warned by his friends not to go, left for his rendezvous with death in Dallas, more than one Irish editorial writer drew a sorrowful comparison between Cuchulainn and this first Irish-American to

[3] Note the similarity to the name of the Akkadian God of the Moon, Acu.

transcend, if only briefly, boundaries of race and religion in the New World.

The comparison becomes more vivid as one studies the legends concerning Cuchulainn. He was of an older strain than the Knights of the Red Branch, the protagonists of the second, the so-called "Heroic" or "Ulster" Cycle, yet he agreed to serve them. In his rigid adherence to duty, he slew both his closest friend and his adored only son. When his son was dead, he gathered up his body and placed it at the feet of the King of Ulster, whose name contains in it an element that emphasizes the basic conflict suggested in these pages between the Temmites or Ishmaelites, and those descended from Abraham and Sarah who identified themselves by the Eber name. The name of the King of Ulster was

Conchobar: pronounced Konk-*abar.*

George Stewart's *Names on the Land* is a dangerous book to wander into if you are trying to disengage yourself from this subject. On page 7 of the 1958 edition, he refers, in terms of the world of spirits, to the suffix *wakan*, which has been presented herein as a blending of Hawa/Ok/Ana, and to *manito*, presented herein as a blending of Mana/Ata/Hawa, or Manitowa. He then continues:

"The Cherokees had a belief in a race of huge snakes. Each was great as a tree-trunk, horned, with a bright blazing crest. Even to see one was sure death. Where they were thought to lurk, in deep river-pools and lonely passes in high mountains, the Cherokees called *Where-the-Uktena-stays.*"

The relationship of Uk to Oc seems reasonable. If you will turn to the entry under "Thames" from *The Concise Oxford Dictionary of English Place-Names* included in Chapter 3, you will see that the Tema "Rivers of Darkness" names are related to the Latin *tenebrae* and so on. *Tenebra* in Latin means literally "darkness," hence "tenebrous," or "dark, gloomy, obscure." On the afternoon of Holy Wednesday the office of matins and lauds called Tenebrae begins in the Roman Catholic Church, and continues on Holy Thursday and Good Friday, during which candles are gradually extinguished to commemorate the Crucifixion.

The legend of Tenes in classical mythology rightfully belongs in the Tema legends mentioned above. Tenes was banished by his father, Cycnus, and set adrift in a chest when he was wrongfully accused by his stepmother, Phylonome, of trying to seduce her. This side channel of research has not been explored to any length, although a number of Tena place-names that appear to be corruptions of Tema have been observed. In the Cherokee name for their huge, horned snakes—Uktena—is a blending of Oc with Tema of such stature that it cannot be bypassed. The name Cherokee itself suggests Asch and Ok joined together by an *ara*. The evidence from all directions indicates that snakes must have been the most dreaded and dangerous enemy of early mankind on this planet.

One of the earliest maps of eastern North America (Plate 54), included in the *Theatrum Orbis Terrarum* of Abraham Ortelius, published in 1574, less than a hundred years after Columbus crossed the Atlantic, features prominently four place-names each of which adds another block to the overall premise of *The Key*. Between them they embrace the entire mid western portion of this continent:

> Avacal: in the general area of the Ohio River; Ava/Oc, as in our starting point, "havoc," joined by the third key name, Ala from Eloah.
> Chilaga: laid across the upper stretches of the Mississippi. Asch/Ala/Og?
> Calicvas: covering the lower stretches of the Mississippi. Oc/Ala/Oc/Ava/Asa? Four of the six key names, with Oc appearing twice.
> Tagil: a bit southeast of Calicvas. Ata/Og/Ala?

In Baron de Lahontan's *Nouveaux Voyages . . . dans l'Amérique Septentrionale*, first published in 1703, two of the best

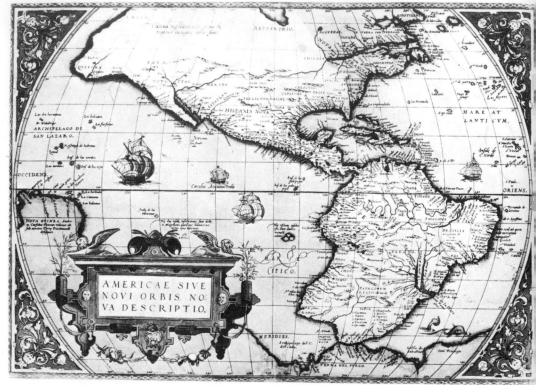

PLATE 54. North America: The *Theatrum Orbis Terrarum* map of
Abraham Ortelius. Published in 1574, less than a century after Columbus crossed the Atlantic, the map features prominently in eastern
North America four names built out of primary elements discussed
in *The Key:* Chilaga, Avacal, Calicvas, Tagil. Other pertinent names
include: farther west in North America, Quivara and Tototeac; and,
in the Far North, Sagvenam; in South America, Paguana and Bre-
silia.

*Print: British Museum Map Room,
courtesy Radio Times Hulton Picture Library*

250

known names in North America appear in intriguing early forms:

> Chegakou: with a vowel fore and aft, as Aschegakoua, a melding of Ash/Og/Ok/Hawa. Today the name is Chicago.

> Ouaricon: containing both an Hawwah and an Oc, *Ouaricon*, this name has been put forward as the origin point for Wisconsin as well as Oregon.

Quentowic

Here is a name that belongs in the same category with the *que* names covered in Chapter 16. While the ending suggests some of the Indian names in Wisconsin, it was actually the name of one of the most famous seaports in Europe when history began. Quentowic was directly across the English Channel from the mouth of the Thames River, a major trading and manufacturing center, possessing a mint, and of such importance that in A.D. 842 it underwent an assault with terrible slaughter and plunder by the Vikings, at the same time that there was an equally bloody attack on London. In the name Quentowic, with a preceding vowel added, as Oquentowic, one finds Oc/Hawa (Akhaiwa)/Ana/Ata/Hawa/Oc (Hawa/Oc as in "havoc").

Which brings us to the etymology of the name, *Viking*s, whose legendary banquet hall of the immortals, Valhalla, has already been proposed as Ava/Ala/Alla. In his incredible feat of scholarship combined with swift-moving readability, *A History of the Vikings*, Gwyn Jones discusses the name Viking at some length:

"There is still less than full agreement as to the original meaning of the two Norse nouns *viking* and *víkingr*. In the written sources they certainly mean, *viking*, piracy or a pirate raid, and *víkingr*, a pirate or raider. The first element of the words, *vík-*, has been explained in various ways. A viking was one who lay up or lurked in or came from a bay, fjord, or creek (*vík*); he was a man of the camp (O.E. *wíc*, *wícing*), i.e. a soldier or fighter; or a man of the town (*wíc*, Latin *vícus*), i.e. a seafaring man or trader."[4]

The use of the verb, in the sense to go *vik*ing, to go raiding and plundering, runs parallel to the verb in English, to go *havoc*ing, to go raiding and plundering. In English it is possible to trace back to the two full names Haue and Oc ancient "Godys." It appears logical that in the forgotten past *Vik*, once *A*vic, also had its origin in Hawwah (Avvah) and Oc. Havok and Avik?

The universality of these names in prehistoric times is further illustrated by two names associated with one of the most daring of all the Viking raids. In 845 they struck far inland in Spain and attacked the Moorish stronghold at Seville. For a week they held the city, except for the citadel, slaughtered the men, and carried off the women and children as slaves to their island base at the mouth of the river. The name of the river up which they knifed, showing an audacity defying imagination, was

Guadalquivir.

Once, as the Oguatalaquavara, a blending of Og/Hawa/Ata/ Ala/Oc/Hawa/Ara, containing two Akhaiwa's? (Ada is a corruption of Ata frequently encountered in historic times.) The name of the island base to which the Vikings transported their prisoners, today the Isla Menor, was then called Qubtil. As Ocuabtil, another Akhaiwa name?

Viewed from the twentieth century, the enormous, sudden surge outward from Scandinavia of the Vikings, extending along the coastal areas of half the earth, penetrating to the Mediterranean coasts of France and Italy, far down the rivers of Russia, engulfing Normandy and Britain and the seaports of Ireland, crossing the Atlantic via Iceland to Newfoundland and Canada, appears like a later-day version of the ferocious assault of the Akhaiwa "Sea People" two thousand years earlier, upon the Mediterranean. If this research is valid, then both names, Ak-

[4] New York: Oxford University Press, 1968, footnote to page 76.

haiwa and Viking, would have been originally dedicated to Hawwah and Oc, or, if you prefer, to Oc and Hawwah.

In a panoramic section of his book on the Vikings dealing with Scandinavian mythology, Gwyn Jones discusses a number of geographical, tribal, and personal names of monumental proportions that appear to support a Hawwah/Ok origin for the name Viking. First, the most dramatic example I have found of an earlier people worshiping Og/Oc being superseded by a later people whose name seems to be based on an Eber/Abar/Hebri origin:

Egill and Eofor

The name of the legendary King Egill in the Scandinavian myths is identical etymologically to Oigle, Achill, and so on, in pre-Christian Ireland. (See Cruagh Oigle, presently Croagh Patrick, above.) King Egill is slain by Eofor, the "Boar," "Egill's blood reddening the boar's snout."

If you will examine the entry "York" in *The Concise Oxford Dictionary of English Place-Names*, you will find that this Scandinavian name Eofor is related to the Abor element in the earliest recorded spelling of York, *Abor*icum. This has already been presented as a conceivable placing of an Eber/Abar name in front of an earlier Og/Oc name, Aboricum, also found in a number of other early key place-names in Europe and elsewhere.

In the Scandinavian legend of Egill's death through Eofor, the inference is strong that an Egill (Og/Ala) people are subjugated by an Eofor/Abor people but that the bloodstreams of the two peoples were mixed together. One of the most prominent regional names in Viking Scandinavia featured the same Og/Ala elements. The entire northernmost portion of Norway was called Halogaland (Ala/Og/Ala). The positioning suggests that the earlier people were pushed northward by the later people. (See map opposite page 60, *A History of the Vikings*.) The name Halogaland has disappeared today, but the name Heligoland for the island and bay off the northern coast of

Germany appears to be related. For good measure King Egill had a close relation called King Ali.

Huiglaucus or Hygelac

Another mighty champion of the early Scandinavians was named King Huiglaucus or Hygelac. Leaving off the Latinized *us* ending, one finds in the two variants a conceivable blending of Hawa/Og/Ala/Oc in Huigelac. It was said of this king that he was "so huge that from the age of twelve no horse could carry him." He was slain in a "piratical naval raid" against the Frisian people who bore the tribal name Attuarii (another Atta/ Hawa, "Ottawa," name?). His skeleton was "preserved on an island at the mouth of the Rhine, and for a long time was displayed there to the curious as a marvel of the human creation." (See page 30, *A History of the Vikings.*) The etymology of the word "huge" returns to mind.

Kvan

Kvan, kvaen, gen. plural *kvenna*, is an Old Norse word for woman. Here one finds a *k* preceding an Ava/Ana blending identical to the name of the compassionate goddess of the Orient, *Kwan*yin or *Kuan*yin. Note also the Scandinavian tribal name *Kven*ir, *Kvaen*ir, or *Cwen*a, once Ocawana? Oc/Awa (Akhaiwa)/Ana. Also *Kven*land on the western shore of the Gulf of Bothnia, which, because of confusion with the Old Norse word for "woman," "became mistakenly a land of Amazons, Adam of Bremen's *terra feminarum.*" (See page 25, *A History of the Vikings.*)

Floki Vilgerdason

One of the three semilegendary discoverers of Iceland, credited with bestowing on it the name Island, was called Floki Vilgerdason. Here both the first and last names are conceivable blends of Hawa/Ala/Ok as in *Avalok*itesvara. Afa/ Ala/Ok: *Flok*i, the same elements proposed for the word "folk"; Ava/Ala/Og: *Vilg*erdason.

Dan

Closely intertwined in Scandinavian mythology with the Og/
Oc and Eber/Abar names is a powerful strain of names that
appear related to the Danaid legend. Dan was the one "from
whom, so saith antiquity, the pedigrees of our kings have flowed
in glorious series, like channels from some parent spring." Dan
was the father of the most famous of the Norse gods, *Odin*. In
turn they were both descended from the most powerful of the
early gods, Bor, whose name is preserved in such other names
as the Aurora *Bor*ealis. From the name Dan traditionally
stemmed the name *Den*mark, or, more properly *Dan*mark. The
name of Dan's father, Ypper, looks and sounds suspiciously like
a corruption of Eber.

*   *   *

I would be remiss if I failed to acknowledge the great debt
owed to three outstanding classical scholars for information
regarding the Akhaiwa "Sea People." The first two have been
briefly mentioned in Chapter 3: A. R. Burn, *Minoans, Philistines,
and Greeks;*[5] R. A. Stewart Macalister, *The Philistines, Their
History and Civilization;*[6] and B. H. Warmington, *Carthage.*[7]
Rereading the pages of these authors after nearly four years,
several names of epic proportions come onstage, which meant
nothing to me when I last saw them. A. R. Burn provides the
name of the Akhaiwa ruler as

Tawagalawas, titled The Ayawalawas.

Could one ask for a name of more profound significance in
terms of the data presented herein? Ata/Awa/Og/Ala/Awa/
Asa, The Aya/Awa/Ala/Awa/Asa. One's mind centers on the
Pueblo sun-god Tawa and on the early English expletive
Walawa!

The same author reflects on the name of the southeast corner
of Asia Minor which, six centuries after the attacks of the "Sea

[5] London: Routledge, 1930.
[6] The Schweich Lectures, British Academy, 1911; Oxford: Oxford
University Press, 1913.
[7] London: Robert Hale, 1960.

People," about 658 B.C., was recorded as Kuweh. He sees it as "resembling Akhhiyawa and Achaia." So I am obviously not the first to add initial vowels to names.

Dr. Macalister presents five tribal names of the "Sea People" from Egyptian inscriptions which meant nothing to me at first but which now appear to be variations on the same theme:

> Lukku: as *A*luk*o*ku*a* (Ala/Ok/Ok/Hawa), an Akhaiwa ending.
> Kelekesh: as *O*kelekesh (Ok/Ala/Ok/Ash).
> Shekelesh: as *A*shekelesh (Ash/Ok/Ala/Ash).
> Zakkala: As *A*zak*o*kala (Aza/Ok/Ok/Ala).
> Washasha: as *A*washasha or *Ha*washasha (Hawa/Ash/ Asha).

What is so remarkable is that working with only four key elements, five tribal names of such individual distinction evolved. The same thing held true all across the face of the earth. The prehistoric pattern of place-names, tribal names, mythological names was intelligible and meaningful far beyond that of historic times. Elsewhere in the same lectures this scholar presents a word that features the same blended names found in *Avalok*itesvara. It is a Sanskrit word with the highly relevant meaning "white":

> *V*al*ak*sa. Once *A*valak*a*sa? As in the nomadic Vlach, once *A*v*a*lach people of Romania?

*   *   *

Abandoning terrestrial for celestial suroundings, the time has come to rise above ourselves, to survey our mortal predicament from the perspective of the universe around us. Soaring up into the heavens, leaving behind the yolk and the egg, following in reverse the route down which Zoutem-que plunged in his cataclysmic fall from grace, we can use as our two chief navigational stars those that were used by the three astronauts who circled the moon, once *mona*, in their stupendous voyage last Christmas. These stars are named

*Ach*enar and *Ach*emar.

It was an extremely helpful young man, Martin Steinbaum, at the Hayden Planetarium, in New York, who advised me about the importance of these two Oc-named stars the day before the epic voyage began. An appropriately named vantage point from which to survey the boundless space around us is the star Aquila, another blending of the three key names Oc/Hawa/Ala. Far below us spins the earth, and around its middle we can see the hypothetical band dividing the earth into two halves, a dividing line that someone before history began named the

Aequator (Oc/Hawa), today the Equator.

Among the stars are other familiar names:

Aquarius, a constellation, signifying water, but again a blending of the two fertility deities Hawwah, "mother of all living," and Oc, founder of the cult of Ashtaroth.

Capricorn, part of the Zodiac, which in the very beginning was named

Aegipan,

the goat/man deity, a name found in Greek for goat, *aeg*, earlier *aiyog* (Hawa/Og).

In another direction burns the bright star the Romans referred to as the shield bearer:

Aegiochus (Og and Oc).

There is one little-known name that cannot be overlooked. It is the name "given to patches in the Milky Way distinguished by extraordinary blackness, owing to the absence of even dim stars, especially to one near the Southern Cross, formerly called also the Black Magellanic Cloud" (*Oxford English Dictionary*). It received this latter name because it was first historically observed by Magellan's crew on the first historic voyage around the world in the sixteenth century, a little over four hundred years ago. No one knows where the other name for these black patches came from. It has been used by navigators for an indefinite period and has outlasted the name Black Magellanic Cloud. In the overall context it seems likely that the ancient Mexicans believed that it was through these huge "empty" spaces that Zoutem-que and his band of fallen angels arrived on this planet. The name is made up of all but one of the elements found in the name of the great plumed serpent Quetzalcoatl. Only the two t's or Ata's are missing:

Oc/Hawa/Ala/Aza/Ock
Ocoalazock, Ocoalasock
Coalsock
Coalsack

If you choose, you can go along with those who believe this name of undetermined origin came into being because English sailors thought these great black spaces looked like "sacks of coal." When one observes the scores of place-names all over the earth beginning with Coal, many in countries like Mexico where coal isn't called "coal," it appears more logical that our prehistoric ancestors, possessing an incredible knowledge of astronomy, charted out, with this name Coalsack, the route by which they believed their ancestors found their way to earth.

*   *   *

In a book of this nature there is no true ending. What is expounded in these pages is merely a beginning. However, during the past few weeks, while double-checking the spellings of the various names from all parts of the world, I could not help noticing scores of names that fall into the basic patterns of the key names included herein. But I believe that the time has come to call a halt to citing additional examples and that there is sufficient evidence here on which to rest the case. Nonetheless, I want to echo the hope expressed by Cyrus Gordon, Frederick Santee, and Walter Wood that *The Key* will encourage and inspire others to explore far beyond the horizons of this particular work.

There seems to be no more fitting note on which to close than the lines already quoted from George R. Stewart's *Names on the Land*:

"One might venture to apply a principle so nearly universal that it has even been called a law, that is, the unintelligible but repeated elements in names are to be referred back to some generic term in an earlier language."

Epilogue

SINCE *The Key* was published in New York during the autumn of 1969 three developments have been of particular interest to me: the reception the book received in America; certain works by other writers which have substantiated the basic premise of *The Key*; a number of 'key' names and words which have resulted from further research or, in most cases, have come from authorities or general readers.

On the first score, the reception, the underlying note was struck by a reviewer in the Columbus, Ohio, *Dispatch* who described it as "a book for those whose minds are wide open." Almost without exception the admittedly highly controversial material and methods were so greeted by American authorities and reviewers.

Hugh Kenner, the distinguished author critic, and Professor of English at the University of Southern California in Santa Barbara, wrote:

"To doubt if any man alive has the erudition to evaluate it definitively is simply to say that its originality locates it in a terrain where erudition has not yet been developed. If only it isn't brushed aside as a crank book, it should spur learning for decades."

259

John O'Brien, Associate Professor of English at Georgia Tech, writing in the *Atlanta Constitution*, stated:

"It may indeed be 'The Key' to unlock the riddle of man's past . . . (it) offers a groundwork, a hypothesis to be tested."

Carrying this question of a 'hypothesis to be tested' a step further, Marilyn Vittert Lipman made a most pertinent suggestion in the *St. Louis Post-Dispatch*:

"There is no doubt in the author's mind that these key words appear much more frequently than they would by mere chance. That is the crux of the theory. One of the early studies should be a mathematical analysis to determine if this is true."

Others have suggested such an analysis might be undertaken by means of computers. Professor Van L. Johnson, Department of Classics, Tufts University, member of the American Philological Association, commenting in the *Boston Globe* on my closing verdict that "in a book of this nature, there is no true ending" added: "Nor will there be until someone puts together rules and principles about the possible interplay of primitive languages, and develops what might be called Prehistoric—as opposed to Historical and to Structural —Linguistics."

Professor Johnson, in my opinion, was getting at the very heart of the matter. That other specialists have been influenced by the unorthodox research methods was brought home by a letter received in April, 1972, from Professor Victor L. Strite, Department of English, Baylor University, Waco, Texas, who wrote in part:

"As a medievalist/philologist who is interested in interdisciplinary studies, your suggestions have supported many of my hunches about world migratory patterns which came from formal university exposure. . . . It should be stimulating to a scholarly community which is reluctant to stick its neck out of footnotes. Perhaps someday it will footnote your book."

I like particularly Professor Strite's use of the word 'suggestions' for that indeed is what I am presenting. Employing such research methods it seemed inevitable that a certain amount of chaff would turn up among the wheat. I figured that if only 50 per cent or 60 per cent of the material stood up under critical examination, the project would be worth the time and effort. On the basis of evidence to date the percentage of relevant material appears to be considerably higher. I will come back to this point in a moment.

On the second score, certain works by other writers which have substantiated the basic premise of *The Key*, two books which are related and which indicate close links between ancient Egypt and ancient Britain, are Gerard Hawkin's *Stonehenge Decoded* and Peter Tompkins' *Secrets of The Great Pyramid* (see Bibliography). Above everything else, these works point up the general conclusion of Cyrus Gordon's *Before Columbus* (Turnstone Books, London, 1972):

"for thousands of years men have been in contact with other men at the ends of the earth, influencing each other's ways of life, and producing thereby an intertwined network of developed regional cultures. . . . Sea Peoples in remote antiquity established and maintained sea lanes so extensively that from the start all high civilizations formed one ecumene."

Each month during the past three years, in archaeological discoveries as well as in printed matter, it has become more and more obvious that the traditionalist concept of man's prehistory must undergo drastic re-evaluation. (The discovery in 1971 of a prehistoric highly sophisticated village beneath an ancient graveyard on the shore of County Mayo, in the opinion of many authorities is alone going to require such a re-evaluation in Ireland and Britain.)

Three additional books that bear on this are: *No Longer on the Map*, Raymond H. Ramsay, Viking Press, New York, 1972. Pierre Honore's *In Quest of the White God* which is discussed at some length in *Before Columbus* . . . and Ronald and Catherine Berndt's *World of the First Australians*, which concludes, among many other fascinating conclusions, that the 750 or more current aboriginal dialects in Australia stem from at most three or possibly four languages brought in from outside. There are other pertinent books but the above five stand out in my mind.

On the third and last score, of certain words and names that have turned up since the American edition of *The Key*, there are over two thousand which fit into the formula, most of them representing wheat not chaff, helping to strengthen at least in my own mind and those who submitted them the basic premise of the book. After the barrage of words and names you have been subjected to herein, one hesitates to submit any more but a few are of such a nature they can not be ignored:

> Wo-Kwok: Japan is so called in the Cantonese dialect on the coast of China. In an annotation to the *Arabian Nights*, Sir Richard Burton suggests a relationship to the mythical island of El Wakwak which is mentioned in this classic. It hardly seems necessary to point out that Wo-Kwok conceivably stems from Awa/Ok/ Awa/Ok.

> Koal Hill: The name of the sacred hill outside Peking on which the Chinese Emperor and his astronomers maintained an observatory and where each year in elaborate ceremonies they plotted the seasonal patterns, planting, reaping, etc. (See Coalsack and other similar names and words in text.)

> Hoyuk: In Turkish generic for 'ancient hill or mound.' See Catal Hoyuk and other archaeological sites. From Hawa/Ok?

> Ayasoluk: The name of the hill near the ancient site of Ephesus in Turkey where the earliest ornamental finds, 13th century B.C. Mycenean, have been excavated. Awa/Asa/Ala/Ok?

Robert F. Scott, Director of the Library of Science in New York, points out that in Turkish *Ok* for 'arrow' and *Hava* for 'air' seem symbolically pertinent to the 'key' premise.

> Echua: The Mayan God of Travel. See the *Larousse Encyclopedia of Mythology*. A transatlantic Akhiawa?

Loa: The Haitian generic name for all voodoo gods. See
Aloa, Loa, etc. in text.

Ogou: The name of one of the most powerful of these
Haitian gods, a fearsome central figure in a cult of
fertility.

Ochun: The name of a prominent Cuban fertility god.
Some years ago, in the late 1950s, the Cuban singer,
Xiomara Alfaro, recorded a traditional native song in
which a barren woman seeks the intercession of Ochun.

Oxun: The name of another fertility deity in Latin
America, this one in Brazil. Specialists believe the two
names, Ochun and Oxun, are of common origin.

These three 'fertility' names—Ogou (Haitian) . . . Ochun
(Cuban) . . . Oxun (Brazilian)—are thought to have been
transported into the New World by black African slaves. Still
surviving in primitive transatlantic cultures, they are in my
opinion additional pieces of evidence that Og, the legendary
survivor of the Great Flood, founder of the fertility cult of
Bashan, deserves further examination by objective scholars.
Another discovery in the Old World bolstered considerably
my feelings on this score:

Oegir: The terrible Norse God of the Sea. Oegir has
been related to the Latin *Oceanus*. May not both stem
from Og? (For Oegir see E. Cobham Brewer's
Dictionary of Phrase and Fable.)

I am grateful to my British publisher, Alick Bartholomew,
for pointing out an omission from the original edition that
particularly concerns British and Irish place names. He states
that the standard reference for British place names, Bartholomew's *Gazetteer of the British Isles* (first published by
his great-grandfather in 1887) lists 129 names with the prefix
Ach and 162 with *Auch*, the majority of which are river or
water names.

Ahua: Several correspondents have pointed out that in
northern Mexico 'Ahua' is a standard component in
many native songs, interposed as an expletive or con-

ceivably as an invocation between sentences. The origin
and the meaning of this name or word are unknown.

Chucagua: The Indian name for the Rio Grande. See
George R. Stewart's *Dictionary of American Place
Names*. Again one finds the *agua* element in an
important pre-Colombian name. Note also *Aqua*shicola,
the native Indian name bestowed on a town in eastern
Pennsylvania.

The above handful of names alone strengthened the conviction that the surface had only been scratched in this study.
One last name deserves mention.

Since 1969 I have done some further research on the question
of vowels dropped or added in place names that once might
have been comparable—Tarifa, Trafalgar, etc. Working
among Ash- place names I discovered:

*A*sha and Sha seventeen miles apart in Cyprus.

*A*shah and a number of Shah place names in Syria.

*A*schach and a number of Schach place names in Austria.

*A*chennini, Saskatchewan, and *Chen*equa, Wisconsin . . .
*Chen*oa, Illinois . . . *Chen*oa, Kentucky, etc. Chazy in
up-state New York and the *A*chazi river in Canada.

Eventually I arrived at Ashaway, Rhode Island, which could
not be in a more highly strategic location. It is nine miles by
water from *Acoa*xtet on the island which the native Indians
called *Aque*theneck (Rhode Island). Two and a half miles
from Ashaway is another village with the name Shannock,
once *A*shannock?

If the initial A is dropped from Ashaway, one is left with
Shaway and a conceivable linguistic link to:

*Shaway*miyah Cape on the southern coast of Arabia . . .
*Shuway*hatiyah water course, Arabia . . . *Shuway*man,
Arabia . . . *Shuway*kah, Jordan . . . *Shuway*kh,
Kuwait . . . conceivably related to the ancient ruins of
*Shawa*k in Saudi Arabia.

After working with detailed local maps of Wisconsin,
Iowa, Pennsylvania, New Jersey, Connecticut, Rhode Island,

New Jersey, Massachussets, Oregon and Washington, I became convinced of one thing: if all the Indian place names that feature 'key' elements were plotted on the map of any one of these states, the result would be quite startling. And, coming back to Miss Lipman's point above, it is impossible to attain comparable results with any other combination of elements.

*   *   *

I had been working for over two years on the material which was finally incorporated into *The Key* before I discovered I had stepped all unwittingly into a vicious academic battle as to what role the Mediterranean and especially Semitic peoples played in the prehistory and ancient history of Ireland and Britain. What this amounts to was most succinctly summed up in several letters from one of Europe's most distinguished Celtic scholars who has asked to remain anonymous. I quote in part:

"On the British Isles people do not like the idea that there could be connections between Northern Africa and their beloved country. But they exist, and Celtic mythology is full of early Mediterranean elements. I have been told that Morris-Jones' article (an appendix to *The Welsh People* by John Rhys and David Brnmor-Jones, first published in the late 1890s) was very badly received in Wales as well as in Ireland when it appeared. It is never being quoted. . . .

"During the thirties of this century German scholars tried to prove that Germanic is an archaic Indo-European language and tried to locate the home of the Indo-Europeans in central Germany. Now Irish, Welsh and some American scholars seem to do the same kind of nonsense for Celtic. . . .

"Nationalism and counter-nationalism play a big part in this game of life, as well as political doctrines. Fortunately there are always people who do not follow the general pattern, and those are the only ones who really search for the truth."

The single plausible reason why the traditionalists stubbornly refuse to admit there were any early links between

Britain, Ireland and the Mediterranean is that there must follow inevitably the admission that at least one important element in the blood stream of the English, Irish, Scottish and Welsh is very likely Semitic. Admit one chink into the façade and the whole structure might crumble. This was brought forcibly home several years ago when a testimonial dinner was tended in Bonn to Dr. Professor Julius Pokorny of Zurich University, accepted as the 'Dean' of Celtic scholars, on his eightieth birthday. Columns appeared in the Irish newspapers lauding Dr. Pokorny on his accomplishments but nowhere, in any newspaper, was it mentioned that his chief objective over the past decades has been to establish that both the English and Irish languages have a common sub-stratum closely related to Berber dialects, Egyptian and Hebrew. It wasn't the fault of the newspaper editors. They didn't know this; they weren't told by those who did.

There is only room here for one specific example of how this 'Iron Curtain' of sophistry works, how it has been built up both deliberately and in some instances unknowingly over the past several hundred years. As a prelude to this example I should explain that I first became interested in Irish archaeology when certain place names convinced me that somewhere near the Curragh, the legendary gathering place and present leading race course of the Irish people, there must be the site of an earlier Tara (palace) of the Irish high kings than the accepted one in County Meath.

Returning to Ireland from Rome in 1967 my initial attempt to find this site drew a blank. The second landed squarely on Dun Ailinne or Knockaulan, a huge mound that dominates the Curragh, situated a few miles from Old Kilcullen in Co. Kildare. Having tried without success to interest a number of highly placed Irish officials and authorities in bringing an American university into a joint excavating project at the untouched site, I approached Mr. Charles J. Haughey, then Minister for Finance, whose name appears in the Acknowledgements. When he heard the facts he stated: "To hell with

what people think or believe! Let's find out the truth."
Within 24 hours he set wheels in motion which resulted in five
summers of excavating by the University of Pennsylvania in
conjunction with the Irish Government and work is being
projected for several more summers.

Whether or not Dun Ailinne is an earlier Tara is still a
moot question. The point is that the 'official' attitude should
have prepared me for the 'official' attitude towards the Burren,
an attitude that prevails not only in Ireland but in Britain.
The Burren, an area about fifty miles in diameter located near
Corofin in West Clare, is one of the archaeological treasure
houses of Europe. Within this area are more than 700 prehistoric 'forts' and megalithic ruins or dolmens. They are
related to the ancient remains on the Aran Islands discussed
in the text. This now desolate, brooding region was obviously
once the centre of intense human activity. Further southwest
in County Clare within a twenty-mile-long triangle bounded
by Querren, Kilkee and Loophead, between the Shannon river
and the Atlantic Ocean, on what was once called in Irish
Magh Fhearta (presently Moyarta), the 'Plain of the Graves,'
are nearly two hundred prehistoric mounds, many of which
contain underground passages and chambers. As in the case
of the ruins in the Burren, these mounds are slowly being
obliterated and forgotten. It is almost impossible to find some
of the most important remains in either related area.

Almost the first question that comes to mind wandering
through West Clare is: Where did the people come from who
lived here thousands of years ago? I could find nothing
published during the past seventy years that sheds any light
on this subject. It is only when one goes back seventy-five
years that an answer is set forth in detail which has been
ignored in this century, obliterated as badly as the remains
themselves.

In 1897 W. Copeland Borlase, President of the Royal
Institution of Cornwall and Vice-President of the Society of
Antiquaries of London, set forth his views on the origin of the

Burren's megalithic remains in a three-volume work: *The Dolmens of Ireland* (Chapman and Hall, London). Those who followed Borlase have quoted him extensively but nowhere have I found a single mention of the fact that he devoted over sixty pages in his definitive work to the conviction that these extensive structures were built by seafarers from the Mediterranean. Borlase believed the dolmens were constructed to resemble the prows of ships; with diagrams and illustrations he related them to such prehistoric stone artifices as the Gallarus Orator on the Dingle Peninsula in Kerry, and in turn to the ancient stone navitas found on islands throughout the Mediterranean including Crete and Majorca. These navitas are believed to have been built to resemble ships which seafarers at an even earlier date had beached and used inverted as shelters against the elements.

Contemplating the manner in which Borlase's theory has been shuffled into obscurity, even more than in the treatment of Maurice-Jones's conclusions, I felt certain that our concept of prehistory has been and still is being sadly manipulated. Shortly after finishing *The Key*, staying in a thatched cottage at Doonaha on the Plain of the Graves, I discovered that a number of place names, which today have lost their resemblance to one another through anglicization, still feature in Irish the identical 'key' element, one that in my opinion links them directly to the Mediterranean, to Ulysses and his companions, supporting the theories of Borlase and Maurice-Jones.

These place names are: Kilkee . . . Quilty . . . Querren . . . Quin. The one significant element in the Irish versions of all four names is the same. It is:

Chaoi or interchangeably *Caoi*

which in the above text has already been related to the Homeric name for the Mycenean Greeks: Achaoi and the mysterious ancient sea people from the West: Akhiawa.

These place names grow in importance when one notes the name of the principle 'druid' who in Irish legends was in opposition to St. Patrick. His name was:

*Chaoi*lte: identical to the Irish name for Quilty.

And one should not pass over the name of the 'mythical' Christian saint who long ago performed extraordinary feats in this part of Ireland. His name was:

Cuan

which linguistically is identical to Chaoin, as in the 1311 version of what is today Glenquin: Glennchaoin.

If you visit West Clare, it is well worth taking a look at Kilkee, Querren, Quilty and certain Quin places. They could not be more perfectly situated in terms of the Borlase theory. Coming along the Atlantic coast from Loophead, navigators would have been faced with towering cliffs, still a menace to shipping, until they arrived at the sheltered, crescent-shaped, splendid strand of Kilkee (Cill Chaoi, Cill or Kill meaning 'church'), today a favourite summer resort for the Irish. Cill Chaoi or Chaoi must have been a welcome haven to early storm-tossed mariners travelling in ships that could be beached.

Directly opposite to Kilkee on the Shannon is Querren (Chaoiran). This is presently an almost abandoned area along an estuary which flows across to within a mile or so of Kilkee, making the Plain of the Graves almost an island separated from the rest of Ireland. Kilkee and Querren would have been the two principal ports for those who inhabited that plain in prehistoric times.

Continuing up the Atlantic coast from Kilkee, the next principal haven is the snug, picturesque village of Quilty or Chaoilte, tucked behind a string of small off-shore islands. Continuing up the Shannon, such places as the ancient village of Quin or Chaoin with its exquisite medieval abbey, situated on a stream that reaches the Shannon, and outside Corofin fabled Lake Inchi*quin* (in Irish the 'Isle of Quin or Chaoin') lead directly into the heart of the Burren. For centuries this has been O'Brien country and today Lord Inchiquin is an O'Brien title, but before the ancient O'Briens were there the ancient Chaoi (Quin) people were there.

My zest for exploring West Clare was heightened the very

first day when at one of the largest of the mysterious mounds, only a few hundred yards from the justly famed pub in Doonaha of genial John Lynch (who by some quirk of modern migratory patterns was born across the Atlantic on the island the Indians once called *Aque*theneck), I encountered by chance a Norwegian archaeologist who was spending several weeks in the region. As he and I stood on the rim of the mound with the equally genial local farmer, John Downes, who owns this land and who, unlike countless ancestors, is not afraid to investigate these sites, the latter-day Norseman peered off in the distance towards the Shannon where several other mounds were faintly visible and exclaimed indignantly: "What are they doing with these priceless, five-thousand-year-old monuments? They are letting them disappear from the face of the earth. They are idiots!"

Who he meant by "they" became quite evident several months later in Dublin when at one of the principal 'official' sources I was told that certain typewritten manuscripts dealing with West Clare, which have never been published and which I had consulted on a previous occasion, were "not available." Despite considerable pressures, local and otherwise, the mounds in the Kilkee/Querren/Loophead triangle and the megalithic ruins in the Burren remain unposted, well-nigh impossible to find unless one consults the maps which accompanied the papers of T. J. Westropp published in the *Journal of the Royal Society of Antiquaries of Ireland* over a thirty-year period from the 1890s to about 1920.

And that brings one back at this second ending of *The Key* to the words of Francis Bacon quoted at the beginning:

"For as God was the help of our reason to illuminate us, so should we turn it every way, that we may be more capable of understanding His mysteries; provided only that the mind be enlarged, according to its capacity, to the grandeur of the mysteries, and not the mysteries contracted to the narrowness of the mind."

Bibliography

Acosta, José de, *Historia Natural y Moral de Las Indias* (translated by E. G.). London, 1604.

Apollonius of Rhodes, *The Voyage of Argo*, E. V. Rieu translation. Penguin, London, 1959.

Arbman, Holger, *The Vikings*, Thames & Hudson, London, 1961.

Akurgal, Ekrem, *Ancient Civilizations and Ruins of Turkey*, 1969.

Ardrey, Robert, *African Genesis*. Fontana, London.

Astour, M. C., *Hellenosemitica: An ethnic and cultural study in West Semitic impact on Mycenaean Greece*. Leiden, 1965.

Atkinson, R. J. C., *Stonehenge*. Hamish Hamilton, London, 1956.

Ausubel, Nathan, *A Treasury of Jewish Folklore*. Crown Publishers, New York, 1948.

Bacon, E., Editor, *Vanished Civilizations of the Ancient World*. Thames & Hudson, London, 1963.

Baldwin, John Denison, *Prehistoric Nations*. London and New York, 1869.

Bancroft, H. H., *Native Races*. London, 1875.

Bartholomew's *Gazetteer of the British Isles*. 9th ed. Bartholomew, Edinburgh, 1966.

Bass, George Fletcher, *Archaeology Under Water*. Thames and Hudson, London, 1966.

Batut, Guy de la, and Georges Friedman, *A History of the French People*. Methuen, London, 1923.

Berndt, Ronald M. & Catherine H., *The World of the First Australians*, Angus & Robertson, London, 1964.

271

Bhaldraithe, Tomás de, *English-Irish Dictionary*. Dublin, 1959.

Bibby, Geoffrey, *Four Thousand Years Ago*. Collins, London, 1962.

Bible, The Holy, King James Version.

Birket-Smith, Kaj, *The Paths of Culture*. University of Wisconsin, Madison, 1966.

Bisschop, Eric de, *Tahiti Nui*. Collins, London, 1959.

Bizonfy, Franz De Paula, *English-Hungarian, Hungarian-English Dictionary*. "Szabadsag" Hungarian Daily, Cleveland, Ohio.

Bonner, C., *A Study of the Danaid Myth*. Harvard Studies in Classical Philology. Harvard University Press, Cambridge, Mass. (n.d.)

Borlase, William C., *The Dolmens of Ireland*. 3 vols. Chapman & Hall, London, 1897.

Brewer, E. Cobham, *A Dictionary of Phrase and Fable*, revised edition. Cassell, London, 1963.

Brogan, Olwen, *Roman Gaul*. Bell & Sons, London, 1953.

Brown, Lawrence, *The Might of the West*. Astor-Honor, New York, 1962.

Bulfinch, Thomas, *The Golden Age of Myth and Fable*, London, 1915.

Burland, Cottie, *North American Indian Mythology*. The Hamlyn Group, Middlesex, 1965.

Burn, A. R., *Minoans, Philistines, and Greeks*. Routledge, London, 1930.

————, *The Lyric Age of Greece*. St. Martin's Press, London, 1960, 1961.

————, *Persia and the Greeks*. St. Martin's Press, London, 1962.

————, *The Pelican History of Greece*. Penguin Books, London, 1966.

Bushnell, G. H. S., *The First Americans*. Thames & Hudson, London, 1968.

Candolle, Alphonse de, *The History of Cultivated Plants*. Paris, 1893.

Casson, L., *The Ancient Mariners: Seafarers and Sea-fighters of the Mediterranean in Ancient Times*. London, 1959.

Cassell's Dutch, French, German, Italian, Latin, and Spanish dictionaries. Cassell and Co.

Cates, W. L. R. *See* Woodward, B. B.

Catling, H., *Cypriot Bronze Work in the Mycenaean World*. Oxford, 1964.

Chadwick, John, *The Decipherment of Linear B*. Penguin, London, 1961.

Clarke, Graham, *Prehistoric England*. B. T. Batsford, London, 1962.

Colum, Padraic, Editor, *A Treasury of Irish Folklore*. Crown Publishers, New York, 1954.

Concise Encyclopedia of Archaeology, The. Editor, Leonard Cottrell. Hutchinson, London, 1960.

Concise Oxford Dictionary of English Place-Names, The. Editor, E. Eckwall. Oxford University Press, London, 1960.

Cottrell, Leonard. See *Concise Encyclopedia of Archaeology*.

Cork Historical and Archaeological Society, Journal of the, 1892–1968. Guy and Co., Cork; John English and Co., Wexford.

Culican, William, *The First Merchant Venturers: The Ancient Levant in History and Commerce*. Thames and Hudson. London, 1966.

Curtis, Edmund, *A History of Ireland*. Methuen, London, 1960.

Curwen, E. C., *The Archaeology of Sussex*. Methuen, London, 1954.

Daniel, G. E., *The Prehistoric Chamber Tombs of England and Wales*. Cambridge University Press, 1950.

Darlington, C. D., *The Evolution of Man and Society*. Allen & Unwin, London, 1969.

Darwin, Charles, *Animals and Plants Under Domestication*. London, 1885.

———, *Voyage of the Beagle*. Surrey, 1959.

Desborough, V. R. d'A., *The Last Mycenaeans and Their Successors, An Archaeological Survey, c. 1200–1000 B.C.* Oxford, 1964.

Diringer, D., *The Alphabet: A Key to the History of Mankind*. London, 1947.

Donnelly, Ignatius, *Atlantis: The Antediluvian World*. London, 1889.

Driver, G. R., *Canaanite Myths and Legends*. Edinburgh, 1956.

Dunbabin, T. J., *The Greeks and their Eastern Neighbours*. London, 1957.

Dunlop, D. M., *The History of the Jewish Khazars*. Princeton University Press, Princeton, N.J., 1954.

Durant, Will, *The Life of Greece*. Simon & Schuster, New York, 1939.

Elderkin, George W., *Archaeological Papers*. Martha Kilbourne Fund, Springfield, Mass., 1932.

Encyclopaedia Britannica, The. 1796 and 1968 editions.

Evans, Arthur, *The Palace of Minos.* Biblo & Tannen, New York,

Evans, Arthur, *The Palace of Minos.* 4 vols. Macmillan, London, 1921–36.

1921.

Evans, E. Estyn, *Prehistoric and Early Christian Ireland.* Barnes & Noble, New York, 1966.

Ferguson, J., *Rude Stone Monuments.* London, 1872.

Finley, M. I., *The World of Odysseus.* Chatto and Windus, London, 1956.

Förster, Max, *Keltisches Wortgut in Englischen.* Halle, 1921.

———, *Der Flussname Temse und seine Sippe.* Munich, 1941.

———, *Zur Geschichte des Reliquienkultus in Altengland.* Munich, 1943.

Freeman, E. A., *Sicily: Phoenician, Greek and Roman.* Unwin, London, 1894.

Freeman, William, *A Concise Dictionary of English Slang.* English Universities Press, London, 1955.

Garcilaso De La Vega, *Royal Commentaries of the Incas and General History of Peru*, two volumes. Translation and introduction by Harold V. Livermore. University of Texas Press, 1969.

Glyn, Daniel. *See* O'Riordin, S. P.

Gordon, Cyrus H., *The Living Past.* John Day, New York, 1941.

———, *Ugaritic Grammar*, 1941; *Ugaritic Handbook*, 1947; *Ugaritic Manual*, 1955; *Ugaritic Textbook*, 1965: Pontificum institutum biblicum, Rome.

———, *Introduction to Old Testament Times.* Ventnor Publications, Ventnor, N.J., 1953.

———, *Adventures in the Nearest East.* London, 1957.

———, *Before the Bible: The Common Background of Greek and Hebrew Cultures.* Collins & Sons, London, 1962.

———, *Evidence for the Minoan Language.* Ventnor Publications, Ventnor, N.J., 1966.

———, *Homer and the Bible: The Origin and Character of East Mediterranean Literature.* Ventnor Publications, Ventnor, N. J., 1967.

——— *Ugarit and Minoan Crete: The Bearing of Their Texts on the Origins of Western Culture.* W. W. Norton, New York, 1966.

———, *Forgotten Scripts: The Story of their Decipherment.* Thames

& Hudson, London, 1968.

———, *Before the Bible: The Common Background of Greek and Hebrew Civilizations.* Collins, London, 1962.

———, *Before Columbus: Links between the Old World and Ancient America.* Turnstone, 1972.

Graves, Robert, *The Greek Myths.* Penguin, London, 1955.

Grinsell, L. V., *The Archaeology of Wessex.* London, 1958.

Grollenberg, L. H., *Atlas of the Bible.* Thomas Nelson and Sons, London, 1956.

Hale, Susan, *Mexico.* Unwin, London, 1891.

Harrison, Michael, *London Beneath the Pavement.* (Peter) Davies, London, 1961.

Hawkes, Jacquetta and Christopher, *Prehistoric Britain.* Chatto and Windus, London, 1951.

Hawkins, Gerald S., *Stonehenge Decoded.* Souvenir, London, 1966.

Hawkins, Quail. *See* Von Hagen, Victor W.

Hazlitt, W. Carew, *Dictionary of Faiths and Folklore.* Reeves and Turner, London, 1905.

Hencken, Hugh O'N., *Indo-European Languages and Archaeology.* American Anthropological Association, 1955.

———, *The Archaeology of Cornwall.* Methuen, London, 1932.

Herodotus, *The Histories.* Penguin, London, 1954.

Heyerdahl, Thor, *Kon-Tiki.* Allen & Unwin, London, 1951.

———, *Aku-Aku.* Allen and Unwin, London, 1958.

———, *Sea Routes to Polynesia.* Allen & Unwin, London, 1968.

Hoagland, Kathleen, *One Thousand Years of Irish Poetry.* London, 1947.

Homer, *The Iliad,* E. V. Rieu translation. Penguin Books, London, 1950.

———, *The Odyssey,* E. V. Rieu translation. Penguin Books, London, 1946.

Honore, Pierre, *In Quest of the White God.* Hutchinson, London, 1963.

Hutchinson, R. W., *Prehistoric Crete.* Penguin Books, London, 1962.

Irwin, Constance, *Fair Gods and Stone Faces.*

Jackson, K. H., *The Oldest Irish Tradition: A Window on the Iron Age.* Cambridge University Press, 1964.

Jones, Gwyn, *A History of the Vikings*. Oxford University Press, London, 1968.

Jones, H. P., *Dictionary of Foreign Phrases and Classical Quotations*. John Grant, Edinburgh, 1939.

Joyce, P. W., *The Origin and History of Irish Names and Places*. Longmans, Green, London, 1922.

Kendrick, T. D., *A History of the Vikings*. Methuen, London, 1930.

Kingsborough, Lord (Edward King), *Antiquities of Mexico* (nine volumes). London, 1830–1848.

Lahontan, Baron de, *Nouveaux Voyages . . . dans l'Amérique Septentrionale*. Paris, 1741.

Lahovary, N., *La Diffusion des langues anciennes du Proche-Orient, leurs relations avec le Basque, le Davidien, et les parlers Indo-European primitive*. Francke, Bern, 1957.

Larousse Encyclopedia of Mythology, The. Batchworth Press, London, 1959.

Leemans, W. F., *Foreign Trade in the Old Babylonian Period*. Leiden, 1960.

Leesburg, A. C. M., *Comparative Philology, Semitic and North Indian Dialects*. Leiden, 1903.

Lhote, Henri, "The Fertile Sahara," in *Vanished Civilizations of the Ancient World*, E. Bacon, Editor. Thames and Hudson, London, 1963.

Limerick Field Club, Journal of the, 1892.

Lons, Veronica, *Egyptian Mythology*. The Hamlyn Group, Middlesex, 1965.

Lynch, F. J., two-part article, *Journal of the Limerick Field Club*, 1892.

Macalister, R. A. Stewart, *The Philistines: Their History and Civilization* (Schweich Lectures, British Academy, 1911). Oxford University Press, London, 1913.

McClure, Edmund, *British Place-Names in Their Historical Settings*. London, 1910.

MacManus, Seumas, *The Story of the Irish Race*. Devin-Adair, New York, 1967.

Malet, Hugh, *In the Wake of the Gods*. Chatto & Windus, London, 1970.

Mallowan, M. E. L., *Early Mesopotamia and Iran*. Thames & Hudson, London, 1965.

Malo, David, *Hawaiian Antiquities*. Bernice Pauahi Bishop Museum, Honolulu, 1951.

Maury, Alfred, "Déluge," *La Encyclopédie Moderne*. Paris, 1860.

Mavor, James, Jr., *Voyage to Atlantis*. G. P. Putnam's Sons, New York, 1969.

Meyer, Kuno, *Contributions to Irish Lexicography*. David Nutt, London, 1906.

————, *The Death Tales of the Irish Heroes*. Dublin, 1906.

Morris, E. E., *Austral English*. London, 1898.

Morris-Jones, John, *A Welsh Grammar: Historical and Comparative*. Oxford University Press, London, 1913.

Moscati, S., *Ancient Semitic Civilizations*. London, 1957.

Müller, Max, *Comparative Mythology*. London, 1881.

Nettleship, Henry, and J. E. Sandys, *A Dictionary of Classical Antiquities: Mythology, Religion, Literature and Art* (translated from the German of Oskár Seyffert). William Glaisher, London, 1894.

Oakley, K. P., *Man the Toolmaker*. British Museum (Natural History), 1949.

Odyssey World Atlas, The. Golden Press Odyssey Books, New York, 1966.

O'Riordin, S. P., *Antiquities of the Irish Countryside*. Barnes & Noble, New York, 1964.

————, and Daniel Glyn, *New Grange and the Bend of the Boyne*. Praeger, New York, 1965.

Ortelius, Abraham, *Theatrum Orbis Terrarum*. 1574.

Osborn, Fairfield, *Limits of the Earth*. Little, Brown and Company, Boston, 1953.

————, *Our Plundered Planet*. London, 1948.

Owens, R. J., *Peru*. Oxford University Press, 1963.

Oxford Classical Dictionary, The. Oxford University Press, 1970.

Oxford Companion to Classical Literature, The. Oxford University Press, 1937.

Oxford English Dictionary, The. Oxford University Press, 1933.

Pendlebury, J., *Aegyptica; Catalogue of Egyptian Objects in the Aegean Area*. Cambridge, 1930.

Piggott, Stuart, *Ancient Europe*. Edinburgh University Press, 1965.

————, *British Prehistory*. Oxford University Press, 1949.

Pilot Books of the World, The (series). The British Admiralty.

Powell, T. G. E., *The Celts.* Thames & Hudson, London, 1958.

Prescott, William H., *Conquest of Mexico.* London, 1848.

———, *Conquest of Peru.* London, 1847.

Rafinesque, C. S., *The American Nations.* Philadelphia, 1836.

Ragozin, Z. A., *Vedic India: as embodied principally in the Rig-Veda.* Unwin, London, 1895.

Random House Dictionary of the English Language, (unabridged edition). Random House, New York, 1966.

Reed, Alma, *The Ancient Past of Mexico.* Hamlyn, London, 1966.

Reed, T. D., *The Battle for Britain in the Fifth Century.* Methuen, London, 1944.

Rees, Alwyn and Brinley, *Celtic Heritage.* Thames and Hudson, London, 1961.

Royal Irish Academy, Proceedings (later Transactions) of the. Dublin, 1798–1968.

Royal Society of Antiquaries of Ireland, The Journal of the, 1849–1968.

Sandys, J. E. *See* Henry Nettleship.

Schleimann, H., *Mycenae and Tiryns.* London, 1878.

Seyffert, Oskar. *See* Henry Nettleship.

Sieveking, Gale, "Migration of the Megaliths," chapter in *Vanished Civilizations of the Ancient World.* Thames and Hudson, London, 1963.

Skene, W. F., Editor, *Chronicles of the Picts, Chronicles of the Scots, and other Early Memorials of Scottish History.* Edinburgh, 1867.

Smith, William, Editor, *Dictionary of Greek and Roman Antiquities.* London, 1869.

Stewart, George R., *American Place Names.* Oxford University Press, 1970.

Stone, J. F. S., *Wessex Before the Celts.* Thames & Hudson, London, 1958.

Sutherland, C. H. V., *Gold.* Thames and Hudson, London, 1959.

Swan, Michael, *Temple of the Sun and Moon: A Mexican Journey.* Jonathan Cape, London, 1954.

Taylour, William, *The Mycenaeans.* Thames & Hudson, London, 1964.

Thurneysen, Rudolf, *A Grammar of Old Irish.* Dublin Institute for Advanced Studies, 1946.

Times Index-Gazetteer of the World, The. The Times Publishing Company, London, 1965.

Tompkins, Peter, *Secrets of the Great Pyramid.* Weidenfeld & Nicolson, London, 1971.

Tornoe, J. K., *Early American History: Norsemen Before Columbus.* Allen and Unwin, London, 1965.

Turville-Petre, E. O. G., *Myth and Religion of the North.* Weidenfeld and Nicolson, London, 1964.

Vernadsky, G., *The Origins of Russia.* Oxford University Press, New York, 1959.

———, *Ancient Russia.* Yale Univeristy Press, New Haven, 1943.

Von Hagen, Victor W., *The Ancient Sun Kingdoms of the Americas.* Thames & Hudson, London, 1964.

Warmington, B. H., *Carthage.* Robert Hale, London, 1960.

Wood, Eric, *Collins Field Guide to Archaeology in Britain,* Collins, London, 1963.

Wood-Martin, W. G., *Traces of the Elder Faiths in Ireland.* Longmans, Green, London, 1902.

Woodward, B. B., and W. L. R. Cates, *Encyclopedia of Chronology-Historical and Biographical.* Longmans, Green, London, 1872.

Woolley, C. L., *Alalakh: an account of Excavations at Tell Atchana in the Hatay, 1937–1949.* Oxford, 1955.

Index

P